MTEL 22 Physical Education
Teacher Certification Exam

By: Sharon Wynne, M.S
Southern Connecticut State University

"And, while there's no reason yet to panic, I think it's only prudent that we make preparations to panic."

XAMonline, INC.
Boston

Copyright © 2007 XAMonline, Inc.
All rights reserved. No part of the material protected by this copyright notice may be reproduced or utilized in any form or by any means, electronic or mechanical, including photocopying, recording or by any information storage and retrievable system, without written permission from the copyright holder. To obtain permission(s) to use the material from this work for any purpose including workshops or seminars, please submit a written request to:

XAMonline, Inc.
21 Orient Ave.
Melrose, MA 02176
Toll Free 1-800-509-4128
Email: info@XAMonline.com
Web www.xamonline.com
Fax: 1-781-662-9268

Library of Congress Cataloging-in-Publication Data / Sharon A. Wynne. -2nd ed.
ISBN 978-1-58197-886-5
1. Physical Education 22   2. Study Guides.   3. MTEL
4. Teachers' Certification & Licensure.   5. Careers

Disclaimer:
The opinions expressed in this publication are the sole works of XAMonline and were created independently from the National Education Association, Educational Testing Service, or any State Department of Education, National Evaluation Systems or other testing affiliates.

Between the time of publication and printing, state specific standards as well as testing formats and website information may change that is not included in part or in whole within this product. Sample test questions are developed by XAMonline and reflect similar content as on real tests; however, they are not former tests. XAMonline assembles content that aligns with state standards but makes no claims nor guarantees teacher candidates a passing score. Testing companies such as NES or ETS determine numerical scores and compare them with individual state standards. A passing score varies from state to state.

Printed in the United States of America   œ-1

MTEL: Physical Education 22
ISBN: 978-158197-886-5

MASSACHUSETTS TESTS FOR EDUCATOR LICENSURE (MTEL) – Physical Education

ABOUT THE MTEL
The MTEL program includes a test of communication and literacy skills as well as tests of subject matter knowledge.

Communication and Literacy Skills Test:
- Consists of two subtests: Reading and Writing.
- Reading subtests contains multiple-choice items and word meaning items.
- Writing subtest contains four sections: written summary, written composition, grammar and usage, and written mechanics.

Pre K-12 Subject Matter Tests:
- Consists of multiple-choice items and open-response items.

MTEL PASSING REQUIREMENTS
A candidate's performance on a test is evaluated against an established standard. The scores are converted to a common scale to provide consistency. A score of 70 represents the qualifying, or passing, score. Candidates who do not achieve the passing score may retake the test at any of the subsequent test administrations.

LICENSURE TEST REQUIREMENTS
Educators seeking a first Massachusetts PreK-12 license must achieve a passing score on the Communication and Literacy Skills test AND any relevant PreK-12 subject matter test.

Table of Contents

DOMAIN I. PHYSICAL DEVELOPMENT AND MOTOR LEARNING

COMPETENCY 1.0 UNDERSTAND COMPONENTS AND FUNCTIONS OF THE MAJOR BODY SYSTEMS 1

SKILL 1.1 General organization of the skeletal, muscular, circulatory, respiratory, and nervous systems, common disorders of the systems, and physiological processes involving the systems............1

COMPETENCY 2.0 UNDERSTAND PHYSICAL GROWTH AND DEVELOPMENT 11

SKILL 2.1 Phases and characteristics of physical development during infancy, childhood, adolescence, and adulthood 11

SKILL 2.2 Developmental issues during the phases of human growth 12

SKILL 2.3 Factors that influence physical growth and development 13

COMPETENCY 3.0 UNDERSTAND SEQUENCES AND CHARACTERISTICS OF MOTOR DEVELOPMENT 15

SKILL 3.1 Sequences and characteristics of motor skill development during infancy, childhood, adolescence, and adulthood 15

SKILL 3.2 Relationship of motor development to physical, cognitive, psychosocial, and emotional development 15

SKILL 3.3 Factors that influence motor development and performance 18

COMPETENCY 4.0 UNDERSTAND PRINCIPLES OF PERCEPTUAL-MOTOR DEVELOPMENT 19

SKILL 4.1 Visual, auditory, tactile, and kinesthetic discriminations and their relationships to motor development and performance 19

SKILL 4.2 Perceptual-motor development activities, materials, and equipment that are appropriate for students at various developmental levels 19

TEACHER CERTIFICATION STUDY GUIDE

COMPETENCY 5.0 UNDERSTAND PRINCIPLES OF MOTOR LEARNING 21

SKILL 5.1 Theories and models of motor learning 21

SKILL 5.2 Principles of practice, retention, readiness, feedback, observational learning, and transfer of learning as they relate to motor skill acquisition 22

SKILL 5.3 Methods for promoting recognition and use of similar movement concepts and elements in a variety of skills 23

SKILL 5.4 Techniques for detecting errors in motor performance and providing cues and corrective feedback 23

SKILL 5.5 Techniques for modifying sports and games to promote the use of combinations of motor skills 25

DOMAIN II.   HEALTH-RELATED PHYSICAL FITNESS

COMPETENCY 1.0 UNDERSTAND COMPONENTS OF PHYSICAL FITNESS AND PRINCIPLES OF TRAINING 26

SKILL 1.1 Basic components of physical fitness and principles of training 26

SKILL 1.2 Aerobic versus anaerobic conditioning 27

SKILL 1.3 Short- and long-term effects of physical activity on the cardiorespiratory, muscular, skeletal, neural, and endocrine systems 28

SKILL 1.4 Interactions among these systems in producing movement 29

SKILL 1.5 Energy systems used during exercise 30

SKILL 1.6 Factors that affect physical fitness and performance 30

SKILL 1.7 Potential health risks and injury prevention techniques associated with exercise and training 31

PHYSICAL EDUCATION

COMPETENCY 2.0 UNDERSTAND THE DEVELOPMENT AND MAINTENANCE OF CARDIORESPIRATORY ENDURANCE 34

SKILL 2.1 Principles and activities for developing aerobic endurance 34

SKILL 2.2 Techniques for assessing and monitoring heart rate and endurance levels 35

SKILL 2.3 Appropriate aerobic activities for various developmental levels and purposes 36

COMPETENCY 3.0 UNDERSTAND THE DEVELOPMENT AND MAINTENANCE OF MUSCULAR STRENGTH AND ENDURANCE 38

SKILL 3.1 Principles and activities for developing strength and endurance in various muscle groups 38

SKILL 3.2 Principles, safety practices, and equipment for progressive resistance exercise 52

SKILL 3.3 Techniques for assessing muscular strength and endurance 52

SKILL 3.4 Appropriate activities for various developmental levels and purposes 53

COMPETENCY 4.0 UNDERSTAND THE DEVELOPMENT AND MAINTENANCE OF FLEXIBILITY 55

SKILL 4.1 Principles and activities for developing flexibility in the major joints of the body 55

SKILL 4.2 Techniques for assessing flexibility 57

COMPETENCY 5.0 UNDERSTAND HOW TO DEVELOP AND MAINTAIN LEVELS OF BODY COMPOSITION THAT PROMOTE GOOD HEALTH 58

SKILL 5.1 Principles of nutrition and weight control 58

SKILL 5.2 Relationships between physical activity and body composition and ways in which nutrition and eating habits may affect physical development and health 60

SKILL 5.3 Relationships between body type and body composition 61

SKILL 5.4 Techniques for assessing body composition 61

SKILL 5.5 Appropriate activities for developing and maintaining levels of body composition that promote good health 62

DOMAIN III. MOVEMENT SPORTS ACTIVITIES

COMPETENCY 1.0 UNDERSTAND PRINCIPLES OF BIOMECHANICS AND THEIR APPLICATION TO MOVEMENT ACTIVITIES 63

SKILL 1.1 Principles related to motion, stability and balance, force projection and absorption, buoyancy, rotation, speed, acceleration, and other biomechanical concepts 63

SKILL 1.2 The application of these principles in the context of various movement activities 65

COMPETENCY 2.0 UNDERSTAND FUNDAMENTAL MOVEMENT CONCEPTS AND SKILLS 72

SKILL 2.1 Concepts of time, space, direction, speed, and force 72

SKILL 2.2 Techniques for promoting students' application of these movement concepts through exploration of shapes, levels, and pathways 72

SKILL 2.3 Body awareness 73

COMPETENCY 3.0 UNDERSTAND PRINCIPLES AND ACTIVITIES FOR DEVELOPING LOCOMOTOR, NONLOCOMOTOR, AND BODY CONTROL SKILLS 75

SKILL 3.1 Types and characteristics of locomotor, nonlocomotor, and body control skills 75

SKILL 3.2 Techniques for assessing these skills 77

SKILL 3.3 Developmentally appropriate activities for promoting these skills 78

SKILL 3.4 Strategies for integrating these skills in various combinations and activities 80

COMPETENCY 4.0 UNDERSTAND PRINCIPLES AND ACTIVITIES FOR DEVELOPING OBJECT CONTROL SKILLS 81

SKILL 4.1 Throwing, catching, dribbling, kicking, and striking skills 81

SKILL 4.2 Combinations of object control skills 82

SKILL 4.3 Techniques for assessing these skills and developmentally appropriate activities for promoting these skills 82

SKILL 4.4 Strategies for integrating locomotor, nonlocomotor, and object control skills 83

COMPETENCY 5.0 UNDERSTAND PRINCIPLES AND ACTIVITIES FOR DEVELOPING RHYTHMIC AND DANCE SKILLS 84

SKILL 5.1 Basic elements of rhythm 84

SKILL 5.2 Appropriate activities for rhythmic skill development 84

SKILL 5.3 Techniques for assessing rhythmic skills 85

SKILL 5.4 Strategies for integrating rhythmic skills with locomotor, nonlocomotor, body control, and object control skills 85

SKILL 5.5 Techniques, sequences, and skills for various forms of dance 87

COMPETENCY 6.0 UNDERSTAND TECHNIQUES, SKILLS, ORGANIZATIONAL STRATEGIES, AND SAFETY PRACTICES FOR TUMBLING AND GYMNASTICS 90

SKILL 6.1 Skills, activities, skill progressions, organizational strategies, safety practices and proper use of equipment for tumbling and gymnastics 90

SKILL 6.2 Techniques for assessing tumbling and gymnastic skills...................91

SKILL 6.3 Appropriate activities for various developmental levels and purposes......91

COMPETENCY 7.0 UNDERSTAND TECHNIQUES, SKILLS, ORGANIZATIONAL STRATEGIES, AND SAFETY PRACTICES FOR AQUATICS 93

SKILL 7.1 Techniques, skill progressions, safety practices, organizational strategies, emergency pool procedures, and proper use of equipment......93

SKILL 7.2 Techniques for assessing aquatic skills............................94

SKILL 7.3 Activities appropriate for various developmental levels and purposes......94

COMPETENCY 8.0 UNDERSTAND TECHNIQUES, SKILLS, STRATEGIES, RULES, ETIQUETTE, AND SAFETY PRACTICES FOR INDIVIDUAL AND DUAL SPORTS, RECREATIONAL ACTIVITIES, AND OUTDOOR PURSUITS 95

SKILL 8.1 Techniques, skill progressions, strategies, rules, etiquette, safety practices, and types and uses of equipment for individual and dual sports......95

SKILL 8.2 Recreational activities, and outdoor pursuits 116

SKILL 8.3 Techniques for assessing skills in these activities 120

SKILL 8.4 Activities appropriate for various developmental levels and purposes......121

COMPETENCY 9.0 UNDERSTAND TECHNIQUES, SKILLS, STRATEGIES, RULES, ETIQUETTE, AND SAFETY PRACTICES FOR TEAM SPORTS 122

SKILL 9.1   Techniques, skill progressions, strategies, rules, safety practices, equipment, and types of lead-up activities for team sports (e.g., volleyball, team handball, football, floor hockey, track and field) 122

SKILL 9.2   Techniques for assessing skills in these sports 134

SKILL 9.3   Activities appropriate for various developmental levels and purposes 135

DOMAIN IV.   COGNITIVE, SOCIAL, AND PERSONAL DEVELOPMENT

COMPETENCY 1.0 UNDERSTAND COGNITIVE, SOCIAL, AND PERSONAL DEVELOPMENT IN RELATION TO PHYSICAL EDUCATION 138

SKILL 1.1   Characteristics of cognitive, psychosocial, and emotional development during childhood and adolescence 138

SKILL 1.2   Influence of peers and others in determining social attitudes and behaviors 142

SKILL 1.3   Influence of expectations related to gender, physical appearance, and skill level on the development of self-image 142

SKILL 1.4   Causes and effects of anxiety related to performance 143

SKILL 1.5   Stress management principles and strategies 143

SKILL 1.6   Relationships between physical activity and the development of personal identity and psychological well-being 145

SKILL 1.7   Strategies for promoting creative expression through sports and dance 147

COMPETENCY 2.0		UNDERSTAND THE ROLE OF PHYSICAL EDUCATION IN THE DEVELOPMENT OF HIGHER-ORDER THINKING AND EVALUATION SKILLS 148
	SKILL 2.1	Techniques and activities for developing problem-solving, decision-making, self-assessment, goal-setting, and monitoring skills in relation to physical activity and health-related lifestyle decisions 148
	SKILL 2.2	Techniques and activities to promote critical evaluation of claims and advertisements about commercial products 150
COMPETENCY 3.0		UNDERSTAND THE ROLE OF PHYSICAL EDUCATION IN THE DEVELOPMENT OF POSITIVE PERSONAL AND SOCIAL BEHAVIORS AND TRAITS 151
	SKILL 3.1	Role of physical education in fostering enjoyment of aesthetic and creative aspects of skilled performance and in respecting the physical and performance limitations of self and others 151
	SKILL 3.2	Potential social-cultural benefits of participation in physical activities 151
	SKILL 3.3	Ways in which physical education activities can promote positive personal behaviors and traits as well as ways in which physical education activities can promote positive social behaviors and traits 153

DOMAIN V. PROFESSIONAL KNOWLEDGE AND THE PHYSICAL EDUCATION PROGRAM

COMPETENCY 1.0		UNDERSTAND THE HISTORY AND PHILOSOPHIES OF PHYSICAL EDUCATION 154
	SKILL 1.1	Significant events in the historical development of physical education 154
	SKILL 1.2	Past and present philosophies of physical education and their effects on the goals, scope, and practices of physical education programs 156
	SKILL 1.3	Current issues and trends that affect the field 158
	SKILL 1.4	Contributions of noteworthy physical educators 160

COMPETENCY 2.0 UNDERSTAND THE STRUCTURE, GOALS, AND PURPOSES OF PHYSICAL EDUCATION PROGRAMS 161

SKILL 2.1 Structure, organization, goals, and purposes of physical education programs 161

SKILL 2.2 Procedures and components of curriculum development and appropriate scope and sequence in the physical education curriculum 162

SKILL 2.3 Criteria and procedures for evaluating physical education programs 162

SKILL 2.4 Ways to adapt or modify physical education programs based on program evaluation results 163

SKILL 2.5 Relationships between physical education and other areas of instruction 164

SKILL 2.6 Ways to integrate physical education into the overall school curriculum 165

SKILL 2.7 Methods for communicating and maintaining positive relations with students, families, and community members 165

COMPETENCY 3.0 UNDERSTAND INSTRUCTIONAL STRATEGIES IN PHYSICAL EDUCATION 166

SKILL 3.1 Physical education instructional methods and their characteristics 166

SKILL 3.2 Appropriate instructional methods and activities for various objectives, situations, and developmental levels and appropriate methods of instruction for students with special needs and students from diverse cultural or linguistic backgrounds 167

SKILL 3.3 Techniques for modifying rules, equipment, and settings to conform to the needs of students 169

SKILL 3.4 Strategies for consulting and collaborating with teachers, special education personnel, administrators, and other school personnel 171

SKILL 3.5 Strategies for consulting and collaborating with teachers and other school personnel 174

COMPETENCY 4.0 UNDERSTAND PHYSICAL EDUCATION ASSESSMENT METHODS AND INSTRUMENTS 175

SKILL 4.1 Types, characteristics, advantages, and limitations of various assessment methods and instruments (e.g., observational checklists, performance assessments, portfolios, journals, peer assessments, standardized tests) 175

SKILL 4.2 Sources of standards of physical fitness 177

SKILL 4.3 Techniques for selecting, constructing, adapting, and implementing formal and informal assessments 179

SKILL 4.4 Appropriate assessment methods for various objectives and situations 180

SKILL 4.5 Use of technology for analysis of student fitness and performance 183

SKILL 4.6 Development of exercise prescriptions based on assessment results 184

SKILL 4.7 Appropriate interpretation and communication of assessment results 185

COMPETENCY 5.0 UNDERSTAND THE MANAGEMENT OF PHYSICAL EDUCATION ENVIRONMENTS AND PROGRAMS 186

SKILL 5.1 Techniques for organizing and managing physical education classes and environments and benefits and limitations of various management and discipline practices 186

SKILL 5.2 Logistics related to the availability and use of facilities, supplies, equipment, staff, and other resources 187

SKILL 5.3 Financial issues related to physical education programs 188

SKILL 5.4 Care and maintenance procedures for facilities and equipment 188

SKILL 5.5 Procedures for maintaining a safe physical education environment 191

COMPETENCY 6.0 UNDERSTAND PRINCIPLES AND PROCEDURES OF INJURY PREVENTION AND EMERGENCY FIRST AID ASSISTANCE 192

SKILL 6.1 Types and characteristics of injuries common to physical activities and principles and techniques of injury care and prevention 192

SKILL 6.2 Purposes and procedures for CPR 192

SKILL 6.3 First-aid procedures related to the control of emergency situations 192

SKILL 6.4 Safety precautions in administering emergency care procedures 195

COMPETENCY 7.0 UNDERSTAND LEGAL AND ETHICAL ISSUES RELATED TO PHYSICAL EDUCATION PROGRAMS 196

SKILL 7.1 Legal requirements and responsibilities associated with teaching physical education 196

SKILL 7.2 Issues related to lifeguarding and pool safety 198

SKILL 7.3 Issues related to supervision, safety, liability, and negligence 198

SKILL 7.4 State and federal laws and guidelines regarding gender equity, special education, religious issues, and other aspects of students' rights 200

SKILL 7.5 Application of ethical issues and guidelines in various physical education situations 201

ANNOTATED LIST OF RESOURCES 202

SAMPLE TEST 204

ANSWER KEY 231

RATIONALES WITH SAMPLE QUESTIONS 232

SAMPLE WRITTEN ASSIGNMENT WITH RESPONSE 273

Great Study and Testing Tips!

What you study in order to prepare for the subject assessments is the focus of this study guide, but equally important is *how* you study.

You can increase your chances of truly mastering the information by taking some simple but effective steps.

Study Tips:

1. Some foods aid the learning process. Foods such as milk, nuts, seeds, rice, and oats help your study efforts by releasing natural memory enhancers called CCKs (*cholecystokinin*) composed of *tryptophan*, *choline*, and *phenylalanine*. All of these chemicals enhance the neurotransmitters associated with memory. Before studying, try a light, protein-rich meal of eggs, turkey, and fish. All of these foods release the memory enhancing chemicals. The better the connections, the more you comprehend.

Likewise, before you take a test, stick to a light snack of relaxing and energy boosting foods. A glass of milk, a piece of fruit, or some peanuts release various memory-boosting chemicals and help you to relax and focus on the subject at hand.

2. Learn to take great notes. A by-product of our modern culture is that we have grown accustomed to getting our information in short doses (e.g. TV news sound bites or USA Today style newspaper articles).

Consequently, we've subconsciously trained ourselves to assimilate information better in neat little packages. If your notes are scrawled all over the paper, it fragments the flow of the information. Strive for clarity. Newspapers use a standard format to achieve clarity. You can make your notes much clearer by using proper formatting. A very effective format is the *"Cornell Method."*

Take a sheet of loose-leaf lined notebook paper and draw a line all the way down the paper about 1-2" from the left-hand edge.

Draw another line across the width of the paper about 1-2" up from the bottom. Repeat this process on the reverse side of the page.

Look at the highly effective result. You have ample room for notes, a left hand margin for special emphasis items or inserting supplementary data from the textbook, a large area at the bottom for a brief summary, and a little rectangular space for just about anything you want.

3. **Get the concept then the details.** Too often we focus on the details and don't gather an understanding of the concept. However, if you simply memorize only dates, places, or names, you may well miss the whole point of the subject.

A key way to understand things is to put them in your own words. If you are working from a textbook, automatically summarize each paragraph in your mind. If you are outlining text, don't simply copy the author's words.

Rephrase them in your own words. You remember your own thoughts and words much better than someone else's, and subconsciously tend to associate the important details to the core concepts.

4. **Ask Why?** Pull apart written material paragraph by paragraph and don't forget the captions under the illustrations.

Example: If the heading is "Stream Erosion", flip it around to read, "Why do streams erode?" Then answer the questions.

If you train your mind to think in a series of questions and answers, not only will you learn more, but it also helps to lessen the test anxiety because you are used to answering questions.

5. **Read for reinforcement and future needs.** Even if you only have 10 minutes, put your notes or a book in your hand. Your mind is similar to a computer; you have to input data in order to have it processed. *By reading, you are creating the neural connections for future retrieval.* The more times you read something, the more you reinforce the learning of ideas.

Even if you don't fully understand something on the first pass, *your mind stores much of the material for later recall.*

6. **Relax to learn, so go into exile.** Our bodies respond to an inner clock called biorhythms. Burning the midnight oil works well for some people, but not everyone.

If possible, set aside a particular place to study that is free of distractions. Shut off the television, cell phone, and pager and exile your friends and family during your study period.

If you really dislike silence, try background music. Studies show that light classical music played at a low volume aids in concentration.

Music that evokes pleasant emotions without lyrics is highly suggested. Try just about anything by Mozart. It relaxes you.

7. Use arrows not highlighters. At best, it's difficult to read a page full of yellow, pink, blue, and green streaks.

Try staring at a neon sign for a while and you'll soon see my point. The horde of colors obscures the message.

A quick note, a brief dash of color, an underline, and an arrow pointing to a particular passage is much clearer than a horde of highlighted words.

8. Budget your study time. Although you shouldn't ignore any of the material, *allocate your available study time in the same ratio that topics may appear on the test.*

Testing Tips:

1. Get smart, play dumb. **Don't read anything into the question.** Don't assume that the test writer is looking for something else than what is asked. Stick to the question as written and don't read extra things into it.

2. Read the question and all the choices *twice* before answering. You may miss something by not carefully reading and re-reading both the question and the answers.

If you really don't have a clue as to the right answer, leave it blank the first time through. Go on to the other questions, as they may provide a clue as to how to answer the skipped questions.

If later on, you still can't answer the skipped ones . . . ***Guess.***
The only penalty for guessing is that you *might* get it wrong. One thing is certain; if you don't put anything down, you will get it wrong!

3. Turn the question into a statement. Look at the wording of the questions. The syntax of the question usually provides a clue. Does it seem more familiar as a statement rather than as a question? Does it sound strange?

By turning a question into a statement, you may be able to spot if an answer sounds right, and it may also trigger memories of material you've read.

4. Look for hidden clues. It's actually very difficult to compose multiple-choice questions without giving away part of the answer in the options presented.

In most multiple-choice questions, you can often readily eliminate one or two of the potential answers. This leaves you with only two real possibilities, and automatically your odds go to fifty-fifty with very little work.

5. Trust your instincts. For every fact that you have read, you subconsciously retain something of that knowledge. On questions that you aren't certain about, go with your basic instincts. **Your first impression on how to answer a question is usually correct.**

6. Mark your answers directly on the test booklet. Don't bother trying to fill in the optical scan sheet on the first pass through the test.

Just be very careful not to miss-mark your answers when you eventually transcribe them to the scan sheet.

7. Watch the clock! You have a set amount of time to answer the questions. Don't get bogged down trying to answer a single question at the expense of 10 questions you can more readily answer.

TEACHER CERTIFICATION STUDY GUIDE

DOMAIN I.   **PHYSICAL DEVELOPMENT AND MOTOR LEARNING**

COMPETENCY 1.0   **UNDERSTAND COMPONENTS AND FUNCTIONS OF THE MAJOR BODY SYSTEMS**

SKILL 1.1   **General organization of the skeletal, muscular, circulatory, respiratory, and nervous systems, common malfunction of these systems, and the physiological processes of these systems.**

A basic understanding of the body (skeletal, muscular, circulatory, respiratory, and nervous systems) and the body processes involved will help you develop a safe and efficient fitness program. In this competency section (1.0) we will take a brief look at how the body functions work together to enable physical activity.

MUSCULAR SYSTEM

The function of the muscular system is to provide optimal movement for the parts of the human body. The specific functions of each muscle depend on its location. In all cases, however, muscle action is the result of the actions of individual muscle cells. Muscle cells are unique in that they are the only cells in the body that have the property of contractility. This gives muscle cells the ability to shorten and develop tension. This is extremely important for human movement.

Muscles are classified in three categories:

1. Skeletal: muscles that attach to the bone
2. Visceral: muscles that are associated with an internal body structure
3. Cardiac: muscles that form the wall of the heart

Skeletal muscles are the only voluntary muscles, meaning they contract as initiated by the will of a person.
Visceral and cardiac muscles are both involuntary muscles, meaning they are governed by nerve impulses found in the autonomic nervous system.

Skeletal and cardiac muscles are striated or band-like, whereas visceral muscles are smooth.

SKELETAL SYSTEM

The skeletal system has several functions:

1. Support: The skeleton acts as the framework of the body. It gives support to the soft tissues and provides points of attachment for the majority of the muscles.

PHYSICAL EDUCATION

2. Movement: The fact that the majority of the muscles attach to the skeleton and that many of the bones meet (or articulate) in moveable joints, the skeleton plays an important role in determining the extend and kind of movement that the body is capable of.
3. Protection: Clearly, the skeleton protects many of the vital, internal organs from injury. This includes the brain, spinal cord, thoracic, urinary bladder and reproductive organs.
4. Mineral Reservoir: Vital minerals are stored in the bones of the skeleton. Some examples are calcium, phosphorus, sodium and potassium.
5. Hemopoiesis or blood-cell formation: After a mother gives birth, the red marrow in specific bones produces the blood cells found in the circulatory system.

The human skeletal is composed of 206 individual bones that are held in position by strong fibrous ligaments. These bones can be grouped into two categories:
1. Axial skeleton: total 80 bones (skull, vertebral column, thorax)
2. Appendicular skeleton: total 126 bones (pectoral, upper limbs, pelvic, lower limbs)

The ENDOCRINE SYSTEM

The endocrine system is not a clearly defined anatomical system but rather is composed of various glands that are located throughout the body. The main function of this system is to aid in the regulation of body activities by producing chemical substances we know as hormones. Through a complicated regulation system, the bloodstream distributes hormones throughout the body with each hormone affecting only specific targeted organs.

The primary endocrine glands are the pituitary, thyroid, parathyroids, adrenals, pancreas and gonads. Additionally, the kidneys, gastrointestinal and placenta exhibit endocrine activity but to a lesser extent than the primary glands.

The hormones produced by the endocrine system do not fall into an easily defined class of chemical substances. Some are steroids (such as cortisol), others are proteins (such as insulin), and still others are polypeptides and amino acids (such as parathyroid hormone and epinephrine).

Irregardless of the specific chemical substance, the hormones produced by the endocrine system play a critical role in aiding in the regulation and integration of the body processes.

IMMUNE SYSTEM

The immune system's function is to defend the human body against infectious organisms and other attacking forces, such as bacteria, microbes, viruses, toxins and parasites. Simply put, the immune system strives every day to keep human beings healthy and free of disease and illness.

The immune system is made up of two main fluid systems, intertwined throughout the body, that are responsible for transporting the agents of the immune system, the blood stream and the lymph system. White blood cells are considered to be the most important part of your immune system.

Different types/names of white blood cells are:

- Leukocytes – this is often used as the primary term for white blood cells
- Lymphocyte
- Monocytes
- Granulocytes
- B-cells
- Plasma cells
- T-cells
- Helper T-cells
- Killer T-cells
- Suppressor T-cells
- Natural killer cells
- Neutrophils
- Eosinophils
- Basophils
- Phagocytes
- Macrophages

A foreign substance that invades the body is referred to as an antigen. When an antigen is detected, the immune system goes into action immediately through several types of cells working together. These initial cells try to recognize and respond to the antigen, thereby triggering white blood cells to release antibodies. Antigens and antibodies have been referred to as fitting like a "key and a lock" throughout the scientific community. Once these antigens have been produced in the body they stay in the body, meaning if this same antigen enters the body again, the body is immune and protected.

Vaccines are antigens given in very small amounts. They stimulate both humoral and cell mediated responses. After vaccination, memory cells recognize future exposure to the antigen so the body can produce antibodies much faster.

There are three types of immunity:

1. Innate Immunity: the immunity (general protection) we are all born with
2. Adaptive Immunity: immunity that develops throughout our lives (antibodies) as we are exposed to diseases and illnesses
3. Passive Immunity: this is an immunity that comes from outside ourselves (outside antibiotics...)

There are two defense mechanisms in the immune system: non-specific and specific.

The **non-specific** immune mechanism has two lines of defense. The first line of defense is the physical barriers of the body. These include the skin and mucous membranes. The skin prevents the penetration of bacteria and viruses as long as there are no abrasions on the skin. Mucous membranes form a protective barrier around the digestive, respiratory, and genitourinary tracts. In addition, the pH of the skin and mucous membranes inhibit the growth of many microbes. Mucous secretions (tears and saliva) wash away many microbes and contain lysozyme that kills microbes.

The second line of defense includes white blood cells and the inflammatory response. **Phagocytosis** is the ingestion of foreign particles. Neutrophils make up about seventy percent of all white blood cells. Monocytes mature to become macrophages, which are the largest phagocytic cells. Eosinophils are also phagocytic. Natural killer cells destroy the body's own infected cells instead of the invading the microbe directly.

The other second line of defense is the inflammatory response. The blood supply to the injured area increases, causing redness and heat. Swelling also typically occurs with inflammation. Basophils and mast cells release histamine in response to cell injury. This triggers the inflammatory response.

The **specific** immune mechanism recognizes specific foreign material and responds by destroying the invader. These mechanisms are specific and diverse. They are able to recognize individual pathogens.

CIRCULATORY SYSTEM

The function of the closed circulatory system (**cardiovascular system**) is to carry oxygenated blood and nutrients to all cells of the body and return carbon dioxide waste to the lungs for expulsion. Or paraphrased simply, to transport blood leaving the heart to all parts of the body, permitting the exchange of certain substances between the blood and body fluids and ultimately returning the blood to the heart.

The circulatory system is composed of veins, arteries and capillaries. Arteries carry blood away from the heart, veins return blood to the heart and capillaries allow for the exchange of substances between the blood and the cells of the body. Capillaries are the most important vessels of the blood vascular system. Arteries must be able to withstand the greatest pressure and veins are the largest vessels of the system.

The heart, blood vessels, and blood make up the cardiovascular system, which clearly is closely related to the circulatory system.

The following diagram shows the structure of the heart, noting the specific arteries and veins:

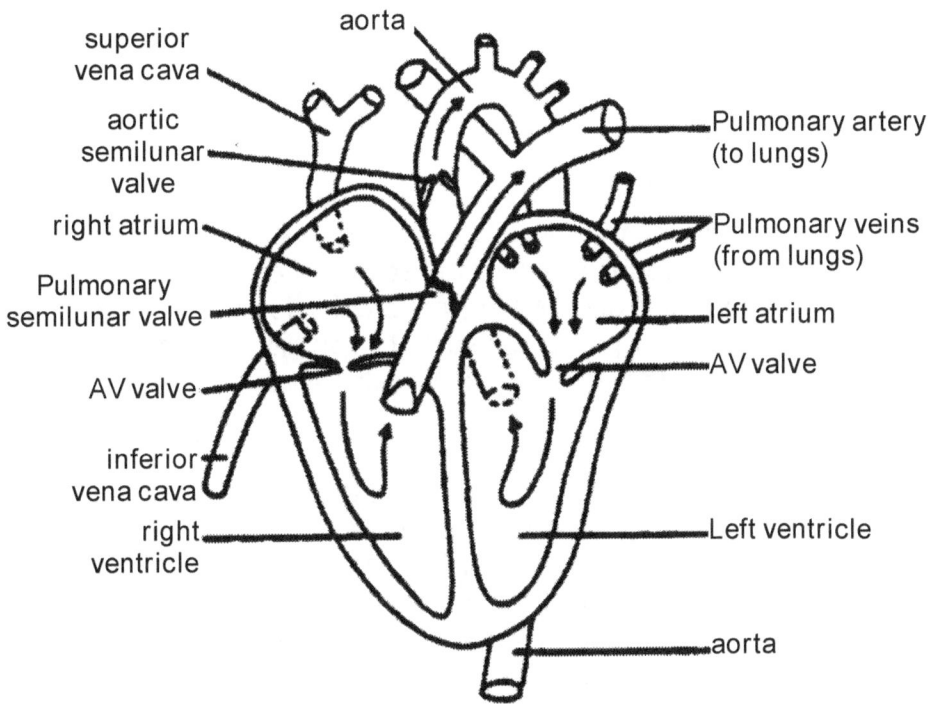

THE RESPIRATORY SYSTEM

The function of the respiratory system is, as oxygen is brought into the body through normal breathing or aerobic activity, carbon monoxide is removed, with the assistance of the circulatory system. The respiratory system also makes vocalization possible. We are able to speak, sing and laugh by varying the tension of the vocal cords as exhaled air passes over them.

The lungs are the respiratory surface of the human respiratory system. A dense net of capillaries contained just beneath the epithelium form the respiratory surface. The surface area of the epithelium is about $100m^2$ in humans. Based on the surface area, the volume of air inhaled and exhaled is the tidal volume. This is normally about 500mL in adults. Vital capacity is the maximum volume the lungs can inhale and exhale. This is usually around 3400mL.

To describe the respiratory more thoroughly, air enters the mouth and nose, where it is warmed, moistened and filtered of dust and particles. Cilia in the trachea trap and expel unwanted material in mucus. The trachea splits into two bronchial tubes and the bronchial tubes divide into smaller and smaller bronchioles in the lungs. The internal surface of the lung is composed of alveoli, which are thin walled air sacs. These allow for a large surface area for gas exchange. Capillaries line the alveoli. Oxygen diffuses into the bloodstream and carbon dioxide diffuses out of the capillaries and is exhaled from the lungs due to partial pressure. Hemoglobin, a protein containing iron, carries the oxygenated blood to the heart and all parts of the body.

The thoracic cavity holds the lungs. The diaphragm muscle below the lungs is an adaptation that makes inhalation possible. As the volume of the thoracic cavity increases, the diaphragm muscle flattens out and inhalation occurs. When the diaphragm relaxes, exhalation occurs.

THE DIGESTIVE SYSTEM

The function of the digestive system is to break food down into nutrients, absorb them into the blood stream, and deliver them to all cells of the body for use in cellular respiration. Every cell in the body requires a constant source of energy in order to perform its particular function(s). The digestive system breaks down or alters food ingested by mechanical and chemical processes so that it can ultimately cross the wall of the gastrointestinal tract and enter the blood vascular and lymphatic (circulatory) systems.

The digestive system consists of a tube called the gastrointestinal tract (alimentary canal) that extends from the mouth to the anus. As long as food remains in the gastrointestinal tract it is considered to still be outside of the body. To "enter" the body, it must cross the wall of the digestive tract. Emptying into the digestive tube are the secretions of the salivary glands, gastric glands, intestinal glands, liver and pancreas, all of which assist in the digestion of food. These regions include the mouth, esophagus, stomach, small and large intestines.

The digestive system activities can be divided into six parts:

1. ingestion of food into the mouth
2. movement of food along the digestive tract
3. mechanical preparation of food for digestion
4. chemical digestion of food
5. absorption of digested food into the circulatory and lymphatic systems (circulatory system)
6. elimination of undigestible substances and waste products from the body by defecation

REPRODUCTIVE SYSTEM

The reproductive system differs greatly from the other organ systems of the body in that it does not contribute to the survival or homeostasis of a human being. Instead, the organs of the reproductive system ensure the continuance of the species.

The reproductive system produces gametes (germ cells). Through sexual intercourse, the gametes (sperm) of the male joins with a gamete (ovum) of the female. This joining is called fertilization. The organs of the female reproductive system provide a suitable environment in which the fertilized ovum (zygote) can develop into a stage in which it is capable of surviving outside of the mother's body.

The organs that produce the gametes are referred to as the primary or essential sex organs. Specifically, these are the gonads (testes) in the male and the ovaries in the female. Additionally, the organs that produce the gametes also are responsible for producing hormones that influence the development of secondary sex characteristics and regulation of the reproductive system. In the male, specialized cells in the testes produce androgen hormones. The most active of these is testosterone. In the female, the ovaries produce estrogen and progesterone.

The structures that transport, protect and nourish the gamates in both the male and female are referred to as accessory sex organs. In the male, these include:

- the epididymis
- the ductus deferens
- the seminal vesicles
- the prostate gland
- the scrotum
- the penis

Female accessory sex organs include:

- the uterine tubes
- the uterus
- the vagina
- the vulva

PHYSICAL ACTIVITY AND FITNESS ADAPTATIONS

The structure and function of the human body adapts greatly to physical activity and exertion. When challenged with any physical task, the human body responds through a series of integrated changes in function that involve most, if not all, of its physiological systems. Movement requires activation and control of the musculoskeletal system. The cardiovascular and respiratory systems provide the ability to sustain this movement over extended periods. When the body engages in exercise training several times, each of these physiological systems undergoes specific adaptations that increase the body's efficiency and capacity.

When the body works, it makes great demand on every muscle of the body. Either the muscles have to 'shut down' or they have to do work. The heart beats faster during strenuous exercise so that it can pump more blood to the muscles, and the stomach shuts down during strenuous exercise so that it does not waste energy that the muscles need. Exercising makes the muscles work like motor that use up energy in order to generate force. Muscles, also known as 'biochemical motors', use the chemical adenosine triphosphate (ATP) as an energy source.

Physical activity affects the cardiovascular and musculoskeletal systems the most. However, it also helps in proper functioning of metabolic, endocrine, and immune systems.

For all the major organs to function properly, it is imperative that human beings apply a healthy lifestyle in the form of regular physical activity, proper nutrition, adequate rest and sleep, mental, social and emotional well-being and avoidance of substance abuse of any kind and cigarette smoking.

MALFUNCTIONS OF THE BODY SYSTEMS

Malfunctions of the respiratory and excretory systems

Emphysema is a chronic obstructive pulmonary disease (COPD). These diseases make it difficult for a person to breathe. Partial obstruction of the bronchial tubes limits airflow, which makes breathing difficult. The primary cause of emphysema is smoking. People with a deficiency in alpha$_1$-antitrypsin protein production have a greater risk of developing emphysema and at an earlier age. Furthermore, the alpha$_1$-antitrypsin helps protect the lungs from damage due to inflammation. This genetic deficiency of alpha$_1$-antitrypsin is rare and doctors can test for it in individuals with a family history of the deficiency. There is no cure for emphysema, but there are treatments available. The best prevention against emphysema is to refrain from smoking.

Nephritis usually occurs in children. Symptoms include hypertension, decreased renal function, hematuria, and edema. Glomerulonephritis (GN) is a more precise term to describe nephritis.. An antigen-antibody complex, produce nephritis. Nephritis damages normal kidney tissue and, if left untreated, nephritis can lead to kidney failure and death. (Nephritis by Sahar Fathallah-Shaykh, MD located at www.emedicine.com/ped/topic1561.htm)

Malfunctions of the circulatory system

Cardiovascular diseases are the leading cause of death in the United States. Cardiac disease usually results in either a heart attack or a stroke. A heart attack occurs when cardiac muscle tissue dies, usually from coronary artery blockage. A stroke occurs when nervous tissue in the brain dies due to the blockage of arteries in the head.

Atherosclerosis causes many heart attacks and strokes. Plaques form on the inner walls of arteries, narrowing the area in which blood can flow. Arteriosclerosis occurs when the arteries harden from the plaque accumulation. A healthy diet low in saturated fats and cholesterol and regular exercise can prevent atherosclerosis. High blood pressure (hypertension) also promotes atherosclerosis. Diet, medication, and exercise can reduce high blood pressure and prevent atherosclerosis.

Malfunctions of the immune system

The immune system attacks both microbes and cells that are foreign to the host. This is the problem with skin grafts, organ transplantations, and blood transfusions. Antibodies to foreign blood and tissue types already exist in the body. Antibodies will destroy the new blood cells in transfused blood that is not compatible with the host. There is a similar reaction with tissue and organ transplants.

The major histocompatibility complex (MHC) is responsible for the rejection of tissue and organ transplants. This complex is unique to each person. Cytotoxic T-cells recognize the MHC on the transplanted tissue or organ as foreign and destroy these tissues. Suppression of the immune system with various drugs can prevent this reaction. The complication with immune suppression is that the patient is more susceptible to infection.

Autoimmune disease occurs when the body's own immune system destroys its own cells. Lupus, Grave's disease, and rheumatoid arthritis are examples of autoimmune diseases. There is no way to prevent autoimmune diseases. Immunodeficiency is a deficiency in either the humoral or cell mediated immune defenses. HIV is an example of an immunodeficiency disease.

Malfunctions of the digestive system

Gastric ulcers are lesions in the stomach lining. Bacteria are the main cause of ulcers, but pepsin and acid can exacerbate the problem if the ulcers do not heal quickly enough.

Appendicitis is the inflammation of the appendix. The appendix has no known function, but is open to the intestine and hardened stool or swollen tissue can block it. The blocked appendix can cause bacterial infections and inflammation leading to appendicitis. The swelling cuts the blood supply, killing the organ tissue. If left untreated, this leads to rupture of the appendix allowing the stool and the infection to spill out into the abdomen. This condition is life threatening and requires immediate surgery. Symptoms of appendicitis include lower abdominal pain, nausea, loss of appetite, and fever.

Malfunctions of the nervous and endocrine systems

Diabetes is the best-known endocrine disorder. A deficiency of insulin resulting in high blood glucose is the primary cause of diabetes. Type I diabetes is an autoimmune disorder. The immune system attacks the cells of the pancreas, ending the ability to produce insulin. Treatment for type I diabetes consists of daily insulin injections. Type II diabetes usually occurs with age and/or obesity. There is usually a reduced response in target cells due to changes in insulin receptors or a deficiency of insulin. Type II diabetics need to monitor their blood glucose levels. Treatment usually consists of dietary restrictions and exercise.

Hyperthyroidism is another disorder of the endocrine system. Excessive secretion of thyroid hormones is the cause. Symptoms are weight loss, high blood pressure, and high body temperature. The opposite condition, hypothyroidism, causes weight gain, lethargy, and intolerance to cold.

There are many nervous system disorders. The degeneration of the basal ganglia in the brain causes Parkinson's disease. This degeneration causes a decrease in the motor impulses sent to the muscles. Symptoms include tremors, slow movement, and muscle rigidity. Progression of Parkinson's disease occurs in five stages: early, mild, moderate, advanced, and severe. In the severe stage, the person is confined to a bed or chair. There is no cure for Parkinson's disease. Private research with stem cells is currently underway to find a cure for Parkinson's disease.

COMPETENCY 2.0 UNDERSTAND PHYSICAL GROWTH AND DEVELOPMENT

SKILL 2.1 Phases and characteristics of physical development during infancy, childhood, adolescence, adulthood.

Motor development is defined as how spontaneous actions within the structured central nervous system, environmental and social fields assemble temporary linkings of muscle groups to do different and sequential kinds of work. Although the sequence of motor development is fairly uniform across children, differences still may exist individually. A baby may develop slowly in one stage but then "catch up" in the next. Concern arises if a child motor development is delayed in many motor skill areas, not just one.

Listed below are the stages, sequences and characteristics of motor development and motor learning and the general ages each stage occurs:

1. Newborn to 2 months: while laying on the stomach, an infant pushes up on arms and lifts and holds head up
2. 2 to 6 months: Uses hands to support self in sitting, roles from back to tummy, while standing with support, accepts entire weight with legs
3. 7 to 8 months: Sits and reaches for toys without falling, moves from tummy or back into sitting position, creeps on hands and knees with alternate arm and leg movement (crawling)
4. 9 to 11 months: Pulls to stand and cruises along furniture, stands alone and takes several independent steps
5. 12 months on: Walks independently and seldom falls, squats to pick up toy(s)

Age appropriate specific motor skills development:

- By age 3, walking is automatic
- By age 4, the child has mostly achieved an adult style of walking
- By age 4-5, a child can run, stop and turn
- By age 5-6, a child's running is in the style of an adult running
- Between ages 3 and 6, a child should be able to climb using ladders
- By age 6, children can hop and jump longer than before distances

After age six, it becomes increasingly more difficult to describe changes and differences in motor skills among children. Changes are usually to fine motor skills only and are more subtle. By age nine, eye-hand coordination normally has developed to a good point and growth continues on, but slowly from this point. The motor skills that have been achieved are stabilized and perfected.

At the onset of puberty, motor skills of faster running, jumping higher, throwing further and balancing and coordination increase. Of course all of these skills are dependent on body size, weight, age and strength.

Adult physical development (considered, developmentally, to be age 18 and over) is characterized by the completion of the process of physical maturation. This means full adult height has usually been attained by age 18 and all secondary sexual characteristics, such as size of penis and breasts are completed.

Throughout adulthood the ability to increase muscle size, lessen or increase body weight, cardiovascular health and overall quality of life, is immensely dependent on the level of fitness of each adult. As the adult ages, the metabolism decreases as well as many other changes within the internal systems of the body. Having and maintaining a healthy level of fitness throughout one's life is imperative in possessing optimal, overall wellness.

SKILL 2.2 Developmental issues during human growth.

Physical educators need to be aware of developmental issues during student's growth and how these issues may affect a student's physical activities and abilities. Increasingly, osteoporosis is being accepted as a pediatric issue. The prepubertal human skeleton is very sensitive to the mechanics involved in physical activity. Daily, including after school activities as well as during school physical activities combined should not exceed three hours for student's that are prepubertal, usually referring up to age 13. Up to three hours of physical activity will achieve for the student the bone benefits that are needed at the prepubertal age. With this being said, physical activity should and needs to start at this level, prepubertal ages, in order to obtain the maximal peak bone mass that is potentially achievable for the student. Beginning physical activity prior to the pubertal growth spurt stimulates both bone and skeletal hypertrophy (increase) to a greater degree than in normal growth non-physcially active student's.

Prepubertal student's that are non-physically active have been shown to being diagnosed with increasing cases of osteoporosis both in childhood as well as into adulthood.
Entering into the adolescent age sports such as gymnastics and football are recommended to increase peak bone mass. These sports both require muscle strain as well as are both weight bearing. This is no guarantee but certaintly thwarts off the opportunity for osteoporosis developing.

Additional developmental issues to consider during human growth are body image and composition, delayed growth that continues, appetite changes that do not subside and clumsiness or trouble balancing, based on the norm.

SKILL 2.3 Factors that influence growth and development

The effect of factors such as gender, age, environment, nutrition and heredity are crucial in understanding childhood and adolescence development. From a physiological standpoint, specifically in regard to the onset of puberty, girls normal range of onset is ages 8-14 in, while boys normal onset of puberty is ages is 9-15. While environment (social, cultural and ambient) is considered to play a huge role in the age onset of both genders, it is more and more widely accepted and believed that the determination of the onset of puberty is also controlled by interactions between the brain and the pituitary glands.

Environment has and continues to be considered an extremely important contributing factor in of all aspects of childhood and adolescent growth and development. Children that live in environments that include substance abuse tend to exhibit behavioral, emotional and social problems more readily than those that are not. Additionally, without adequate, healthy and appropriate social role models, children tend to have a difficult time forming positive social relationships with their peers. Without positive child-adult patterns, children's social growth and development is impaired. Research indicates without these, children have a much more difficult time acquiring skills needed later in life to carry out adult roles. Also, in adolescence, without proper social skill development through environmental influences, such as mentioned, healthy child-adult patterns, positive adult role models, students tend to have significant behavioral and development, negative consequences (i.e., sexual interactions at any early age, high risk behaviors, substance use/abuse, cigarette smoking, mental health problems). Other environment factors affecting growth and development of children and adolescents are adequate cleanliness, air quality, health care, neighborhood safety, parental involvement and family income.

Children's environments also need to provide or adequate sleep. Sufficient sleep for childred is considered to be 7-8 hours a night and is critical for all areas of childhood growth and development. During sleep, the body performs many important cleansing and restoration tasks. Most importantly, the immune and excretory systems clear waste and repair cellular damage that accumulates in the body each day. Lack of sufficient amount of sleep leaves the body much more vulnerable and susceptable to infections and disease. Additionally, if children do not get a sufficient amount of sleep, their concentration levels, emotional control and equilibrium as well as their energy for activity will be negatively affected.

Proper nutrition positively influences the quality of a child's physical activity level, their cognitive abilities, such as classroom concentration, as well as their emotional and mental growth. Adequate and proper nutrition is vital to encourage and support all aspects of children's development. Obesity, chronic diseases, high blood pressure, type 2 diabetes and even heart disease are just a few of the negative consequences that can result from poor nutrition in children.

Additionally, obese children are at greater risk of becoming obese adults. Daily calorie intact is determined by children's age, size and their activity level. Meals should mainly include whole grains, low-fat or nonfat dairy products, vegetables, fruits and lean meats. It is also recommended introducing fish into children's diets along with reductions in the intake of beverages high in sugar and highly salted foods.

Heredity factors affecting children's growth and development include height, susceptibility to diseases and genetic predispositions to mental illnesses and developmental disabilities.

Societal – We cannot separate students from the societies in which they live. The general perceptions around them about the importance of fitness activities will necessarily have an effect on their own choice regarding physical activity. We should consider the "playground to PlayStation" phenomenon and the rising levels of obesity among Americans negative societal influences on motor development and fitness.

Psychological – Psychological influences on motor development and fitness include a student's mental well being, perceptions of fitness activities, and level of comfort in a fitness-training environment (both alone and within a group). Students experiencing psychological difficulties, such as depression, will tend to be apathetic and lack both the energy and inclination to participate in fitness activities. As a result, their motor development and fitness levels will suffer. Factors like the student's confidence level and comfort within a group environment, related to both the student's level of popularity within the group and the student's own personal insecurities, are also significant. It is noteworthy, though, that in the case of psychological influences on motor development and fitness levels, there is a more reciprocal relationship than with other influences. While a student's psychology may negatively affect their fitness levels, proper fitness training has the potential to positively affect the student psychologically, thereby reversing a negative cycle.

Cultural – Culture is a significant and sometimes overlooked influence on a student's motor development and fitness, especially in the case of students belonging to minority groups. Students may not feel motivated to participate in certain physical activities, either because they are not associated with the student's sense of identity or because the student's culture discourages these activities. For example, students from cultures with strict dress codes may not be comfortable with swimming activities. On the same note, students (especially older children) may be uncomfortable with physical activities in inter-gender situations. Educators must keep such cultural considerations in mind when planning physical education curricula.

COMPETENCY 3.0 UNDERSTAND SEQUENCES AND CHARACTERISTICS OF MOTOR DEVELOPMENT

SKILL 3.1 Sequences and characteristics of motor skill development.

SEE ALSO DOMAIN I., Skill 2.1

The development of motor skills in children is a sequential process. We can classify motor skill competency into stages of development by observing children practicing physical skills. The sequence of development begins with simple reflexes and progresses to the learning of postural elements, locomotor skills, and, finally, fine motor skills. The stages of development consider both innate and learned behaviors.

STAGES OF MOTOR LEARNING

Stage 1 – Children progress from simple reflexes to basic movements such as sitting, crawling, creeping, standing, and walking.

Stage 2 – Children learn more complex motor patterns including running, climbing, jumping, balancing, catching, and throwing.

Stage 3 – During late childhood, children learn more specific movement skills. In addition, the basic motor patterns learned in stage 2 become more fluid and automatic.

Stage 4 – During adolescence, children continue to develop general and specific motor skills and master specialized movements. At this point, factors including practice, motivation, and talent begin to affect the level of further development.

SKILL 3.2 Relationship of motor development to physical, cognitive, psychosocial, and emotional development.

Studies show that physical activity leads to improved motor development in children. Physical activity also enables various other progressions that shape the mind and personality of an individual. Such developments, which are the result of physical activity, include cognitive, psychosocial, and emotional growth.

Physical education in the Cognitive Domain contributes to academic achievement; is related to higher thought processes via motor activity; contributes to knowledge of exercise, health and disease; contributes to an understanding of the human body; contributes to an understanding of the role of physical activity and sport in the American cultures; and contributes to the knowledgeable consumption of goods and services.

Teaching methods that facilitate cognitive learning include:

1. **Problem Solving** - The instructor presents the initial task and students come to an acceptable solution in unique and divergent ways.

2. **Conceptual Theory** - The instructor's focus is on acquisition of knowledge.

3. **Guided Inquiry** – Stages of instructions strategically guide students through a sequence of experiences.

Initially, performing skills will be variable, inconsistent, error-prone, "off-time," and awkward. Students' focus will be on remembering what to do. Instructors should emphasize clear information of the skill's biomechanics and correct errors in gross movement that effect significant parts of the skill. So students will not be overburdened with too much information, they should perform one or two elements at a time. Motivation results from supportive and encouraging comments. Peer to peer encouragement is also very useful and helpful.

Techniques to facilitate cognitive learning include:

1. **Transfer of learning** – Identifying similar movements of a previous learned skill present in a new skill.

2. **Planning for slightly longer instructions and demonstrations** as students memorize cues and skills.

3. **Using appropriate language** for the level of the students.

4. **Conceptual Thinking** - giving more capable students more responsibility for their learning.

Aids to facilitate cognitive learning include:

1. Frequent assessments of student performance

2. Movement activities incorporating principles of biomechanics

3. Laser discs, computers and software

4. Videorecordings of student performance

Physical education in the Affective (Emotional) Domain contributes to self-actualization, self-esteem, and a healthy response to physical activity; contributes to an appreciation of beauty; contributes to directing one's life toward worthy goals; emphasizes humanism; affords individuals the chance to enjoy rich social experiences through play; assists cooperative play with others; teaches courtesy, fair play, and good sportsmanship; contributes to humanitarianism. By improving one's motor development through physical activity, the emotional growth of a student is only increased.

Teaching methods and techniques that facilitate affective development include:

1. **Fostering a positive learning environment** – Instructors should create a comfortable, positive learning environment by encouraging and praising effort and emphasizing respect for others.

2. **Grouping students appropriately** – Instructors should carefully group students to best achieve equality in ability, age, and personalities.

3. **Ensure all students achieve some level of success** – Instructors should design activities that allow students of all ability levels to achieve success and gain confidence.

Physical Education and the Psychosocial Domain:

By participating in physical activities, students develop various aspects of the self that are easily applicable to other settings (e.g., the workplace). Communication is one skill that improves enormously through participation in sports and games. Students will come to understand that skillful communication can contribute to a better all-around outcome, whether it be winning the game or successfully completing a team project. They will see that effective communication helps to develop and maintain healthy personal relationships, organize and convey information, and reduce or avoid conflict.

Physical activities also teach students how to set personal goals. At first, one can set a physical goal such as running one mile in eight minutes. After accomplishing that specific feat, the student will feel capable and will be more willing to set greater goals in various fields within his life.

Finally, physical activities teach perseverance, the importance of following directions, leadership, and teamwork. Recovering from competitive loses and withstanding personal and team setbacks help develop perseverance. All games and sports have rules that participants must follow in order to participate. Leadership and teamwork are both integral parts of team sports. In the team sport setting, participants learn how to work together and lead others to achieve a common goal. These skills are invaluable in real life and the workplace.

Examples of activities that promote cooperation and collaboration are all team sports. Basketball, baseball, softball, volleyball, soccer and football are all team sports. There has to be cooperation and collaboration among the teammates, otherwise there would be absolutely no success. Whereas individual sports such as tennis, swimming, wrestling, track and field (with the exception of relays) and golf are not as dependent on collaboration and cooperation in order for the athletes in these sports achieving successs. Irregardless of a team or individual sports, all organized physical activites involve some element of cooperation and collaboration. Rules, regulations, schedules and sportsmanship are fundamental requirements of physical activity and sports.

SKILL 3.3 Factors that influence motor development and performance.

SEE ALSO DOMAIN I., Skill 2.3

AFFECT OF GENDER ON MOTOR DEVELOPMENT

The differences between males and females in motor performance result from certain biological and environmental influences. Generally, people perceive the males as stronger, faster, and more active than females. This higher activity level can stem from childhood behaviors influenced by certain environmental factors and superior motor performance results largely from the biological make up of males versus females.

In most cases, the male body contains less fat mass and more muscle mass than the female body. In addition, the type of muscle differs between males and females. Males have more fast-twitch muscle fibers allowing for more short duration, high intensity movements such as jumping and sprinting. In addition, males generally, but not always, display better coordination. Females have proved their superiority at certain activities, such as skipping, and tend to display better fine movements, such as neater handwriting.

Certain environmental factors also contribute to the gender differences in motor performance. As children, boys tend to be more physically active. Society expects boys to participate in sports and play games that involve running around, such as tag and foot races. On the other hand, society expects girls to be more social and less active. They participate in activities such as playing with dolls. In addition, parents rarely ask girls to perform tasks involving manual labor.

While these sedentary tasks have value, it is important for both males and females to participate in an adequate amount of physical activity each day. If children develop this type of active lifestyle early in life, they are more likely to maintain it throughout adulthood.

COMPETENCY 4.0 UNDERSTAND PRINCIPLES OF PERCEPTUAL-MOTOR DEVELOPMENT

SKILL 4.1 Visual, auditory, tactile discrimination and their relationships to motor development.

Visual, auditory, and tactile discrimination greatly affects perceptual-motor development. Those students with visual discrimination problems have trouble taking in information visually and translating it into action. For example, such students have difficulty seeing an instructor perform a dance step and copying the appropriate action. Those students with auditory discrimination problems have difficulty taking in verbal information and translating it into action. Such students may not be physically able to hear directions or they may not be able to translate what they hear into appropriate action. Finally, those students with tactile discrimination problems have trouble feeling the difference between objects. Touch and feel are integral parts of many motor skills.

Perceptual-motor development refers to one's ability to receive, interpret, and respond successfully to sensory signals coming from the environment. Because many of the skills acquired in school rely on the child's knowledge of his body and its relationship to the surroundings, good motor development leads directly to perceptual skill development. Development of gross motor skills leads to successful development of fine motor skills, which in turn help with learning, reading, and writing. Adolescents with perceptual-motor coordination problems are at risk for poor school performance, low self-esteem, and inadequate physical activity participation. Without a successful intervention, these adolescents are likely to continue avoiding physical activity and experience frustration and teasing from their peers. Children with weak perceptual-motor skills may be easily distracted or have difficulty with tasks requiring coordination. They spend much of their energy trying to control their bodies, exhausting them so much that they physically cannot concentrate on a teacher-led lesson.

SKILL 4.2 Perceptual-motor development activities.

Perceptual-motor development activities clearly differ from age group to age group. With younger students, activities are directed toward body awareness movements. Specific examples include kickball, tetherball, calisthenics, tag and dance.

Middle school and high school student activities are more directed toward fine motor skill development. Activity examples are the team sports, such as basketball drills and volleyball drills (using basic and advanced fundamentals) and individual sports, such as jogging/running, golf and tennis.

Unfortunately, with some student's perceptual-motor coordination problems do not just go away and they don't self-repair. At this point, physical educator's must use adaptive games to help increase perceptual-motor development. Practice and maturity are necessary for children to develop greater coordination and spatial awareness. Physical education lessons should emphasize activities that children enjoy doing, are sequential, and require seeing, hearing, and/or touching. Discussing with students the actual steps involved in performing a fundamental skill is a great benefit. Activities and skills that instructors can break down and teach in incremental steps include running, dribbling, catching or hitting a ball, making a basket in basketball, and setting a volleyball. Recommended strategies include introducing the most fundamental skill of each activity, practicing in a variety of settings with an assortment of equipment, sequentially introducing the next fundamental, implementing modified lead-up games to ensure practice of the necessary skills, and incorporating students into an actual game situation. Other useful activities are:

- Teacher-directed games and activities that provide the teacher the opportunity to work on specific skills and movements
- Success-oriented tag, chase and dodge games, using a non-threatening, interactive approach to give students a sense of belonging and self confidence regardless of their physical abilities. This in turn will aid in the development

COMPETENCY 5.0 UNDERSTAND PRINCIPLES OF MOTOR LEARNING

SKILL 5.1 Theories and models of motor learning.

Motor learning is defined as understanding how processes that subserve movement are developed and factors that facilitate or inhibit this development. Motor learning also includes a modification and/or improvement of a motor behavior proficiency through practice and experience conditions.

It is important for physical education teachers to understand the process involved in learning and performing motor skills because it enables the teacher to:

1. Design and deliver appropriate activities within the curriculum
2. Conduct more effective practice and rehabbing of motor skills

There are many different theories and models of motor learning. Among all theories there lies a thread of consistency. Motor learning is broken down into three stages:

- Element Learning: Learn elements of a skill- student needs teacher input and observational example
- Associate Stage: Learn how these component skills link together- student needs teacher input and observational example for the correct sequence of skill building (Example: A student understands and can demonstrate a proper forehand on the tennis court. Teacher now introduces the skill of how to hit a top-spin forehand).
- Autonomous Stage: Performance does not require attention. Instruction not needed.

It is important for the physical education teacher to include in developing motor learning of their students, processing information, visual skills, practice, feedback and timing.

SKILL 5.2 Principles of practice, retention, readiness, etc. as they relate to motor skill acquisition.

Motor-development learning theories that pertain to a general skill, activity, or age level are important and necessary for effective lesson planning. Motor-skill learning is unique to each individual, but does follow a general sequential skill pattern, starting with general gross-motor movements and progressing to specific or fine motor skills. Teachers must begin instruction at a level where all children are successful and proceed through the activity to the point where frustration for the majority is hindering the activity. You need to learn the fundamentals or basics of a skill, or subsequent learning of more advanced skills becomes extremely difficult. Students must spend enough time learning beginning skills so they become second nature. Teaching in small groups with enough equipment for everyone is essential. Practice sessions that are too long or too demanding can cause physical and/or mental burnout. Teaching skills over a longer period of time, but with slightly different approaches, helps keep students attentive and involved as they internalize the skill. The instructor can then begin to teach more difficult skills while continuing to review the basics. If the skill is challenging for most students, allow plenty of practice time so that they retain it before having to use it in a game situation.

Visualizing and breaking the skill down mentally is another way to enhance the learning of motor movements. Instructors can teach students to "picture" the steps involved and see themselves executing the skill. Start by teaching the skill with a demonstration of the necessary steps. Beginning with the first skill taught, introduce key language terms and have students visualize themselves performing the skill. For example, when teaching dribbling in basketball, begin by demonstrating the skill and the component steps. Show students how to push the ball down toward the ground, let it bounce back up, and push it down again. Next, give students equipment to practice with while standing still. Then, add movement while dribbling. Finally, demonstrate how to control your dribbling while being guarded by another student.

SKILL 5.3 Methods for promoting recognition and use of similar movement concepts and elements in a variety of skills.

Physical education helps students to develop motor skills and movement patterns that they can use in a variety of physical skills, including different types of sports events. We can identify similar movement patterns in diverse sports skills. For example, there is a similar movement pattern in underhand throwing and underhand volleyball serving.

Various experts have studied movement concepts and elements. To help students and athletes realize the underlying similarities between movements while doing a variety of skills, teachers and instructors often use various techniques. For example, instructors can demonstrate similarity in movement to the students and athletes through effective data collection. They can do this by videotaping the lessons and movements. This helps the performers to recognize visually the similarity in movement between the different skills that they perform.

SKILL 5.4 Techniques for detecting errors in motor performance.

RECOGNIZE ERRORS IN SKILL PERFORMANCE.

Because performing a skill has several components, determining why a participant is performing poorly may be difficult. Instructors may have to assess several components of a skill to determine the root cause of poor performance and appropriately correct errors. **An instructor should have the ability to identify performance errors by observing a student's mechanical principles of motion during the performance of a skill. Process assessment** is a subjective, observational approach to identifying errors in the form, style, or mechanics of a skill.

A strategy to help to correct skill performance is repetition. Assign a peer who has the skill mastered to work with one who does not. By working together and through repetition of the correct skill performance, the struggling student can overcome and develop the skill performance they need the majority of the time. With a fellow peer assisting them, the student's tend to be more motivated to develop the correct skill performance.

RECOGNIZE APPROPRIATE OBJECTIVE MEASUREMENTS OF FUNDAMENTAL SKILLS.

Instructors should use **product assessments**, quantitative measures of a movement's end result, to evaluate objectively fundamental skills. Objective measurements such as , how far, how fast, how high, or how many are the quantitative measures of product assessments.

A **criterion-referenced test** (superior to a standardized test) or a **standardized norm-referenced test** can provide valid and reliable data for objectively measuring fundamental skills.

USE SKILL ASSESSMENT INFORMATION TO PLAN ERROR CORRECTION STRATEGIES.

Instructors can use criterion-referenced standards to diagnose weaknesses and correct errors in skill performance because such performance standards define appropriate levels of achievement. , Instructors, however can also use biomechanical instructional objectives. The following list describes the skill assessment criteria in several representative activities:

- Archery - measuring accuracy in shooting a standardized target from a specified place.

- Bowling - calculating the bowling average attained under standardized conditions.

- Golf - the score after several rounds.

- Swimming - counting the number of breaststrokes needed to swim 25 yards.

Error correction activities examples include, involve re-teaching the non-learned skills, breaking the skill down into individual parts and showing video's of the skill being performed correctly.

SKILL 5.5 Techniques for modifying sports and games to promote the use of combinations of motor skills.

TECHNIQUES TO ENHANCE SKILL PERFORMANCE AND STRATEGY

Playing complex games requires the combination of skills, the use of skills in more complex ways, and relation to others in both offensive and defensive settings. Sequentially progressive activities allow students to acquire the psychomotor, cognitive, and affective skills necessary for participation in complex games. There are four stages of complex skill development.

Stage One concerns **controlling an object.** For striking or throwing objects, students can consistently practice sending objects to a specified location, developing control of the force that accomplishes the objective. For catching or collecting, students can practice control by securing possession of an object from any direction, level, or speed. For carrying and propelling, students can practice maintaining control of an object by moving in different directions and at different paces. Developing control begins with the completion of easily attainable objectives and progresses gradually to more difficult objectives involving movement and different directions, levels, and force.

Stage Two also concerns controlling an object, however, combining skills increases difficulty. Instructors should stress rules to constrain the execution of skills. Drills such as passing and dribbling belong in stage two.

Stage Three focuses on **offense and defense**, utilizing correct skill performance. Students should now be able to control objects; therefore, the focus shifts to obtaining and maintaining possession, as well as offensive and defensive strategies in the midst of opponents. Net activities and keep-away games help develop this stage. In addition, instructors can add more offensive and defensive players, boundaries, scorekeeping, and conduct rules. Students develop by adjusting their responses with each element introduced to the activity.

Stage Four involves **complex activity.** Students execute the complete activity and modified activities that allow participation by all students. Continuous play is important; thus, the instructor may have to modify rules or a part of the activity to keep the flow of the game constant (e.g. eliminating free throws/kicks, substituting volleyball serve with a throw, initiating play out-of-bounds).

DOMAIN II. HEALTH-RELATED PHYSICAL FITNESS

COMPETENCY 1.0 UNDERSTAND COMPONENTS OF PHYSICAL FITNESS AND PRINCIPLES OF TRAINING

SKILL 1.1 Basic components of physical fitness.

There are five health related components of physical fitness: **cardio-respiratory or cardiovascular endurance, muscle strength, muscle endurance, flexibility, and body composition.**

Cardiovascular endurance – the ability of the body to sustain aerobic activities (activities requiring oxygen utilization) for extended periods.

Muscle strength – the ability of muscle groups to contract and support a given amount of weight.

Muscle endurance – the ability of muscle groups to contract continually over a period of time and support a given amount of weight.

Flexibility – the ability of muscle groups to stretch and bend.

Body composition – an essential measure of health and fitness. The most important aspects of body composition are body fat percentage and ratio of body fat to muscle.

Wellness has two major components: understanding the basic human body functions and how to care for and maintain personal fitness, and developing an awareness and knowledge of how certain everyday factors, stresses and personal decisions can affect one's health. Teaching fitness needs to go along with skill and activity instruction. Life-long fitness and the benefits of a healthy lifestyle need to be part of every P.E. teacher's curriculum. Cross-discipline teaching and teaching thematically with other subject matter in classrooms would be the ideal method to teach health to adolescents.

BASIC TRAINING PRINCIPLES

The **Overload Principle** is exercising at an above normal level to improve physical or physiological capacity (a higher than normal workload).

The **Specificity Principle** is overloading a particular fitness component. In order to improve a component of fitness, you must isolate and specifically work on a single component. Metabolic and physiological adaptations depend on the type of overload; hence, specific exercise produces specific adaptations, creating specific training effects.

The **Progression Principle** states that once the body adapts to the original load/stress, no further improvement of a component of fitness will occur without the addition of an additional load.

There is also a **Reversibility-of-Training Principle** in which all gains in fitness are lost with the discontinuance of a training program.

MODIFICATIONS OF OVERLOAD

We can modify overload by varying **frequency, intensity, and time**. Frequency is the number of times we implement a training program in a given period (e.g. three days per week). Intensity is the amount of effort put forth or the amount of stress placed on the body. Time is the duration of each training session.

SKILL 1.2   Aerobic versus anaerobic conditioning.

Physical education is vital for the all-around development of every individual. Rigorous physical training and exercise also burn fats and calories and increases energy and cardiovascular functions within the body. Metabolic training and cardiovascular conditioning refer to physical training exercises that increase the capacity of energy pathways to store and deliver energy for activity. Research reveals the two main types of metabolic training, aerobic and anaerobic conditioning, are the center of controversy and debate.

Aerobic conditioning utilizes oxygen and includes activities performed from low to moderate intensity for more than 2 minutes. Aerobic activities allow oxygen to release energy through metabolism. On the other hand, anaerobic conditioning always takes place without oxygen. It includes activities that take place at medium or high intensity. It also releases energy, but without deriving it from oxygen.

In other words, aerobic conditioning raises the heart rate up to its Target Heart Rate zone, whereas, anaerobic does not raise the heart rate up to this zone. Examples of aerobic conditioning activities are: running, jogging, walking fast, aerobic classes, swimming, continuous bike riding. In other words, any activity that sustains the heart rate in the target zone (220-age times .60 to.80). Examples of anaerobic conditioning activities are weightlifting and golf. These activities do increase the heart rate, however they do not sustain the increased heart rate. In between the increase in heart rate, there are periods of rest.

Aerobic conditioning benefits primarily the cardiovascular system whereas anaerobic conditioning benefits muscle strength.

Aerobic conditioning has a number of advantages. It greatly enhances the oxygen using ability of our heart, lungs, and other systems. It is also the cornerstone of athletic conditioning programs because it serves as a basis for physical conditioning.

SKILL 1.3 Short- and long-term effects of physical activity on the cardiorespiratory, muscular, skeletal, neural, and endocrine systems.

DISEASES AND CONDITIONS CAUSED IN PART BY A LACK OF PHYSICAL ACTIVITY

Physical activity is essential in optimizing both physical and mental health.

Hypertension, atherosclerosis, arteriosclerosis, heart attack, stroke, congestive heart failure, angina, osteoporosis, osteoarthritis, obesity, adult on-set diabetes, gout, gall bladder disorders, ulcers, osteoporosis, cancer, lordosis, poor posture, neck, leg, knee, and foot problems are all diseases and conditions caused in part by a lack of physical activity.

Long-term physiological benefits of physical activity include:
- improved cardio-respiratory fitness
- improved muscle strength
- improved muscle endurance
- improved flexibility
- more lean muscle mass and less body fat
- quicker rate of recovery
- improved ability of the body to utilize oxygen
- lower resting heart rate
- increased cardiac output
- improved venous return and peripheral circulation
- reduced risk of musculoskeletal injuries
- lower cholesterol levels
- increased bone mass
- cardiac hypertrophy and size and strength of blood vessels
- increased number of red cells
- improved blood-sugar regulation
- improved efficiency of thyroid gland
- improved energy regulation
- increased life expectancy
- Increased bone density
- Increased connective tissues strength
- Increased lean body mass
- Anaerobic power and capacity
- Improved blood-lipid ratios
- Aids in body composition management

Studies within the last year have also been shown to prove that physical activity plays a vital role in the management of arthritis. Regular physical activity can keep the muscles around affected joints strong, decrease bone loss and may help control joint swelling and pain. Regular activity replenishes lubrication to the cartilage of the joint and reduces stiffness and pain.

Short term benefits of physical activity on the major systems of the body are:

- the metabolism speeds up, aiding in weight loss
- increased and enhanced energy
- improved sleep
- decreased anxiety
- improved mood and well being
- promotes a state of relaxation
- increased stamina
- decreased fatique

SKILL 1.4   Interactions among the body systems in producing movement.

The structure and function of the human body adapts greatly to physical activity and exertion. When challenged with any physical task, the human body responds through a series of integrated changes in function that involve most, if not all, of its physiological systems. Movement requires activation and control of the musculoskeletal system. The cardiovascular and respiratory systems provide the ability to sustain this movement over extended periods. When the body engages in exercise training several times, each of these physiological systems undergoes specific adaptations that increase the body's efficiency and capacity.

When the body works, it makes great demand on every muscle of the body. Either the muscles have to 'shut down' or they have to do work. The heart beats faster during strenuous exercise so that it can pump more blood to the muscles, and the stomach shuts down during strenuous exercise so that it does not waste energy that the muscles need. Exercising makes the muscles work like motor that use up energy in order to generate force. Muscles, also known as 'biochemical motors', use the chemical adenosine triphosphate (ATP) as an energy source.

Different types of systems, such as the glycogen-lactic acid system, help muscles perform. Such systems help in producing ATP, which is extremely vital to working muscles. Aerobic respiration, which also helps in releasing ATP, uses the fatty acids from fat reserves in muscle and helps produce ATP for a much longer period of time.

The following points summarize the process of bodily adaptation to exercise:

• Muscle cells use the ATP they have floating around in about 3 seconds.

• The phosphagen system initiates and supplies energy for 8 to 10 seconds.

• If exercise continues longer, the glycogen-lactic acid system kicks in.

• Finally, if exercise continues, aerobic respiration takes over. This would occur in endurance events such as an 800-meter dash, marathon run, rowing, cross-country skiing, or distance skating.

Physical activity affects the cardiovascular and musculoskeletal systems the most. However, it also helps in proper functioning of metabolic, endocrine, and immune systems.

SKILL 1.5   Energy systems used during exercise.

SEE ALSO DOMAIN II., Skill 1.4

In order to help muscles perform their duty, there are different types of systems such as the Glycogen-Lactic Acid System that provide energy. Such systems help in producing ATP, which is extremely vital for proper muscle function. Of the systems, aerobic respiration, which also helps in releasing ATP, uses the fatty acids from fat reserves in muscle and helps in producing ATP for the longest period of time.

SKILL 1.6   Factors that affect physical fitness and performance.

SEE ALSO DOMAIN I., Skill 2.3

The effect of factors such as gender, age, environment, nutrition, heredity and substance abuse is also crucial in understanding adolescent fitness performance. Girls mature earlier than boys do, but boys quickly catch up and grow larger and stronger. Age, combined with maturity level, influences a child's physical strength, flexibility, and coordination. Good nutrition positively influences the quality of a child's physical activity level, while poor nutrition has the opposite effect. Adverse environmental conditions such as high heat or poor air quality strongly affect activity level. Students that inherit favorable physical characteristics will perform better and with more ease than those who aren't so fortunate. Substance abuse of any sort – alcohol, tobacco, or drugs – is a detriment to physical performance.

Dealing with factors that are out of the teacher's control requires both structure and flexibility. When necessary, make adjustments amongst the students and/or the activity. For example, when teaching a student how to throw a softball, the teacher should not hesitate to pair girls with boys if their maturity and strength levels are similar. If the distance is too far for some pairs, move them closer. If some pairs are more advanced, challenge them by increasing the partner's distance while continuing to work on accuracy and speed. Add a personal challenge to see how many times they can toss without dropping the ball. Finally, having more advanced students teach their peers that aren't as competent will benefit all students.

SKILL 1.7   Potential health risks and injury prevention techniques.

STRATEGIES FOR INJURY PREVENTION

Participant screening – evaluate injury history, anticipate and prevent potential injuries, watch for hidden injuries and reoccurrence of an injury, and maintain communication.

Standards and discipline – ensure that athletes obey rules of sportsmanship, supervision, and biomechanics.

Education and knowledge – stay current in knowledge of first aid, sports medicine, sport technique, and injury prevention through clinics, workshops, and communication with staff and trainers.

Conditioning – programs should be year long and partipants should have access to conditioning facilities in and out of season to produce more fit and knowledgeable athletes that are less prone to injury.

Equipment – perform regular inspections, ensure proper fit and proper use.

Facilities – maintain standards and use safe equipment.

Field care – establish emergency procedures for serious injury.

Rehabilitation – use objective measures such as power output on an isokinetic dynamometer.

Weather Conditions- use common sense and always err on the side of caution in extreme heat/cold or possible stormy condition weather

PREVENTION OF COMMON ATHLETIC INJURIES

Foot – start with good footwear, foot exercises.

Ankle – use high top shoes and tape support; strengthen plantar (calf), dorsiflexor (shin), and ankle eversion (ankle outward).

Shin splints – strengthen ankle dorsiflexors.

Achilles tendon – stretch dorsiflexion and strengthen plantar flexion (heel raises).

Knee – increase strength and flexibility of calf and thigh muscles.

Back – use proper body mechanics.

Tennis elbow – lateral epicondylitis caused by bent elbow, hitting late, not stepping into the ball, heavy rackets, and rackets that are strung too tight.

Head and neck injuries – avoid dangerous techniques (i.e. grabbing face mask) and carefully supervise dangerous activities like the trampoline.

CARE OF COMMON ATHLETIC INJURIES

The most common injuries that physical education instructors will encounter include muscle sprains and strains, soft tissue injuries, and cuts and bruises. Instructors should apply the RICE principle when caring for muscle sprains, strains, and soft tissue injuries. The RICE principle stands for: rest, ice, compression, and elevation.

- **Rest** – injured students should stop using the injured body part immediately

- **Ice** – the instructor should apply ice to the injured area to help reduce swelling

- **Compression** – the instructor should wrap the injured area to help reduce swelling

- **Elevation** – the student should raise the injured area above the level of the heart

In addition, physical education instructors should have a well-stocked first aid kit that allows the treatment of routine cuts and bruises. Finally, instructors must recognize more serious injuries that require immediate medical attention. For example, injuries to the head or neck require medical attention and extreme caution.

TECHNIQUES AND BENEFITS OF WARMING UP AND COOLING DOWN

Warming up is a gradual 5 to 10 minute aerobic warm-up in which the participant uses the muscles needed in the activity to follow (similar movements at a lower activity). Warm-ups also include stretching of major muscle groups after the gradual warm-up.

The benefits of warming up are:

- preparing the body for physical activity
- reducing the risk of musculoskeletal injuries
- releasing oxygen from myoglobin
- warming the body's inner core
- increasing the reaction of muscles
- bringing the heart rate to an aerobic conditioning level

Cooling down is similar to warming up - a moderate to light tapering-off vigorous activity at the end of an exercise session.

The benefits of cooling down are:

- redistributing circulation of the blood throughout the body to prevent pooling of blood
- preventing dizziness
- facilitating the removal of lactic acid

COMPETENCY 2.0 UNDERSTAND THE DEVELOPMENT AND MAINTENANCE OF CARDIORESPIRATORY ENDURANCE

SKILL 2.1 Principles and activities for developing aerobic endurance.

The term aerobic refers to conditioning or exercise that requires the use of oxygen to derive energy. Aerobic conditioning is essential for fat loss, energy production, and effective functioning of the cardiovascular system. Aerobic exercise is difficult to perform for many people and participants must follow certain principles and activities in order to develop aerobic endurance.

Slow twitch muscle tissue, fueled by oxygen, power aerobic activities. For the body to sustain aerobic activity for an extended period of time, the heart must pump oxygen-rich blood to the muscles of the body. When the heart tires due to insufficient cardiorespiratory fitness, the quantities of oxygen delivered to the muscles decreases to levels that cannot sustain the activity.

Other physiological processes involved in aerobic endurance include the respiratory system (which must take sufficient air into the body and efficiently supply oxygen to the blood), the blood itself (which must efficiently carry oxygen), the circulatory system (that takes blood to the muscles and then returns it to the heart), and the muscles themselves (which must efficiently extract oxygen from the blood).

Tips that aid in developing and building aerobic endurance include working out for extended periods at the target heart rate, slowly increasing aerobic exercises, exercising for three or four times per week, and taking adequate rest to help the body recover. Exercising in the target heart rate zone for 30-45 minute periods is the most important principle in the development of aerobic endurance. Submaximal intensity activities, such as walking and slow jogging, are effective aerobic activities that improve aerobic endurance without unnecessary strain on the body.

The amount of overload required to maintain or improve an individuals fitness level is based on the following components:

- **Frequency** = Fitness requires regular exercise. Depending on the individual's fitness level and fitness goals, the frequency varies. The minimum frequency starts at 3 days per week
- **Intensity** = The intensity level increases when an individual exercises harder than the normal routine or level of activity. Intensity includes various levels such as exercising in or above the normal target heart-rate zone
- **Time** = The time or duration occurs when you exercise for a specific period of time. The minimum duration is 20 minutes

Progression for cardiovascular fitness:

- begin at a frequency of 3 days/week and work up to no more than 6 days/week

- begin at an intensity near the target heart rate (THR) threshold and work up to 80% of THR

- begin at 20 minutes and work up to 60 minutes

Examples of activities that develop aerobic endurance (keeping the heart rate in the Target Heart Rate zone for at least 20 minutes* 220-age times .60 * include:

- running or jogging
- brisk walking
- swimming
- biking

SKILL 2.2   Techniques for assessing and monitoring heart rate and endurance levels.

We can measure cardiorespiratory fitness in a number of ways. The simplest way is for the students to check their resting heart rate. To do this, the students should:

- Find their pulse in any point of the body where an artery is close to the surface (e.g., wrist [radial artery], neck [carotid artery], or the elbow [brachial artery]).

- Count the number of beats felt within one minute..

We usually express resting heart rate in "beats per minute" (bpm). For males, the norm is about 70 bpm. For women, the norm is about 75 bpm. This rate varies between people and the reference range is normally between 60 bpm and 100 bpm. It is important to note that resting heart rates can be significantly lower in athletes, and significantly higher in the obese.

Another way to measure cardiorespiratory fitness is by having students determine their Target Heart Rate (THR). The Target Heart Rate, or Training Heart Rate, is a desired heart rate range that is reached during aerobic exercise. This range allows a student's heart and lungs to receive the most benefit from a workout. There are three methods used to measure a student's THR discussed in SKILL 3.2. Students should check their heart rates frequently during activity to ensure they train within their THR zones.

VALID PHYSICAL FITNESS TESTS TO MEASURE CARDIORESPIRATORY FITNESS

Cardiorespiratory fitness tests – maximal stress test, sub maximal stress test, Bruce Protocol, Balke Protocol, Astrand and Rhyming Test, PWC Test, Bench Step Test, Rockport Walking Fitness Test, and Cooper 1.5 Mile Run/Walk Fitness Test.

TARGET HEART RATE ZONE AND HEART RATE MONITORS

The target heart rate (THR) zone is another common measure of aerobic exercise intensity. Participants find their THR and attempt to raise their heart rate to the desired level for a certain period of time. Students can use electronic heart rate monitors that constantly track heart rate during physical activity. Such monitors often alert students when they enter and leave their THR, allowing for adjustment of activity level. There are three ways to calculate the target heart rate.

1. METs (maximum oxygen uptake), which is 60% to 90% of functional capacity.

2. Karvonean Formula = [Maximum heart rate (MHR) – Resting heart rate (RHR)] x intensity + RHR.

MHR= 220 - Age

Intensity = Target Heart Range (which is 60% - 80% of MHR - RHR + RHR).

THR = (MHR - RHR) x .60 + RHR to (MHR - RHR) x .80 + RHR

3. Cooper's Formula to determine target heart range is:

THR = (220 - AGE) x .60 to (220 - AGE) x .80.

Cooper's Formula is the most widely used method among physical educators.

SKILL 2.3   Appropriate aerobic activities for various developmental levels and purposes.

Aerobics are a fundamental component of every physical education or training program. Aerobic activities are necessary for everyone because they are central to weight reduction, cardiovascular fitness, muscular strength development, and performance in all sports events.

Appropriate aerobic activities for various developmental levels vary from low and moderate intensity exercises to high intensity ones. Low and moderate intensity activities include doing household work, walking, playing with children, and working on the lawn. High-intensity aerobic activities include jogging, cycling, participating in sports such as ice or roller-skating, downhill skiing, and swimming. Treadmills and other equipment help create strenuous aerobic exercises.

Instructors and students must take care while undertaking such high-intensity aerobic exercises, because they can be highly strenuous and taxing on muscles, especially during the initial stages. At this beginning stage, the exercise intensity must be low. With passage of time and development towards higher stages, the student can increase the level and intensity of aerobic exercises.

Whether the goal is to develop the body's ability to undergo high levels of muscular activity or just to remain fit, there are aerobic activities suited to every developmental stage and for every person.

CARDIOVASCULAR ACTIVITIES

Walking is a good generic cardiorespiratory activity for promoting basic fitness. Instructors can incorporate it into a variety of class settings (not only physical education instructors – for example, a Biology class might include a field trip to a natural setting that would involve a great deal of walking). Walking is appropriate for practically all age groups, but can only serve as noteworthy exercise for students who lead a fairly sedentary lifestyle (athletic students who train regularly or participate in some sport will not benefit greatly from walking).

Jogging or **Running** is a classic cardiorespiratory activity in which instructors can adjust the difficulty level by modifying the running speed or the incline of the track. It is important to stress proper footwear and gradual increase of intensity so as to prevent overuse injuries (e.g. stress fractures or shin splints).

Bicycling is another good cardiorespiratory activity that is appropriate for most age groups. Obviously, knowing how to ride a bicycle is a prerequisite, and it is important to follow safety procedures (e.g. ensuring that students wear helmets). An additional benefit of bicycle riding is that it places less strain on the knee joints than walking or running.

Swimming is an excellent cardiorespiratory activity that has the added benefit of working more of the body's muscles, more evenly than most other exercises, without excessive resistance to any one part of the body that could result in an overuse injury. To use swimming as an educational cardiorespiratory activity, there must be qualified lifeguards present, and all students must have passed basic tests of swimming ability.

There are many alternatives for cardiorespiratory activities, for example, **inline skating** and **cross-country skiing**. More importantly, instructors should modify the above exercises to match the developmental needs of the students – for example, younger students should receive most of their exercise in the form of games. An instructor could incorporate running in the form of a game of tag, soccer, or a relay race.

COMPETENCY 3.0 UNDERSTAND THE DEVELOPMENT AND MAINTENANCE OF MUSCULAR STRENGTH AND ENDURANCE

SKILL 3.1 Principles and activities for developing strength and endurance in various muscle groups.

The following displays fitness principle and example applications pertaining to overload, progression, and specificity to muscular strength and endurance development program design.

Overloading for muscle strength:

- **Frequency** = every other day
- **Intensity** = 60% to 90% of assessed muscle strength
- **Time** = 3 sets of 3 - 8 reps (high resistance with a low number of repetitions)

Progression for muscle strength:

- begin 3 days/week and work up to every other day
- begin near 60% of determined muscle strength and work up to no more than 90% of muscle strength
- begin with 1 set with 3 reps and work up to 3 sets with 8 reps

Specificity for muscle strength:

- to increase muscle strength for a specific part(s) of the body, we must target that/those part(s) of the body

MUSCLE ENDURANCE:

Overloading for muscle endurance:

- **Frequency** = every other day
- **Intensity** = 30% to 60% of assessed muscle strength
- **Time** = 3 sets of 12 - 20 reps (low resistance with a high number of repetitions)

Progression for muscle endurance:

- begin 3 days/week and work up to every other day
- begin at 20% to 30% of muscle strength and work up to no more than 60% of muscle strength
- begin with 1 set with 12 reps and work up to 3 sets with 20 reps

Specificity for muscle endurance:

- same as muscle strength

EXERCISES THAT BENEFIT THE MAJOR MUSCLE GROUPS OF THE BODY

Physical fitness activities utilize the following major muscle groups: trapezius, deltoid, pectoralis, latissimus dorsi (lats), obliques, abdominals (abs), biceps, quadriceps, hamstrings, adductors, triceps, biceps, and gluteals or gluteus maximus (gluts).

Dumbbell Shoulder Shrug
(Trapezius)

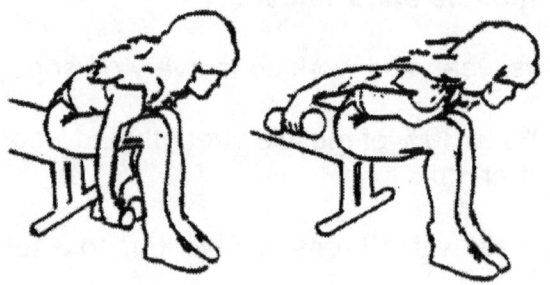

Seated Bent-Over Rear Deltoid Raise
(Rear Deltoids)

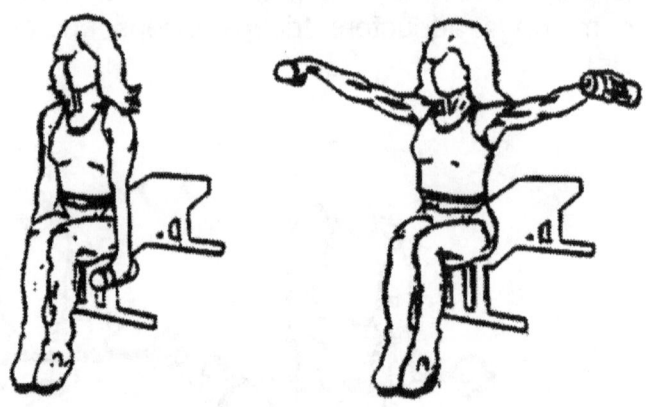

Seated Side Lateral Raise
(Front and Outer Deltoids)

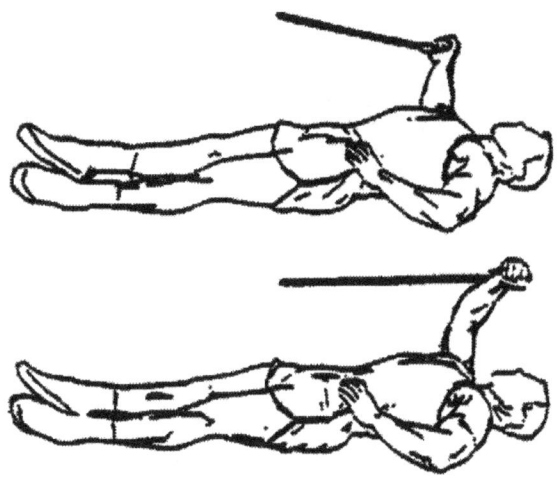

Lying Low-Pulley One-Arm Chest
(Lateral Pectorals)

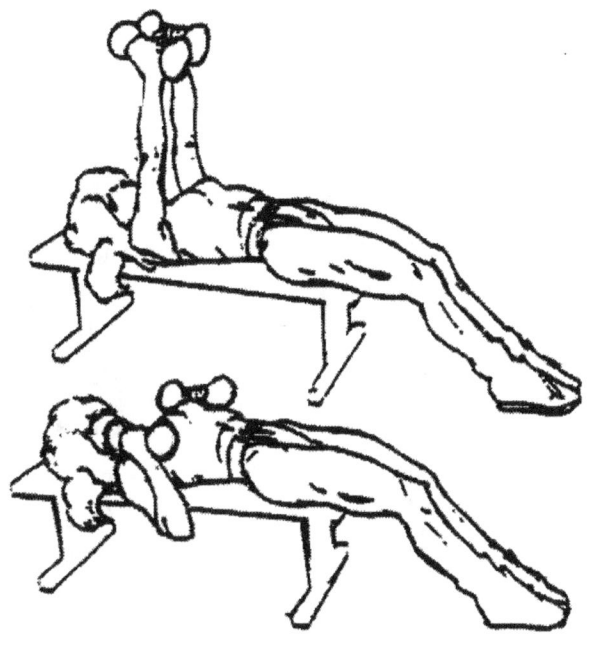

Flat Dumbbell Press
(Pectorals)

Medium-Grip Front-to-Rear Lat Pull Down
(Lats)

Straight-Arm Close-Grip Lat Pull Down
(Lats)

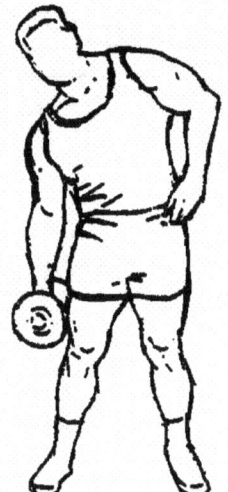 

Dumbbell Side Bend
(Obliques)

Seated Barbell Twist
(Obliques)

Leg Pull-In
(Lower Abdominals)

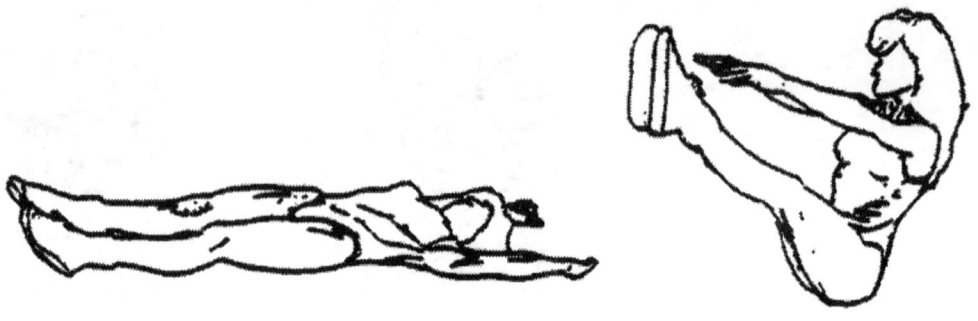

Jackknife Sit-Up
(Upper and Lower Abdominals)

Standing Alternated Dumbbell Curl
(Biceps)

Standing Medium-Grip Barbell Curl
(Biceps)

Standing Close-Grip Easy-Curl-Bar Triceps Curl
(Triceps)

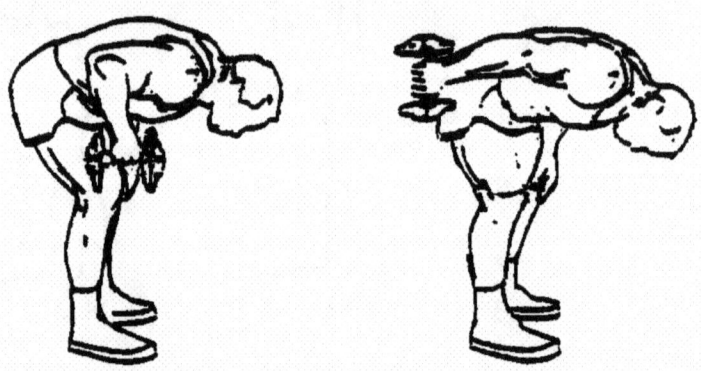

Standing Bent-Over One-Arm-Dumbbell Triceps Extension
(Triceps)

Flat-Footed Medium-Stance Barbell Half-Squat
(Thighs)

Freehand Front Lunge
(Thighs and Hamstrings)

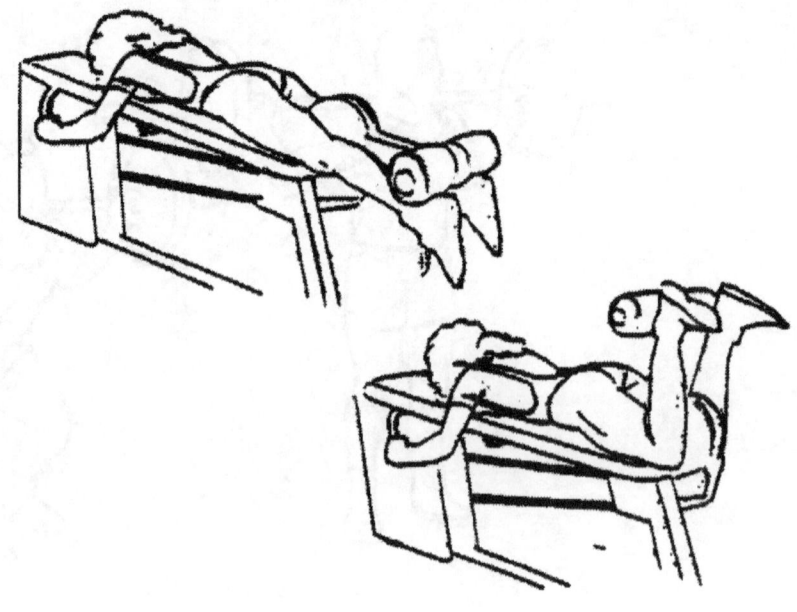

Thigh Curl on Leg Extension Machine
(Hamstrings)

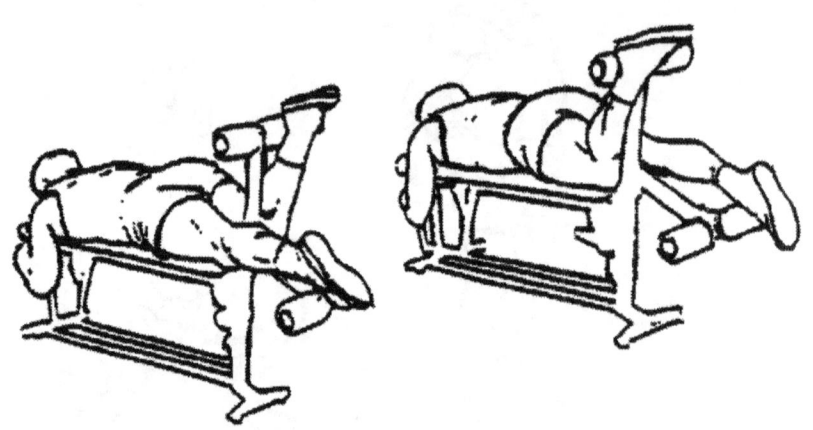

One-at-a-Time Thigh Curl on Leg Extension Machine
(Hamstrings)

Hip Abduction
(Hips)

Hip Adduction
(Inner Thigh)

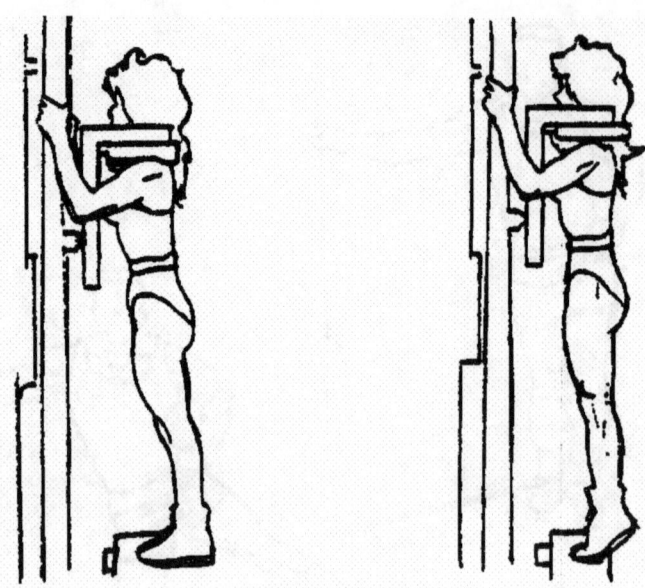

Standing Toe Raise on Wall Calf Machine
(Main Calf Muscles)

Standing Barbell Toe Raise
(Main Calf Muscles)

Hip Extension
(Hips and Thighs)

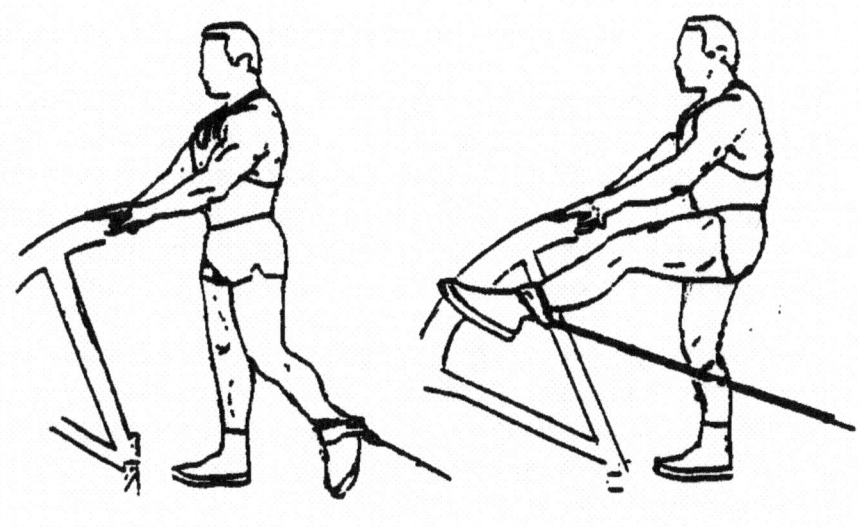

Hip Flexion
(Hip Flexors)

SKILL 3.2 Principles, safety practices, and equipment for progressive resistance exercise

The practice of progressive resistance is an integral part of individual physical development and training programs. As with all other forms of exercise, participants should always follow certain principles and safety practices when performing progressive-resistance exercises.

Principles and safety guidelines that participants should follow include:
- Warm-up prior to performing resistance exercises
- Begin with a low resistance effort, gradually increasing over time (Do not attempt to lift a heavy weight when beginning. Start with lower weights/resistance).
- Gradually increase the number of repetitions for each exercise
- Exercise at least two days and receive adequate rest to achieve proper muscle development
- Perform exercises in a controlled manner
- Perform each exercise through a functional range of motion
- Work in conjunction with instructors who provide adequate feedback and guidance
- Use spotters as necessary

Examples of resistance equipment that can be used for this type of exercise are weights, such as dumbbells and weight machines, stretch ropes, such as seen commonly in Pilates classes and any immovable object can also be used.

SKILL 3.3 Techniques for assessing muscular strength and endurance.

Muscular strength is the maximum amount of force that one can generate in an isolated movement. Physical education teachers can easily assess an improvement or not in a student's muscular strength by making note of the beginning amount of weight a student starts an exercise with and then, in 4 weeks, check and see if the amount of weight the student can left in that same exercise has improved or not. Muscular strength refers to the "max out" weight.

Example: At the beginning of the six weeks, John's maximum amount of weight he can bench press is 110 pounds. After four weeks of gradually increasing the number of reps and weights, John is tested by the teacher and can now bench press a maximum weight of 135 pounds. This type of technique of assessment can be used on all muscle groups.
On the other hand, muscular endurance is the ability of the muscles to perform a sub-maximal task repeatedly or to maintain a sub-maximal muscle contraction for extended periods. In other words, how many times can John, in the example above, consistently, without stopping, bench press 65 pounds? Since his maximum weight is 135 pounds, 65 pounds is a much lower weight and thus a good technique to check his muscle endurance level.

VALID PHYSICAL FITNESS TEST ITEMS TO MEASURE MUSCULAR STRENGTH AND ENDURANCE

Muscle strength tests – dynamometers (hand, back, and leg), cable tensiometer, the 1-RM Test (repetition maximum: bench press, standing press, arm curl, and leg press), bench-squat, sit-ups (one sit up holding a weight plate behind the neck), and lateral pull-down.

Muscle endurance tests – squat-thrust, pull-ups, sit-ups, lateral pull-down, bench-press, arm curl, push-ups, and dips.

SKILL 3.4 Appropriate activities for various developmental levels and purposes.

Physical education instructors should employ a variety of instructional strategies, techniques, and teaching methods to promote student learning. Instructors must also tailor their methods to match the age and developmental level of their students.

STRATEGIES THAT PROMOTE COMPETENCE IN PHYSICAL ACTIVITIES

Instructors must employ a variety of techniques to promote competence in physical activities. Instructors should use verbal instruction, demonstration, practice, and assessment.

Applying techniques that allow students to measure their competence is a very useful strategy for physical education teachers to use. Examples would be mapping, checklist of skills broken down into parts where students would be able to check off a "step" once they have mastered that level of an activity of skill and rewards of stars and so forth by their names on a master, posted chart.

It is important that instructors tailor their techniques to fit the age and skill level of their students. For example, activities for a third grade class will be much simpler than activities for a high school class. In addition, older, more developed students are better able to handle competitive situations than are younger students. Younger and less talented students require a cooperative, stress-free environment to maximize learning.

STRATEGIES THAT PROMOTE POSITIVE ATTITUDES TOWARD FITNESS

One of the most important tasks for physical education instructors is to instill in their students an appreciation of and a positive attitude toward physical fitness. Creating a safe and cooperative learning environment is the best strategy for fostering positive attitudes. Allowing students to explore activities, plan fitness goals, improve personal fitness levels, and generally take responsibility for their own physical selves promotes a positive attitude toward lifelong fitness. Additionally, students need to be taught and have an understanding of the many benefits being physical fit provides. Providing opportunities for many different types of physical activities allows for students to, hopefully find a sport or activity that they enjoy and can continue throughout their lives.

STRATEGIES THAT INVOLVE STUDENTS WITH VARYING INTERESTS AND ABILITIES

SEE SKILL 3.1

A major challenge that physical education instructors face is planning a curriculum that appeals to students of different ability levels and with different interests. Instructors should provide students with a choice of activities to appeal to different interests. Instructors must use a creative approach to inspire students that may not have a natural interest in sports and fitness. Finally, instructors must tailor their lessons to accommodate students of varying abilities and developmental stages. Not all students will be able to perform the same skills and tasks.

COMPETENCY 4.0   UNDERSTAND THE DEVELOPMENT AND MAINTENANCE OF FLEXIBILITY

SKILL 4.1   Principles and activities for developing flexibility.

Flexibility is the range of motion around a joint or muscle. Flexibility has two major components: static and dynamic. Static flexibility is the range of motion without a consideration for speed of movement. Dynamic flexibility is the process of using a desired range of motion at a desired velocity. Flexibility exercises are useful for most athletes.

Good flexibility can help prevent injuries during all stages of life and can keep an athlete safe. To improve flexibility, you can lengthen muscles through activities such as swimming, a basic stretching program, or Pilates. These activities improve your muscles' range of motion, since muscles are the main target of flexibility training. Muscles are the most elastic component of joints while ligaments and tendons are less elastic and resist elongation. Overstretching tendons and ligaments can weaken joint stability and lead to injury.

Coaches, athletes and sports medicine personnel use stretching methods as part of their training routine for athletes. Flexibility exercises help the body to relax and help muscles warm-up for more intense fitness activities.

COMPONENTS OF FLEXIBILITY

Muscles – Muscle is the body's contractile tissue. Its function is to produce force and cause motion (movement within the internal organs and, especially for our purposes, locomotion). Muscles are generally split into Type I (slow twitch) and Type II (fast twitch). Type I muscles carry more oxygen and sustains aerobic activity, whereas, Type II muscles carry less oxygen and powers anaerobic activity. Muscles that are too short can limit flexibility. Individuals who fail to stretch after resistance training can cause the muscles to shorten. The stretch reflex, whereby the opposing muscle will contract in order to prevent over-expansion, can also curtail flexibility (this contraction is generally premature, and part of flexibility training is to re-train the opposing muscle not to contract as quickly).

Joints – Joints allow bones to connect. Their construction allows movement and provides functional mechanical support. Joints are classified as fibrous (connected by collagen), cartilaginous (connected by cartilage), or synovial (capped by cartilage, supported by ligaments, enveloped by the synovial membrane, and filled with synovial fluid). Joint flexibility is limited of range of motion that is imposed by the joint's physical structure orby the lack of flexibility of the muscles, ligaments and tendons.

Ligaments – A ligament is a short band of tough fibrous connective tissue composed mainly of long, stringy collagen fibers. They connect bones to other bones to form a joint. Ligaments can limit the mobility of a joint or prevent certain movements altogether. Ligaments are slightly elastic and under tension they will gradually lengthen. Ligaments that are too short may curtail flexibility by limiting a joint's range of motion.

Tendons – A tendon (or sinew) is a tough band of fibrous connective tissue (similar in structure to ligaments) that connects muscle to bone or muscle to muscle. Tendons are composed mainly of water, type-I collagen, and cells called tenocytes. Most of the strength of tendons stems from the parallel, hierarchical arrangement of densely packed collagen fibrils, which have great strength, little extensibility, and no ability to contract.

EVALUATING FLEXIBILITY

Standard methods of evaluating flexibility include the sit and reach test and having students try to touch their hands behind their backs. Instructors can devise additional flexibility tests to evaluate the range of motion of specific joints. In these cases, the tests should reflect practical function.

VALID PHYSICAL FITNESS TEST ITEMS TO MEASURE FLEXIBILITY

Flexibility tests – Flexibility tests include sit and reach, Kraus-Webber Floor Touch Test, trunk extension, forward bend of trunk, Leighton Flexometer, shoulder rotation/flexion, and goniometer.

DEVELOPING FLEXIBILITY

Overloading for flexibility:

- **Frequency**: 3 to 7 days/week

- **Intensity**: stretch muscle beyond its normal length

- **Time**: 3 sets of 3 reps holding stretch 15 to 60 seconds

Progression for flexibility:

- begin 3 days/week and work up to every day

- begin stretching with slow movement as far as possible without pain, holding at the end of the range of motion (ROM) and work up to stretching no more than 10% beyond the normal ROM

- begin with 1 set with 1 rep, holding stretches 15 seconds, and work up to 3 sets with 3 reps, holding stretches for 60 seconds

Specificity for flexibility:

- ROM is joint specific

SKILL 4.2 Appropriate activities for various developmental levels and purposes.

Every student, depending on their developmental level, responds differently to the same flexibility training activities. Through varying the type of activity performed, it is possible that all students can and will progress at a similar rate throughout the school year, based on their own developmental levels.

Keep in mind the definition of flexibility, the ability to move a joint through its full range of movement without experiencing any pain or discomfort. For each flexibility activity that the teacher plans, they need to remind each student to respect their own, individual levels and to not push past the level to pain or discomfort. Remind them, it is not a competition. Flexibility is a progression. Over time, through activities, student's individual flexibility levels will improve. This will aid in overall physical stability and injury prevention.

Any activity that encourages students to bend, stretch and reach are good flexibility activities.

Below are examples of flexibility activities that are appropriate for students of various developmental levels:

- Calisthenics (sit and reach, any and all types of stretching of the body)
- Dancing
- Gymnastics
- Yoga
- Martial Arts
- Balancing activities (students walk on a low-to-the-floor balance beam)

COMPETENCY 5.0 UNDERSTAND HOW TO DEVELOP AND MAINTAIN LEVELS OF BODY COMPOSITION THAT PROMOTE GOOD HEALTH

SKILL 5.1 Knowledge of nutrition and weight control.

The components of nutrition are **carbohydrates, proteins, fats, vitamins, minerals, and water.**

Carbohydrates – the main source of energy (glucose) in the human diet. The two types of carbohydrates are simple and complex. Complex carbohydrates have greater nutritional value because they take longer to digest, contain dietary fiber, and do not excessively elevate blood sugar levels. Common sources of carbohydrates are fruits, vegetables, grains, dairy products, and legumes.

Proteins – are necessary for growth, development, and cellular function. The body breaks down consumed protein into component amino acids for future use. Major sources of protein are meat, poultry, fish, legumes, eggs, dairy products, grains, and legumes.

Fats – a concentrated energy source and important component of the human body. The different types of fats are saturated, monounsaturated, and polyunsaturated. Polyunsaturated fats are the healthiest because they may lower cholesterol levels, while saturated fats increase cholesterol levels. Common sources of saturated fats include dairy products, meat, coconut oil, and palm oil. Common sources of unsaturated fats include nuts, most vegetable oils, and fish.

Vitamins and minerals – organic substances that the body requires in small quantities for proper functioning. People acquire vitamins and minerals in their diets and in supplements. Important vitamins include A, B, C, D, E, and K. Important minerals include calcium, phosphorus, magnesium, potassium, sodium, chlorine, and sulfur.

Water – makes up 55 – 75% of the human body. Essential for most bodily functions. Attained through foods and liquids.

DETERMINE THE ADEQUACY OF DIETS IN MEETING THE NUTRITIONAL NEEDS OF STUDENTS.

Nutritional requirements *vary from person-to-person.* General guidelines for meeting adequate nutritional needs are: *no more than 30% total caloric intake from fats* (preferably 10% from saturated fats, 10% from monounsaturated fats, 10% from polyunsaturated fats), *no more than 15% total caloric intake from protein* (complete), *and at least 55% of caloric intake from carbohydrates* (mainly complex carbohydrates).

Exercise and diet help maintain proper body weight by equalizing caloric intake and caloric output.

RECOGNIZE FALLACIES AND DANGERS UNDERLYING SELECTED DIET PLANS.

High Carbohydrate diets (i.e. Pritikin, Bloomingdale's) can produce rapid or gradual weight loss, depending on caloric intake. Vitamin and mineral supplements are usually needed because protein intake is low. These diets may or may not recommend exercising or permanent lifestyle changes, which are necessary to maintain one's weight.

High-Protein Diets promote the same myths, fallacies, and results as high carbohydrate diets. High-protein diets also require vitamin and mineral supplements. In addition, these diets are usually high in saturated fats and cholesterol because of the emphasis on meat products.

Liquid Formulas that are physician/hospital run (i.e. Medifast, Optifast) provide 800 or fewer calories a day consumed in liquid form. Dieters forgo food intake for 12 to 16 weeks in lieu of the protein supplement. Liquid diets require vitamin and mineral supplements and close medical supervision. Food is gradually reintroduced after the initial fast. These diets can result in severe and/or dangerous metabolic problems in addition to an irregular heartbeat, kidney infections and failure, hair loss, and sensations of feeling cold and/or cold intolerance. These diets are very expensive and have a high rate of failure.

Over-The-Counter Liquid Diets (i.e. Slimfast) are liquid/food bar supplements taken in place of one or more meals per day. Such diets advocate an intake of 1,000 calories daily. Carbohydrate, protein, vitamin, and mineral intake may be so low that the diet can be as dangerous as the medically supervised liquid diets when relied on for the only source of nutrition. Because of the lack of medical supervision, the side effects can be even more dangerous.

Over-The-Counter Diet Pills/Aids and Prescription Diet Pills (appetite suppressants) have as their main ingredient phenyl propanolamine hydrochloride [PPA]. Keeping weight off by the use of these products is difficult. Dizziness, sleeplessness, high blood pressure, palpitation, headaches, and tachycardia are potential side effects of these products. Moreover, prescription diet pills can be addictive.

Low Calorie Diets (caloric restricted) are the most misunderstood method of weight loss. However, restricting the intake of calories is the way most people choose to lose weight. All the focus is on food, creating anxiety over the restriction of food - especially favorite foods. These diets are also difficult to maintain and have a high failure rate. Like the other diets, once the diet is over, dieters regain weight quickly because they fail to make permanent behavioral changes. Side effects of caloric restriction include diarrhea, constipation, Ketosis, a lower basal metabolic rate, blood-sugar imbalances, loss of lean body tissue, fatigue, weakness, and emotional problems. Dietary supplements are needed. Those who choose **fasting** (complete caloric restriction) to lose weight can deplete enough of the body's energy stores to cause death.

SKILL 5.2   Identify the relationship of body type to body composition and motor performance.

Recognizing individual students' physical changes helps with understanding how their physiques affect motor performance. The child's physique has a definite affect on their motor performance. Somatype, another term for body type, deals with how fat, muscular, and linear your body is. The three body types are endomorph, mesomorph, and ectomorph. Everyone is some combination of the three types, with one classification usually prevailing over the others. You cannot change your body type but you can modify it through your eating habits and level of physical exercise, which in turn affects your body-fat percentage. Certain body types are more suited for certain sports, but it doesn't mean you won't be successful if your somatype is different from what's mentioned. Somatype classification is important because it shows how children differ in body physique and how vital it is that instruction accommodates individual differences.

Endomorphs are naturally "large" or "big boned" with a pear-shaped bodies and a slow metabolism. Endomorphs are often very strong, but have little speed. They experience difficulty at most sports, including both aerobic and anaerobic activities. Individual sports such as shot or discus throwing in track, wrestling, and judo are activities well suited for endomorphs.

Mesomorphs are "muscular" with an hourglass figure, broad shoulders, small waist, strong thighs, fast metabolism, and little body fat. Often called "natural athletes," they participate with ease and look forward to physical competition of any sort. These children perform best in team sports that require strength, speed, and agility such as football and baseball, or individual sports such as swimming.

Ectomorphs, often called "skinny," are extremely thin, with very little body fat, little or no muscle development, and an ultra fast metabolism. Ectomorphs have difficulty gaining weight or muscle mass. Because they lack power and strength, they are better suited for aerobic endurance activities such as cross-country running, many track and field events such as the high or long jump, sprints, relays, and middle-distance running.

SKILL 5.3 Ways in which nutrition and eating habits may affect physical development and health.

Nutrition and exercise are closely related concepts important to student health. An important responsibility of physical education instructors is to teach students about proper nutrition and exercise and how they relate to each other. The two key components of a healthy lifestyle are consumption of a balanced diet and regular physical activity. Nutrition absolutely plays an enormous role in physical performance. Proper nutrition produces high energy levels and allows for peak performance. Inadequate or improper nutrition can impair physical performance and lead to short-term and long-term health problems (e.g. depressed immune system and heart disease, respectively). Regular exercise improves overall health. Benefits of regular exercise include a stronger immune system, stronger muscles, bones, and joints, reduced risk of premature death, reduced risk of heart disease, improved psychological well-being, and weight management.

SKILL 5.4 Select valid physical fitness test items to measure body composition.

Body composition includes the relative amount of fat, bone, and other vital parts of the body. The measurement of body composition allows for the estimation of body tissues, organs, and their distribution in a living person without inflicting harm. It is important to recognize that there is no measurement method that is error-free. Rather, the principle is to make every individual aware of body composition evaluation techniques and the fact that monitoring body composition is an exemplary method for maintaining a maximum level of physical fitness. The different methods of evaluating body composition include skinfold tests, electronic impedance, and body mass index.

Skinfold tests estimate body fat percentage by measuring the thickness of skinfolds at specific sights on the body with calipers. While the skinfold test is not a valid measurement of body fat percentage, they are useful in monitoring progress in body fat reduction.

Electronic impedance is a technique that estimates body fat percentage by measuring the conductive potential of the body. A bioimpedance meter sends a small electrical current through the body and measures conductive potential. Lean tissue (i.e. muscle, bone, ligaments) is more conductive than fat tissue because of the higher water content.

Body mass index (BMI) is a measure of body fat based on height and weight. BMI is a generic measurement that is not specific to the individual. BMI labels individuals as underweight, normal, overweight, or obese. While BMI is a useful tool in estimating body fat and determining a target weight, it can overestimate fatness in muscular or athletic people.

SKILL 5.5 Appropriate activities for developing and maintaining levels of body composition that promote good health.

IMPLEMENTING THE PRINCIPLES OF OVERLOAD, PROGRESSION, AND SPECIFICITY TO IMPROVE BODY COMPOSITION

Overloading to improve body composition:

- **Frequency**: daily aerobic exercise
- **Intensity**: low
- **Time**: approximately one hour

Progression to improve body composition:

- begin daily
- begin a low aerobic intensity and work up to a longer duration (see cardio-respiratory progression)
- begin low-intensity aerobic exercise for 30 minutes and work up to 60 minutes

Specificity to improve body composition:

- increase aerobic exercise and decrease caloric intake

THE ROLE OF EXERCISE AND DIET IN THE MAINTENANCE OF PROPER WEIGHT

Exercise and diet maintains proper body weight by equalizing caloric intake and caloric output.

HEALTH RISK FACTORS IMPROVED BY APPROPRIATE BODY COMPOSITION

Health risk factors improved by maintaining an appropriate body composition include cholesterol levels, blood pressure, stress related disorders, heart diseases, over fatness and obesity disorders, early death, certain types of cancer, musculoskeletal problems, mental health, and susceptibility to infectious diseases.

DOMAIN III.   **MOVEMENT SPORTS ACTIVITIES**

COMPETENCY 1.0   **UNDERSTAND PRINCIPLES OF BIOMECHANICS AND THEIR APPLICATION TO MOVEMENT ACTIVITIES**

SKILL 1.1   **Knowledge of mechanical principles of body management.**

CONCEPTS OF EQUILIBRIUM AND CENTER OF GRAVITY APPLIED TO MOVEMENT

As body parts move independently of one another, the body's mass redistributes thus changing the location of the body's center of gravity. Body parts also move to change the body's base of support from one moment to the next to cope with imminent loss of balance.

The entire center of gravity of the body shifts in the same direction of movement of the body's segments. As long as the center of gravity remains over the base of support, the body will remain in a state of equilibrium. The more the center of gravity is situated over the base, the greater the stability. A wider base of support and/or a lower center of gravity enhances stability. To be effective, the base of support must widen in the direction of the force produced or opposed by the body. Shifting weight in the direction of the force in conjunction with widening the base of support further enhances stability.

Constant interaction of forces that move the body in the elected direction results in dynamic balance. The smooth transition of the center of gravity changing from one base of support to the next produces speed.

CONCEPT OF FORCE APPLIED TO MOVEMENT

Force is any influence that changes the state of motion of an object. We must consider the objective of movement.

Magnitude of Force – force must overcome the inertia of the object and any other resisting forces for movement to occur.

For linear movement, force applied close to the center of gravity requires a smaller magnitude of force to move the object than does force applied farther from the center of gravity.

For rotational movement, force applied farther from the center of gravity requires a smaller magnitude of force to rotate the object than does force applied closer to the center of gravity.

For objects with a fixed point, force applied anywhere other than through the point of fixation results in object rotation.

Energy – the capacity to do work. (The more energy a body has the greater the force with which it can move something [or change its shape] and/or the farther it can move it).

Movement (mechanical energy) has two types:

1. Potential energy (energy possessed by virtue of position, absolute location in space or change in shape).

    A. Gravitational potential energy - potential energy of an object that is in a position where gravity can act on it.

    B. Elastic (strain) potential energy - energy potential of an object to do work while recoiling (or reforming) after stretching, compressing, or twisting.

2. Kinetic energy (energy possessed by virtue of motion that increases with speed).

Force Absorption - maintaining equilibrium while receiving a moving object's kinetic energy without sustaining injury or without losing balance while rebounding. The force of impact is dependent on an object's weight and speed. The more abruptly kinetic energy is lost, the more likely injury or rebound occurs. Thus, **absorbing force requires gradually decelerating a moving mass by utilization of smaller forces over a longer period of time**. Stability is greater when the force is received closer to the center of gravity.

Striking resistive surfaces - the force of impact per unit area decreases when the moving object's area of surface making contact increases and the surface area that the object strikes increases.

Striking non-resistive surfaces - the force of impact decreases if the moving object's area of surface making contact decreases because it is more likely to penetrate.

The more time and distance that motion stops for a moving object to strike any surface, the more gradually the surface absorbs the force of impact, and the reaction forces acting upon the moving object decrease.

Equilibrium returns easily when the moving body (striking a resistive surface) aligns the center of gravity more vertically over the base of support.

Angular force against a body lessens when the distance between a contacting object and the body decreases and the contact occurs closer to the center of gravity. By widening the base of support in the direction of the moving object stability is increased.

SKILL 1.2 Apply concept of leverage to movement.

CONCEPT OF LEVERAGE APPLIED TO MOVEMENT

First-class lever - the axis is between the points of application of the force and the resistance.

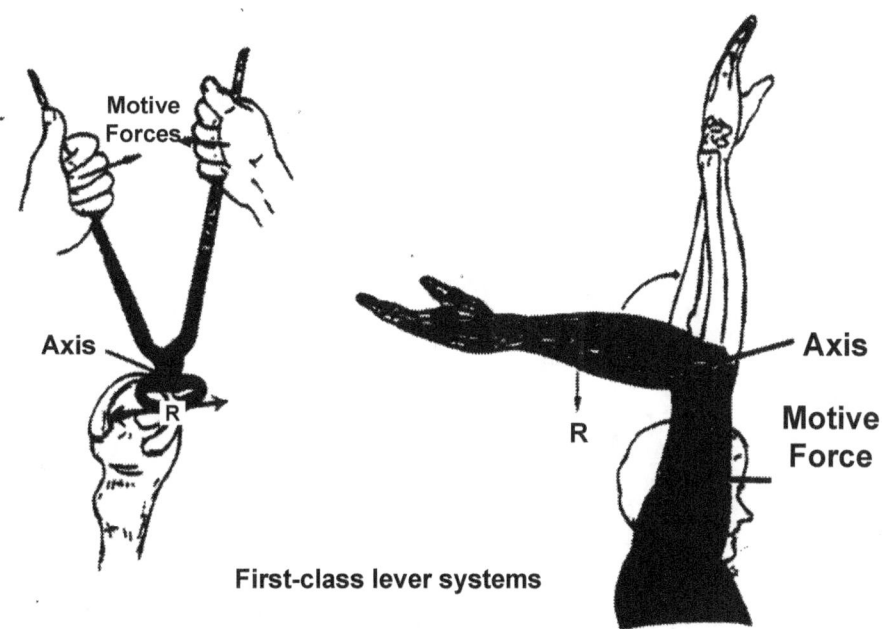

First-class lever systems

Second-class lever - the force arm is longer than the resistance arm (operator applies resistance between the axis and the point of application of force).

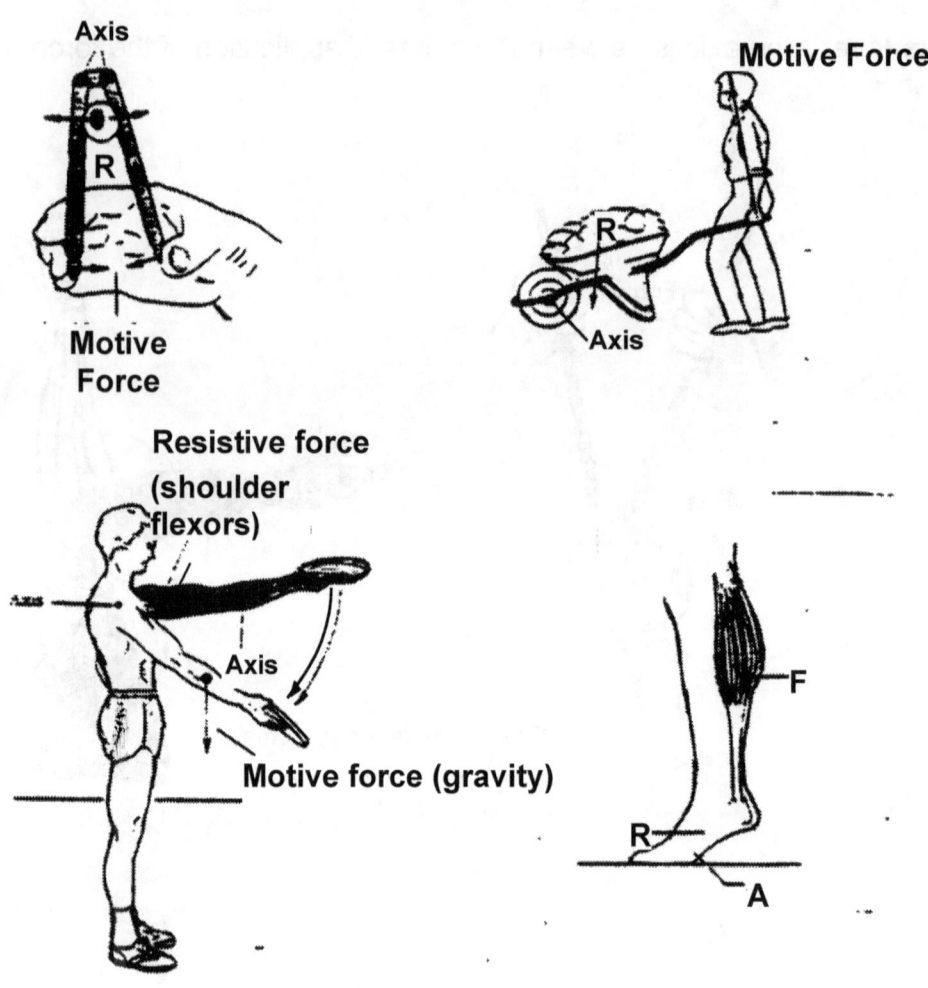

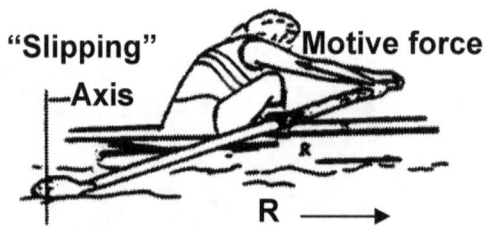

Second-class lever systems

Third-class lever - the force works at a point between the axis and the resistance (resistance arm is always longer than the force arm).

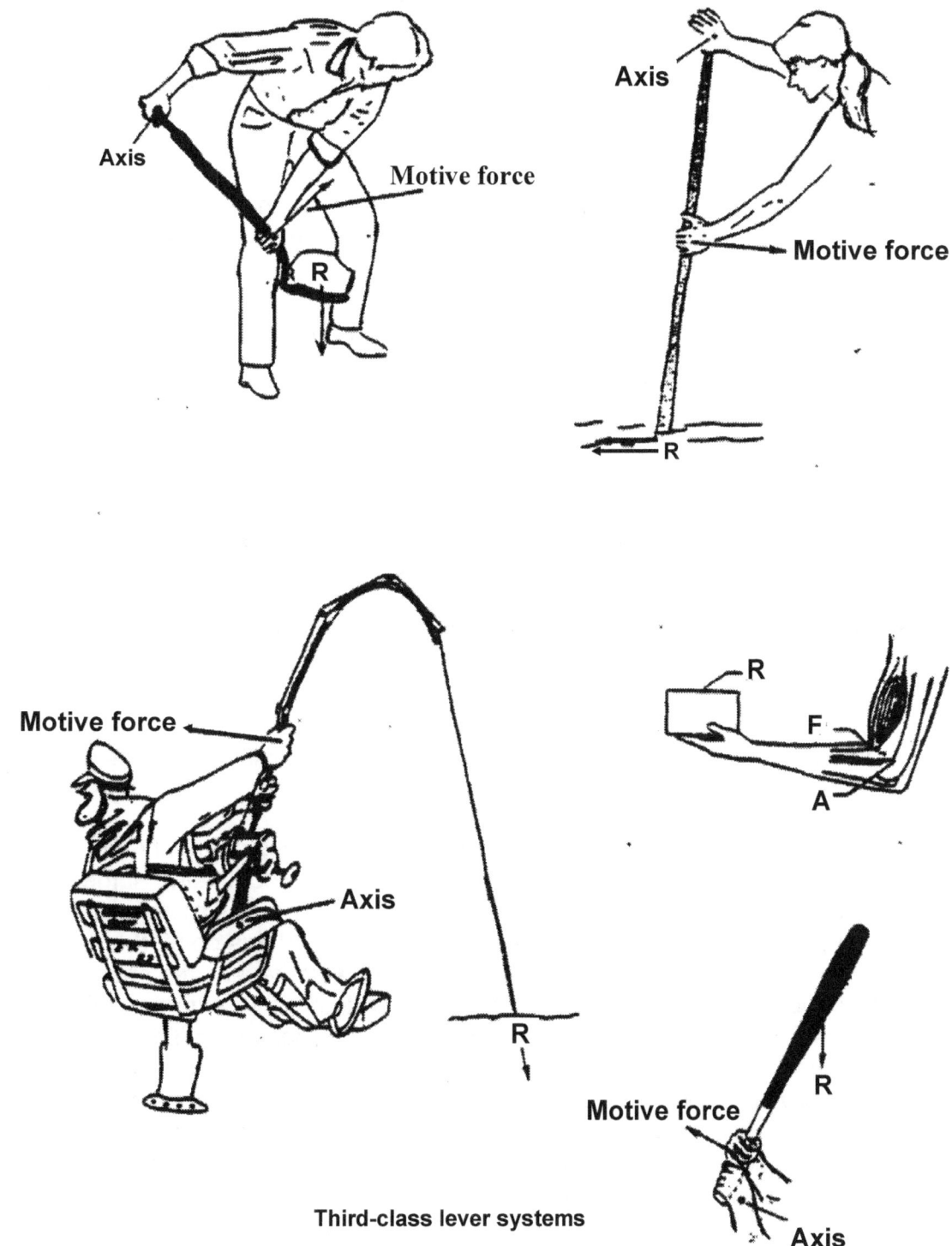

Third-class lever systems

Muscle force is applied where muscles insert on bones.

With a few exceptions, the body consists primarily of third-class levers, with bones functioning as the levers and contracting innervated muscles acting as the fulcrums or by gravity acting on various body masses. As a result, the human body favors speed and range of motion over force.

Because most human body levers are long, their distal ends can move rapidly. Thus, the body is capable of swift, wide movements at the expense of abundant muscle force.

The human body easily performs tasks involving rapid movement with light objects. Very heavy tasks require a device for the body to secure an advantage of force.

Sports instruments increase body levers, thereby increasing the speed of an object's imparting force. However, the use of sports instruments requires more muscle force.

The body's leverage rarely includes one part of the body (a simple, singular lever). Movement of the body is an outcome of a system of levers operating together. However, levers do function in sequence when the force produced by the system of levers is dependent on the speed at the extremity. Many levers function simultaneously for a heavy task (e.g. pushing).

MECHANICAL PRINCIPLES OF MOTION APPLIED TO PHYSICAL EDUCATION ACTIVITIES

1. **Inertia** - tendency of a body or object to remain in its present state of motion; an object will stay in a prescribed straight path and will move at its given speed unless some force acts to change it.

2. **Projecting objects for vertical distance** - the forces of gravity and air resistance prevent vertically projected objects from continuing at their initial velocities. The downward, resistive force of gravity slows a projectile directed upward until it halts (at the peak of vertical path). At this point, the downward force of gravity becomes an incentive force that increases the speed of the object until it confronts another force (the earth or other external object) that slows the object until it stops. When the object stops ascending and begins to descend, gravity alters the object's direction of motion. Air resistance (of still air) always opposes the object's motion. Therefore, an ascending object's air resistance is downward and a descending object's air resistance is upward. An increase in velocity increases air-drag force that decreases the magnitude of the drag as the object moves upward, slowing in velocity. The magnitude of the drag increases as the object moves faster and faster downward. Moreover, the direction and magnitude of the object's acceleration, due to the force of gravity, are constant while direction and magnitude of changes, due to air resistance, are dependent on the object's speed and direction.

An object travels the highest when projected with the greatest velocity, and the object's weight affects neither gravity's upward deceleration nor its downward acceleration. The object's weight, however, is a factor in calculating the net force acting on the object's vertical movement through the air.

- **Projecting the body for vertical distance** - for these activities (e.g. vertical leaping), the height of reach of the hand from the ground is the significant factor. The following three factors determine the body's reach height: 1) the center of gravity's vertical velocity, 2) the center of gravity's height from the ground at takeoff, and 3) the vertical distance of the fingertips relative to the center of gravity at the peak of the jump.

- **Projecting for vertical distance with a horizontal component** - for these activities (e.g. high jumping), a running approach to the point of takeoff produces some horizontal velocity even with a 100% vertical takeoff.

- **Projecting for horizontal distance** - a body will continue to travel horizontally until an external force, usually the ground, halts it. Gravity stops vertical movement while ground friction eventually stops horizontal velocity, preventing any additional horizontal distance. "Air time" increases when the initial upward vertical velocity component is greater. There is a tradeoff between maximum "air time" (determined by vertical velocity) and maximum horizontal distance (determined by horizontal velocity).

- **Horizontal projections where takeoff and landing heights are equal** - maximum horizontal distance occurs when the projection angle is 45-degrees.

- **Horizontal projections where takeoff and landing heights are uneven** – the height of an object's center of gravity depends on a performer's height and his/her location in relation to the ground upon release or impact of the object. The greater the object's travel time forward, the farther the object's distance before landing. Hence, a taller performer has an automatic advantage over a shorter performer who throws with the same projection velocity. In addition, the greater the difference between takeoff and landing heights, the smaller the optimum angle of release - given equal projection velocities.

Projecting objects for accuracy:

- **Vertical plane targets** - accuracy is easiest when using a trajectory that is perpendicular to the target as it coincides with the target face. As projection distance increases, a more curved parabolic path is required.
- **Horizontal plane targets** - the more vertically the projectile arrives at the target (as close to 90 degrees as possible), the greater the likelihood of successfully hitting the target and preventing the object from rolling or sliding away from the target area.

Projecting the body for accuracy - for moving or positioning the body (or its segments) to achieve an ideal/model performance by body maneuvers, the performer projects his body's center of gravity to an imaginary target point in space.

Projecting objects for accuracy when speed may enhance the performance - the performer must increase the angle of projection for slower projection speeds (must consider participant's height).

- **Acceleration** - the movement response (acceleration) of a system depends not only on the net external force applied, but also depends on the resistance to movement change (inertia).

If an object's acceleration is proportional to the applied force, greater force produces greater acceleration. An object's acceleration is inversely proportional to its mass (the greater the mass, the less the acceleration).

- **Angular acceleration** (rate that an object's angular speed or direction changes) - angular acceleration is great when there is a large change in angular velocity in a short amount of time. A rigid body (or segment) encounters angular acceleration or deceleration only when a net external torque is applied. When torque stops, the body reaches and maintains a new velocity until another torque occurs. Acceleration is always in the direction of the acting torque, and the greater the torque, the greater the angular acceleration.

- **Linear acceleration** (time rate of change in velocity) - an object's magnitude of acceleration is significant if there is a large change of velocity in a small amount of time. When the same velocity changes over a longer period of time, acceleration is small. Acceleration occurs only when force is applied. When the force stops, the object/body reaches a new and the object/body continues at the new speed until that a force changes that speed or direction. In addition, the direction of acceleration is the same direction as the applied net force. A large force produces a large acceleration. A small force produces a modest acceleration.

- **Zero/Constant Acceleration** (constant velocity) - there is no change in a system's velocity when the object/body moves at a given velocity and encounters equal, opposing forces. Hence, velocity is constant since no force causes acceleration or deceleration.

- **Acceleration caused by gravity** - a falling object/body continues to accelerate at the rate of 9.8 m/sec. (32 ft/sec.) throughout its fall.

- **Radial acceleration (direction change caused by centripetal force)** - centripetal force is aimed along an illusory line (the circular path) at any instant. Therefore, it is the force responsible for change of direction. The bigger the mass, the greater the centripetal force required. A tighter turn magnifies direction change (radial acceleration), so friction must increase to offset the increased acceleration. Maximum friction (centrifugal force) reduces speed. A combination of the variables mass, radius of curvature, speed of travel, and centripetal force cause radial acceleration.

Action/Reaction - every action has an equal and opposite reaction.

- **Linear motion** - the larger the mass, the more it resists motion change initiated by an outside force.

Body segments exert forces against surfaces they contact. These forces and the reaction of the surfaces result in body movement. For example, a runner propels himself forward by exerting a force on the ground (as long as the surface has sufficient friction and resistance to slipping). The force of the contact of the runner's foot with the ground and the equal and opposite reaction of the ground produces movement. A canoe paddler or swimmer exerts a backward force by pushing the water backwards, causing a specific velocity that is dependent on the stroke's force - as well as the equal and opposite force made by the water pushing forward against the canoe paddle or arm moving the canoe or swimmer forward.

Every torque (angular motion) exerted by one body/object on another has another torque equal in magnitude and opposite direction exerted by the second body/object on the first. Changing angular momentum requires a force that is equal and opposite to the change in momentum.

Performing actions in a standing position requires the counter pressure of the ground against the feet for accurate movement of one or more parts of the body.

COMPETENCY 2.0 UNDERSTAND FUNDAMENTAL MOVEMENT CONCEPTS AND SKILLS

SKILL 2.1 Concepts of time, space, direction, speed, and force.

Research shows that space, direction, and speed are interrelated with movement concepts. Students who understand these concepts will move with confidence and avoid collisions.

A student or player incorporates movement concepts such as space, direction, speed and vision to understand and perform a sport. For instance, a player will determine the appropriate personal space while playing soccer or basketball.

For a player, the concepts are all interconnected. The player has to understand how to maintain or change pathways with speed. This means the player has the ability to change motion and perform well in space or the area that the players occupy on the field.

Time - activities using the concept of time involve students' moving as fast as they can or as slow as they can in specified, timed movement patterns.

Force - activities using the concept of force include students using their bodies to produce an amount of force to move them through space. For example, they can hit balls against the wall with a paddle or jump over objects of various heights.

SKILL 2.2 Techniques for promoting students' application of fundamental movement concepts through exploration of shapes, levels, and pathways.

Movement is the currency of life. Even when at rest, there is movement within our bodies, if only the rise and fall of our chest as we breathe. We move to survive, to learn and to discover. Young students have an insatiable desire for movement. Older students desire for movement may decrease, particularly if it requires physical effort. Using movement concepts through exploration of shapes, levels and pathways, however, involve activities that usually all age students enjoy.

Pathways can be straight, curved or zigzag. Teachers need to explain to the student's that pathways are like designs or shapes that are painted on the floor (feet, legs...) or in the air (hands, head, elbows, arms...) with their body parts. Examples of techniques for using pathways and shapes are:

- instruct students to paint a straight pathway in the air with their hands.
- instruct students to paint a zigzag in the air with their elbows
- instruct students to paint a figure eight on the floor with only their right foot

Additionally example techniques in using just shapes alone are:

- instruct students to make their bodies look like a ball
- instruct students to make their bodies look like a triangle
- instruct students to make their bodies look like a square

Level techniques to promote fundamental movement involve a sequential learning of movement. Beginning with running, hopping, jumping, skipping, catching, throwing, kicking, rolling, balancing, twisting and turning. Through a wide range of activities involving these fundamental levels, students begin to progressively gain control of their movements and can begin to learn to combine them or to build upon them to learn new levels of movements.

SKILL 2.3 Body awareness.

CONCEPT OF BODY AWARENESS APPLIED TO PHYSICAL EDUCATION ACTIVITIES

Body awareness is a person's understanding of his or her own body parts and their capability of movement.

Instructors can assess body awareness by watching students play a game of "Simon Says" and asking the students to touch different body parts. You can also instruct students to make their bodies into various shapes, such as, from straight to round to twisted, to fit into different sized spaces.

In addition, you can instruct children to touch one part of their body to another and to stamp their feet, twist their neck, clap their hands, nod their heads, wiggle their noses, snap their fingers, open their mouths, shrug their shoulders, bend their knees, close their eyes, bend their elbows, or wiggle their toes.

CONCEPT OF SPATIAL AWARENESS APPLIED TO PHYSICAL EDUCATION ACTIVITIES

Spatial awareness is the ability to make decisions about an object's positional changes in space (i.e. awareness of three-dimensional space position changes). Developing spatial awareness requires two sequential phases: 1) identifying the location of objects in relation to one's own body in space, and 2) locating more than one object in relation to each object and independent of one's own body.

An example to increase spatial awareness is plan activities using different size balls, boxes, or hoops. Then, you can have the children move towards and away, under and over, in front of and behind, and inside, outside, and beside the objects.

Common signs of Body Awareness Problems:

Does the student….

- Seem to move awkwardly or stiffly
- Seem to be physically weaker than the other children
- Uses too little or too much force on things (writes way too dark or light, breaks things often..)
- Push, hit or bang other students although he/she is not an aggressive student
- Avoid or crave jumping, crashing, hanging, pulling, pushing
- Always look at what he/she is doing (watches his/her feet when walking/running)
- Chews on clothing or objects more than other children do

COMPETENCY 3.0 UNDERSTAND PRINCIPLES AND ACTIVITIES FOR DEVELOPING LOCOMOTOR, NONLOCOMOTOR, AND BODY CONTROL SKILLS

SKILL 3.1 Types and characteristics of locomotor, nonlocomotor, and body control skills

LOCOMOTOR SKILLS.

Locomotor skills move an individual from one point to another.

1. **Walking** - with one foot contacting the surface at all times, walking shifts one's weight from one foot to the other while legs swing alternately in front of the body.

2. **Running** - an extension of walking that has a phase where the body is propelled with no base of support (speed is faster, stride is longer, and arms add power).

3. **Jumping** - projectile movements that momentarily suspend the body in midair.

4. **Vaulting** - coordinated movements that allow one to spring over an obstacle.

5. **Leaping** - similar to running, but leaping has greater height, flight, and distance.

6. **Hopping** - using the same foot to take off from a surface and land.

7. **Galloping** - forward or backward advanced elongation of walking combined and coordinated with a leap.

8. **Sliding** - sideward stepping pattern that is uneven, long, or short.

9. **Body Rolling** - moving across a surface by rocking back and forth, by turning over and over, or by shaping the body into a revolving mass.

10. **Climbing** - ascending or descending using the hands and feet with the upper body exerting the most control.

NONLOCOMOTOR SKILLS.

Nonlocomotor skills are stability skills where the movement requires little or no movement of one's base of support and does not result in change of position.

1. **Bending** - movement around a joint where two body parts meet.

2. **Dodging** - sharp change of direction from original line of movement such as away from a person or object.

3. **Stretching** - extending/hyper-extending joints to make body parts as straight or as long as possible.

4. **Twisting** - rotating body/body parts around an axis with a stationary base.

5. **Turning** - circular moving the body through space releasing the base of support.

6. **Swinging** - circular/pendular movements of the body/body parts below an axis.

7. **Swaying** - same as swinging but movement is above an axis.

8. **Pushing** - applying force against an object or person to move it away from one's body or to move one's body away from the object or person.

9. **Pulling** - executing force to cause objects/people to move toward one's body.

IDENTIFY AND DEFINE MANIPULATIVE SKILLS.

Manipulative skills use body parts to propel or receive an object, controlling objects primarily with the hands and feet. Two types of manipulative skills are receptive (catch + trap) and propulsive (throw, strike, kick).

1. **Bouncing/Dribbling** - projecting a ball downwards.

2. **Catching** - stopping momentum of an object (for control) using the hands.

3. **Kicking** - striking an object with the foot.

4. **Rolling** - initiating force to an object to instill contact with a surface.

5. **Striking** - giving impetus to an object with the use of the hands or an object.

6. **Throwing** - using one or both arms to project an object into midair away from the body.

7. **Trapping** - without the use of the hands, receiving and controlling a ball.

SKILL 3.2 Techniques for assessing movement skills.

Physical education plays a vital role in developing children's motor and body control skills. These essential skills are what turn today's children into tomorrow's healthy adults.

It is the responsibility of a physical education instructor to identify and assess the mechanics of locomotor, nonlocomotor, and other body control skills. Also, the instructor should role model appropriate motor and body control skills.

A responsible physical education instructor always ensures that students are executing locomotor, nonlocomotor, and body control skills properly. Oftentimes, the student combines these skills while playing sports or engaging in physical activities.

The best way to assess students' performance is to instruct them perform various locomotor skills such as walking, running, and hopping. The instructor can also ask the students to carry out a variety of nonlocomotor skills such as pushing, pulling, stretching, balancing, twisting, and turning.

At the same time, the instructor will have to inspire students to perform difficult locomotor skills. The instructor should monitor how the students are integrating the locomotor and nonlocomotor skills with body control expertise, including balance and weight transfer.

It's also advisable to use music to assess how students are performing locomotor skills. . The assessment will give the teacher a better idea of each student's proficiency. The teacher can also devise innovative games to assess a student's ability to combine locomotor, nonlocomotor, and body control skills.

The evaluation process will identify the student's creative intuition to integrate locomotor and nonlocomotor skills during an individual or group performance.

SKILL 3.3 Knowledge of activities for body management skill development.

KNOWLEDGE OF ACTIVITIES FOR BODY MANAGEMENT SKILL DEVELOPMENT

Sequential development and activities for locomotor skills acquisition

Sequential Development = crawl, creep, walk, run, jump, hop, gallop, slide, leap, skip, step-hop.

- **Activities to develop walking skills** include walking slower and faster in place; walking forward, backward, and sideways with slower and faster paces in straight, curving, and zigzag pathways with various lengths of steps; pausing between steps; and changing the height of the body.

- **Activities to develop running skills** include having students pretend they are playing basketball, trying to score a touchdown, trying to catch a bus, finishing a lengthy race, or running on a hot surface.

- **Activities to develop jumping skills** include alternating jumping with feet together and feet apart, taking off and landing on the balls of the feet, clicking the heels together while airborne, and landing with a foot forward and a foot backward.

- **Activities to develop galloping skills** include having students play a game of Fox and Hound, with the lead foot representing the fox and the back foot the hound trying to catch the fox (alternate the lead foot).

- **Activities to develop sliding skills** include having students hold hands in a circle and sliding in one direction, then sliding in the other direction.

- **Activities to develop hopping skills** include having students hop all the way around a hoop and hopping in and out of a hoop reversing direction. Students can also place ropes in straight lines and hop side-to-side over the rope from one end to the other and change (reverse) the direction.

- **Activities to develop skipping skills** include having students combine walking and hopping activities leading up to skipping.

- **Activities to develop step-hopping skills** include having students practice stepping and hopping activities while clapping hands to an uneven beat.

Sequential development and activities for nonlocomotor skill acquisition

Sequential Development = stretch, bend, sit, shake, turn, rock and sway, swing, twist, dodge, and fall.

- **Activities to develop stretching** include lying on the back and stomach and stretching as far as possible; stretching as though one is reaching for a star, picking fruit off a tree, climbing a ladder, shooting a basketball, or placing an item on a high self; waking and yawning.

- **Activities to develop bending** include touching knees and toes then straightening the entire body and straightening the body halfway; bending as though picking up a coin, tying shoes, picking flowers/vegetables, and petting animals of different sizes.

- **Activities to develop sitting** include practicing sitting from standing, kneeling, and lying positions without the use of hands.

- **Activities to develop falling skills** include first collapsing in one's own space and then pretending to fall like bowling pins, raindrops, snowflakes, a rag doll, or Humpty Dumpty.

Sequential development and activities for manipulative skill acquisition

Sequential Development = striking, throwing, kicking, ball rolling, volleying, bouncing, catching, and trapping.

- **Activities to develop striking** begin with the striking of stationary objects by a participant in a stationary position. Next, the person remains still while trying to strike a moving object. Then, both the object and the participant are in motion as the participant attempts to strike the moving object.

- **Activities to develop throwing** include throwing yarn/foam balls against a wall, then at a big target, and finally at targets decreasing in size.

- **Activities to develop kicking** include alternating feet to kick balloons/beach balls, then kicking them under and over ropes. Change the type of ball as proficiency develops.

- **Activities to develop ball rolling** include rolling different size balls to a wall, then to targets decreasing in size.

- **Activities to develop volleying** include using a large balloon and, first, hitting it with both hands, then one hand (alternating hands), and then using different parts of the body. Change the object as students progress (balloon, to beach ball, to foam ball, etc.)

- **Activities to develop bouncing** include starting with large balls and, first, using both hands to bounce, and then using one hand (alternate hands).

- **Activities to develop catching** include using various objects (balloons, beanbags, balls, etc.) to catch and, first, catching the object the participant has thrown him/herself, then catching objects someone else threw, and finally increasing the distance between the catcher and the thrower.

- **Activities to develop trapping** include trapping slow and fast rolling balls; trapping balls (or other objects such as beanbags) that are lightly thrown at waist, chest, and stomach levels; trapping different size balls.

SKILL 3.4   Strategies for integrating movement skills in various combinations and activities.

Combinations of motor skills, demonstrations of agility and balance, and dance steps and sequences all involve the same key elements of body awareness (proprioception/kinesthesia) and control. Some specific elements include pivot and throw, and a variety of movement sequences that combine traveling, rolling, balancing, and weight transfer.

Pivot and throw are both skills that grow out of the individual's awareness and control of his body's positioning and weight distribution, both at rest and, especially, in motion. To properly execute this movement sequence (i.e., changing direction and continuing to move, maintaining fluid movement throughout the execution), the actor must efficiently distribute his body weight, and manage his weight distribution properly throughout the execution of the pivot. Poor execution will put the individual off-balance, preventing him from continuing the chain of movement without stumbling.

Movement sequences that combine traveling, rolling, balancing, and weight transfer, as with the pivot and throw skills described earlier, rely on the individual's awareness and control of his body's positioning and weight distribution. In order to travel across a space, execute rolls, balancing techniques, and the requisite weight transfers linked to those actions, the athlete must have a keen sense of where their weight is currently distributed, and how to move it in the desired direction with maximum efficiency.

COMPETENCY 4.0 UNDERSTAND PRINCIPLES AND ACTIVITIES FOR DEVELOPING OBJECT CONTROL SKILLS

SKILL 4.1 Throwing, catching, dribbling, kicking, and striking skills.

SEE ALSO DOMAIN I., Skill 5.5

ANALYSIS OF BASIC MOVEMENT PATTERS: OVERHAND THROW, UNDERHAND THROW, KICK

Overhand Throw

The overhand throw consists of a sequence of four movements: a stride, hip rotation, trunk rotation, and forward arm movement. The thrower should align his body sideways to the target (with opposite shoulder pointing towards the target). The overhand throw begins with a step or stride with the opposite foot (i.e. left foot for a right-handed thrower). As the stride foot contacts the ground, the pivot foot braces against the ground and provides stability for the subsequent movements. Hip rotation is the natural turning of the hips toward the target. Trunk rotation follows hip rotation. The hips should rotate before the trunk because the stretching of the torso muscles allows for stronger muscle contraction during trunk rotation. Following trunk rotation, the arm moves forward in two phases. In the first phase the elbow is bent. In the second phase, the elbow joint straightens and the thrower releases the ball.

Development of the overhand throwing motion in children occurs in three stages: elementary, mature, and advanced. In the elementary stage, the child throws mainly with the arm and does not incorporate the other body movements. The signature characteristic of this stage is striding with the foot on the same side of the body as the throwing arm (i.e. placing the right foot in front when throwing with the right hand). In the mature stage, the thrower brings the arm backward in preparation for the throw. Use of body rotation is still limited. Children in the advanced stage incorporate all the elements of the overhand throw. The thrower displays an obvious stride and body rotation.

Underhand Throw

The thrower places the object in the dominant hand. When drawing the arm back the triceps straighten the elbow and, depending on the amount of power behind the throw, the shoulder extends or hyperextends using the posterior deltoid, latissimus dorsi, and the teres major. At the time of drawback, the thrower takes a step forward with the leg opposite of the throwing arm. When coming back down, the thrower moves the shoulder muscles (primarily the anterior deltoid) into flexion. When the object in hand moves in front of the body, the thrower releases the ball. The wrist may be firm or slightly flexed. The thrower releases the object shortly after the planting the foot and the biceps muscle contracts, moving the elbow into flexion during follow through.

Kick

In executing a kick, the object needs to be in front of the body and in front of the dominant leg. The kicker steps and plants with the opposite leg while drawing the kicking leg back. During draw back, the hamstring muscle group flexes the knee. When the kicker plants the opposite foot, the hips swing forward for power and the knee moves into extension using the quadriceps muscle group. The contact point is approximately even with the plant foot and a comfortable follow through completes the action.

SKILL 4.2   Combinations of object control skills.

Object control skills help students remain fit and agile. These skills also help students to become better performers. Physical educators will often combine a number of object control skills to enhance a child's reflexes.

Catch and throw is an ideal example of integrating such skills. This type of skill requires a high level of concentration and nimbleness. A combination of object control skills is always at the heart of any physical activity.

Object control skills make all the difference in successful athletic performance. An ideal combination of these skills keeps students healthy and satisfied.

SKILL 4.3   Techniques for assessing object control skills and developmentally appropriate activities for promoting them.

   SEE ALSO DOMAIN I., Skill 5.4

ASSESSMENT
Instructors can use many of the same methods when assessing object control skills that they use for assessing basic motor skills. In addition, instructors should analyze each component of the skill to determine the root cause of the error or problem. For example, when assessing a student's overhand throw, the instructor should observe the placement and involvement of the legs, body alignment, arm motion, wrist action, and weight transfer. There are certain universal characteristics of immature throwing patterns. These include stepping with the foot on the same side of the body as the throwing arm, using only the elbow to propel the object, and facing the target throughout the throwing process. Conversely, characteristics of a mature overhand throwing pattern include leading with the foot opposite the throwing hand, using the entire body and arm to propel the ball, and starting the throwing motion facing perpendicular to the target. By observing the individual components of the skill, the instructor can determine the developmental level of the student and tailor instruction accordingly.

APPROPRIATE OBJECT CONTROL ACTIVITIES

As with all motor skills, when introducing object control skills, the instructor should begin with the most basic fundamentals and use activities that are simple and easy to perform. For example, when teaching a striking skill, such as batting a ball, the instructor should begin by having the students hit large balls (e.g. beach balls) that are stationary. When introducing catching or volleying, the instructor could first have the students use balloons that are easy to catch and control because they float and move slowly.

As students develop object control skills, the instructor can introduce activities that are more advanced. For example, students can progress from batting a stationary softball or tennis ball to a moving softball or tennis ball.

SKILL 4.4 Strategies for integrating locomotor, nonlocomotor, and object control skills.

Physical education instructors should develop innovative strategies to help students learn the nuances of locomotor, nonlocomotor, and object control skills. Physical education instructors should also present these skills in an entertaining manner for students.

If a teacher starts a training schedule with simple activities, they are more likely to keep the students interested. Once students develop interest, teachers should introduce complex activities such as running and catching, pivoting and throwing, and running and jumping.

Furthermore, physical education is easier for the teachers and students when the student acquires an interest in the physical activity. Finally, traditional sports activities are a perfect venue for the application of combined skills.

COMPETENCY 5.0　UNDERSTAND PRINCIPLES AND ACTIVITIES FOR DEVELOPING RHYTHMIC AND DANCE SKILLS

SKILL 5.1　Basic elements of rhythm.

Rhythmic awareness is another vital aspect of fitness. One of the basic rhythm elements is knowledge of the fundamental movement models.

In teaching students rhythm element basics the instructors have a tremendous role to play. First, instructors must demonstrate how to use suitable terms related to rhythm, movement, and position. The students will have to carry out locomotor movements rhythmically as well as movements such as 45-degree turns. At the next level, teachers should encourage students to integrate movement patterns with music (e.g. dance aerobics).

RHYTHMIC SKILLS

Rhythmic skills include responding and moving the body in time with the beat, tempo, or pitch of music. To develop rhythmic skills, instructors can ask students to clap their hands or stomp their feet to the beat of the music. Dancing and gymnastics requires high levels of rhythmic competency. As with all physical skills, development of rhythmic skills is a sequential process.

SKILL 5.2　Appropriate activities for rhythmic skill development.

Dancing is an excellent activity for the development of rhythmic skills. In addition, any activity that involves moving the body to music can promote rhythmic skill development.

DANCE CONCEPTS AND FORMS

Students of dance acquire many skills during their course of study. The student identifies and demonstrates movement elements in dance performance and uses correct body alignment, strength, flexibility, and stamina (for more demanding performances). Crucial to any form of dance is the concept of coordination in the performance of technical movements. Technical movements must look as though they are easy to perform. The dancer must perform technical dance skills with artistic expression including musicality and rhythm. As the student progresses, he or she will perform more extended movement sequences and rhythmic patterns. The student will then have the experience to introduce his or her own style into the performance. The student will also be able to use improvisation to solve movement problems and adjust choices based on the movement responses of other dancers in the ensemble. Through continued experience, he or she will become a skillful, seasoned dancer whose technique and ability will transcend any form of dance.

Instructors can create rhythmic activities by putting on music with a strong beat and asking students to dance to the beat. Additionally, the instructor should ask students to listen to the beat and move accordingly (e.g. stomping their feet or clapping their hands in time with the beat). It's important for children to learn to move to various sounds and use their bodies to mimic the beat. Another idea is to have the students take turns beating on a coffee can while trying to keep movements in sync with the rhythm. In more structured dance forms, technique or skill comes into play. For instance, in ballet, dancers must have good flexibility, body control, and coordination. Ballet dancers must also have a sense of rhythm, an understanding of music, good turnout and alignment, and a sense of balance and counterbalance. These skills take many years to acquire and, once acquired, take many more years to master and maintain. Ballet dancing may express a mood, tell a story, or simply reflect a piece of music and is the most classical of all dance forms. Other types of music may have similar requirements in terms of a sense of musicality and rhythm. For example, tap dance requires a greater degree of footwork and modern is comparable to ballet, but more flowing and less rigid.

SKILL 5.3 Techniques for assessing rhythmic skills.

There are several proven techniques for the assessment of rhythmic skills. First, an instructor may ask students to demonstrate a known vocabulary of basic movement concepts. Second, instructors should assess the students' ability to respond to verbal commands in the execution of rhythmic skills.

In addition, the instructor can ask students to perform locomotor movements at different levels while going in different directions. This will give the physical educator teacher a better understanding of a student's proficiency. Finally, performance of dance routines is another parameter for assessing rhythmic skills.

SKILL 5.4 Strategies for integrating rhythmic skills with locomotor, nonlocomotor, body control, and object control skills.

It is quite difficult to integrate rhythmic skills with locomotor, nonlocomotor, body control, and object control skills. However, there are strategies for integrating all types of skills that trainers and physical educators can employ.

Activities that integrate different types of skills include traditional gymnastics, rhythmic gymnastics, and balance boards. Such activities help in effectively integrating different skills, such as locomotor and body control skills, with rhythmic movements.

RHYTHMIC GYMNASTICS AND EDUCATIONAL GYMNASTICS

Rhythmic gymnastics is a sport, which combines dance and gymnastics with the use of balls, hoops, ribbons, ropes, and clubs. Gymnasts perform on a carpet to music either individually or in a group of five. In competition, gymnasts perform leaps, pivots, balances, and other elements to demonstrate flexibility and coordination. The gymnast must completely integrate the apparatus into the routine and perform specific moves with each apparatus. Individual routines last from 1 minute and 15 seconds to 1 minute and 30 seconds, while group routines last from 2 minutes 15 seconds to 2 minutes and 30 seconds. The main difference between rhythmic and artistic gymnastics is that rhythmic gymnasts cannot incorporate acrobatic skill. In fact, judges penalize a gymnast for incorporating acrobatic skill into his routine. However, gymnasts may perform pre-acrobatic elements such as forward and backward shoulder rolls, fish-flops, and tah-dahs. In addition, the new Code of Points permits walkovers and cartwheels. Originality and risk are integral parts of this sport, and no two routines are ever the same.

In educational gymnastics, students learn to use and manage their bodies in safe, efficient and creative ways. Educational gymnastics can utilize certain fixed equipment such as mats, bars, ropes, and boxes and is also know as "body management" because the activities provide opportunities for students to learn to manage their own bodies. Instead of a series of gymnastics stunts, they select, refine and perform the six Basic Movement Patterns of Landings, Locomotions, Statics, Rotations, Swings, and Springs in a variety of contexts and environments. Emphasis is on challenges and problem solving. Instructors use the Movement Variables of Body, Space, Effort, and Relationships to design movement-learning experiences. Students work individually, in pairs, and in groups to create movement sequences and structures.

Educational gymnastics does not require elaborate facilities. In fact, many good educational gymnastics programs take place out-of-doors in natural settings. While large-scale gymnastics equipment is not essential for providing students with quality movement-learning experiences, such equipment is certainly advantageous. Another advantage of educational gymnastics is that it provides for the development of the upper body. It is much easier and more common to develop strength in the lower body than in the upper body. Many everyday events such as walking and running and jumping enhance lower body strength. Most team games and sports emphasize lower body strength and tend to neglect upper body development. Gymnastics also help to build overall muscular strength and flexibility. There is also equal development of both left and right sides of the body because most gymnastics activities involve simultaneous use of both arms (e.g. rolls, hangs, swings, supports) or both legs (e.g. springs, tumbling). In contrast, many game activities that involve the use of an implement (e.g., bat, racquet, stick) or object (e.g., beanbag, ball, Frisbee) tend to favor the development of one side of the body more than the other does.

Finally, if educational gymnastics experiences are to be truly "educational," then we must ask in what ways are they educational? In short, these experiences are educational because they start with the needs of students. The instructor presents the students with movement problems, which the students must solve, asks questions to gain the cognitive involvement of students, offers various solutions in the form of movement sequences, and guides students to reflect upon and synthesize their experiences. Students gain knowledge and understandings of the mechanical principles associated with the Basic Movement Patterns of gymnastics and they increase their ability to apply these principles.

SKILL 5.5 Techniques, sequences, and skills for various forms of dance.

DANCE CONCEPTS, FORMS, AND BASIC VOCABULARY – JAZZ AND BALLET

There are several forms of dance including modern, ballet, jazz, country, ballroom, and hip-hop. Though essentially very different from each other, they all have similarities. A sense of musicality is the one constant required for each of the dance forms. Along with that, we can add timing, coordination, flexibility, and, needless to say, an interest in the concept of dance itself. We all know that we will probably experience greater success when we engage in activities that we are interested in and enjoy. Understanding of most dance forms requires knowledge of basic vocabulary. For example, in jazz, turns or kick ball turns; in tap dance, the shuffle or the flap, etc. Ballet has more specialized vocabulary than any other dance form. For example, plie, to bend; tendu, to stretch; degage, to disengage; fouette, to whip; fondu, to melt; ronde jambe, circle of the leg; pirouette, to turn on one leg; port de bras, movement of the arms; and assemble, to assemble.

Integral to dance and particularly ballet are the concepts of balance and counterbalance, pull-up and turnout, weight distribution and alignment, including shoulders down, hips square, legs turned out, and chest lifted.

In ballet, there are many different dance forms and techniques that a dancer can follow. Three of the larger ones are the Cecchetti, Russian Vaganova, and Royal Academy of Dance, (RAD), programmes. They all have levels for all dancers from beginner to advanced and they all have their advantages and disadvantages. The Cecchetti Society developed the Cecchetti technique from the teachings of the great ballet master Enrico Cecchetti. It is a full syllabus designed to train dancers for professional work. One notable emphasis in the Cecchetti syllabus is that the arms flow and blend from position to position more than any other technique. The Cecchetti technique has formed the core of the program at the National Ballet School of Canada. The Russian Vaganova technique derives its name and fundamental elements from the teachings of Agrippina Vaganova, who was the artistic director of the Kirov Ballet for many years. In the Vaganova method, the dancers bring attention to their hands. The hands do not flow invisibly from one position to the, as in the Cecchetti method, rather they are left behind and turn at the last moment. This is where the "flapping" look comes from that many dancers make with their hands. In the Vaganova method, unlike the RAD method, there are no formally established exercises. Each teacher choreographs his own class according to specialized guidelines and the students dance that class in their examinations. The Vaganova method forms the core of the program at the Royal Winnipeg Ballet School. The RAD syllabus is very common. It is well suited to dance classes in community dance schools where the students usually do no more than an average of one class per day. If you go to the ballet school in your community, there is a good chance instructors will use the RAD method. The American School of Ballet teaches the Balanchine method. Created by George Balanchine in the American School of Ballet, the Balanchine method allows dancers to dance Balanchine's choreography much more easily than other dancers can. In the Balanchine method the hands are held differently again from any of the other systems.

DANCE CONCEPTS, FORMS, AND BASIC VOCABULARY – FOLK AND TAP

Folk dance is a term used to describe a large number of dances that originated in Europe and share several common characteristics. Most folk dances practiced today were created before the 20th century, and were practiced by people with little or no training. For this reason, folk dances are usually characterized by a spontaneous style, adaptable movements, and culturally distinctive steps representative of the dance's country of origin. Types of folk dancing include the contra dance, English country-dance, and Maypole dance.

Contra dance is a term used to describe folk dances in which couples dance in two facing lines. A pair of such lines is a set, and these sets are generally arranged to run the length of a long hall. The head of a set is the end of the line closest to the band and caller. At contra dance events where dancers perform several different folk dances, the caller or dance leader teaches the movements of an individual dance to the dancers during the "walk through," a short period of time before the next type of dance begins. During the walk through, all dancers mark the movements following the caller's instructions. At contra dance events in North America, contra dancers traditionally change partners for every dance. On the other hand, in the United Kingdom, dancers remain with the same partner for the entire evening.

Square dance refers to a type of folk dance in which four couples begin and end each sequence in a square formation. When four couples align themselves in such a manner, we call the formation "sets-in-order," and we call dances that use such formations "quadrille." Similar to folk dance, American square dance steps derive from traditional European dances. At every square dance event, the dance caller prompts participants through a sequence of steps to the beat throughout the entirety of each dance, but does not usually participate in the dancing. Steps common to many square dances include allemande left and allemande right, where couples face, take hands, and circle around one another; promenade, where partners cross hands and walk to a counter-clockwise position; and circle right and circle left, where all dancers grasp hands and move round in a circle. Traditionally, the caller explains the steps to each individual square dance at the beginning of a session.

Tap is a form of dance born in the United States during the 19th century in which the dancer sounds out the rhythm by clicking taps on the toes and heels of his shoes. This form of percussive music and dance is believed to have evolved from a fusion of Irish and African Shuffle in New York City during the 1830s. One common characteristic of modern tap dance is "syncopation," where choreographies generally begin on the eighth music beat. Learning to tap dance is a cumulative process in which new information builds on previously learned steps and terms. To teach tap dance successfully, instructors must first teach simple steps that make up the foundation of tap before introducing complex movements. The most basic steps of tap include the walk, step, heel, step-heel, stamp, ball-change, brush, toe tap, shuffle, side shuffle, back shuffle, and cramp roll. Dance instructors can combine these steps to form simple routines for beginners. Once students have mastered these steps, dancers can move on to attempt movements such as the buffalo, Maxi Ford, Cincinnati, pullback, wings, toe clips, and riffs.

COMPETENCY 6.0   UNDERSTAND TECHNIQUES, SKILLS, ORGANIZATIONAL STRATEGIES, AND SAFETY PRACTICES FOR TUMBLING AND GYMNASTICS

SKILL 6.1   Skills, activities, skill progressions, organizational strategies, safety practices, and proper use of equipment for tumbling and gymnastics.

GYMNASTIC MOVEMENTS – STUNTS, TUMBLING, APPARATUS WORK, AND FLOOR EXERCISE

Gymnastics is a sport involving the performance of sequences of movements requiring physical strength, flexibility, and kinesthetic awareness (e.g. handsprings, handstands, and forward rolls).

Proper stretching and strength building exercises are necessary for gymnastics. A useful, brief warm-up can consist of push-ups, sit-ups, and flexibility exercises for hamstrings, back, ankles, neck, wrists, and shoulders. An aerial is one example of a stunt (i.e. difficult physical feat) in which the gymnast turns completely over in the air without touching the apparatus with his or her hands.

Floor exercise and tumbling can include somersaults, backward and frontward rolls, cartwheels, forward straddle rolls, back tucks, back handsprings, and handstands. Gymnasts perform apparatus work on the vaulting horse, balance beam, uneven bars, still rings, and pommel horse. A strong run, dynamism, power, and precision in the rotations are characteristics of an efficient vault. The main characteristics for the beam are a well-developed sense of balance and great power of concentration. The uneven bars demand strength as well as concentration, courage, coordination, precision, and split-second timing. The still rings and pommel horse require upper body strength and balance.

SAFETY PRACTICES

Gymnastics, especially at the advanced level, leaves little room for error to avoid possible serious injury. To avoid injuries from falls, instructors, coaches, and other participants should act as spotters during complex aerial stunts. In addition, proper stretching and strength training is necessary to help prevent muscular and skeletal injuries. Instructors must not require or allow students to perform stunts that are beyond their limitations or abilities.

Additionally, proper equipment, such as mats, landing pads, pulleys, balance beams and bars must be in good condition and checked daily for any lose cables, screws or damage of any kind. Any equipment that is found to not be in good and safe condition for any reason, should not be used until it is fixed or replaced.

SKILL 6.2 Techniques for assessing tumbling and gymnastics.

Tumbling and gymnastics are two specialized skills within the physical education curriculum. To assess competency in tumbling and gymnastics skills, physical education instructors generally ask students to perform various tumbling and gymnastics movements. They should ask the students to perform simple movements in the beginning and progress to more complex movements as the students' skills develop. Through practicing tumbling and gymnastics, a student's movement activity skills will improve. By assessing these skills, teachers will gain insight of the student's ability at gymnastic and tumbling activities.

Balance tests – Bass Test of Dynamic Balance (lengthwise and crosswise), Johnson Modification of the Bass Test of Dynamic Balance, modified sideward leap, and balance beam walk.

SKILL 6.3 Appropriate activities for various developmental levels.

Beginners:

- Helping the children to keep still allows them to explore their balance and body control abilities. Appropriate activities include simple balance activities and making body shapes.

- Next, beginners must learn to maintain body control while moving. An appropriate activity to develop this skill is asking the child to point his/her toes while holding a balance position.

- In order to introduce apparatus work, help the children to find a safe way to interact with the equipment as well as the floor space. For example, the instructor can have all the students roll and jump on mats and slide through apparatuses.

Intermediate:

- At this stage, children should work on improving the quality of their movements. The instructor should ask the children to balance, transfer weight, roll, turn, etc. while concentrating on the precision of their movements.

- Middle-aged children should learn how to link phases of movement. They can do this by moving in and out of positions of stillness (e.g. balance on hands, knees, and elbows and move smoothly into a balanced position on one foot).

- Children of this age should develop a range of actions, body shapes, and balances. Physical education instructors should help their students practice agility activities and actions. They should also have the children perform these movements with a change of speed, level, or direction.

Advanced:

- Advanced students should be able to move from the floor to apparatus, to change levels on the apparatus, and to move safely from the apparatus to the floor. This will help the students perform actions, shapes, and balances consistently and fluently.

- Teachers should talk to their students about the need for accuracy, consistency, and clarity of movement. The students should then share their feedback about successful combinations of actions, shapes, and balances.

- In order to become more fluent and refined, instructors should teach students how to adapt their actions from the apparatus to floor.

COMPETENCY 7.0 UNDERSTAND TECHNIQUES, SKILLS, ORGANIZATIONAL STRATEGIES, AND SAFETY PRACTICES FOR AQUATICS

SKILL 7.1 Techniques, skill progressions, safety practices, organizational, strategies, and emergency pool procedures.

Water safety issues include student familiarity with appropriate medical responses to life-threatening situations. Students should recognize signs that someone needs medical attention (e.g. not moving, not breathing, etc.) and have knowledge of the proper response (e.g. who to contact and where to find them). With older children, the instructor can introduce rudimentary first aid. The instructor must also ensure that students are aware and observant of safety rules (e.g. no running near the water, no chewing gum while swimming, no swimming without a lifeguard, no roughhousing near or in the water, etc.).

Swimming strokes include Butterfly, Breast Stroke, Crawl, Sidestroke, Trudgen, Freestyle, Backstroke, and Dog Paddle. When teaching children how to dive, instructors should emphasize form (arm and body alignment) and safety procedures (e.g. no diving in the shallow end, no pushing students into the water).

Water fitness activities and games should place emphasis on generating a lot of movement in the pool (gross motor activities), and may also incorporate activities that require more coordinated manipulations, like catching a ball (fine motor). Sample games include:

Water Tag – Children can attempt to catch each other in the pool. When someone is caught, he becomes 'it'. Variations include freeze tag (where a caught student isn't allowed to move until someone swims between their legs to free them) and base tag (where some sections of the pool, for example the ladders or the walls, are a safe 'base' – rules must be in place limiting the time that a student can spend on the base). Water tag emphasizes gross motor activities. Safety issue: students may not hold other students or grab other students in the water.

Water Dodgeball – Students divide into two teams, one on either side of the pool. They play dodgeball, throwing a ball from one side to the other. The opposing team captures a student by hitting him with the ball, but if the targeted player catches the ball, the opposition captures the thrower instead. Safety issue: students may not throw the ball at another student's head at close range.

Relay Races – Students divide into teams and perform relay races (i.e. one student swims the length of the pool and back, when he returns the next one does the same, repeating until the whole team has completed the task). This can incorporate various swimming strokes; either all team members use the same stroke or each team member uses a different stroke.

SKILL 7.2　Techniques for assessing aquatic skills.

Aquatic skills are exciting and dangerous. Improper behavior and performance of aquatic skills can lead to serious injury.

Physical education classes usually teach a range of aquatic activities or skills to novices. A series of steps aimed at minimizing the dangers involved with aquatic activities follows the introduction of the basic skills. Finally, after the novice acquires basic aquatic skills, the novice undergoes a series of assessment tests.

The assessment tests may vary from one school or physical education class to another, but the assessment techniques as prescribed by the American Red Cross remain the same. They require the student to float for five seconds on the front as well as back positions. Then, the student's swimming and water treading ability is assessed using a combination of leg and arm movements in the water over a distance of 15 feet.

SKILL 7.3　Activities appropriate for various developmental levels and purposes.

Learning aquatic activities are beneficial and appropriate for children of all developmental levels. Research shows that aquatic activities are important for the body's intellectual and physical development.

Under the parent's supervision, aquatic activities are beneficial for babies. With a combination of motor skill development and endurance, aquatic skills are imperative for the development of all people.

Aquatic skills include swimming, fitness concepts in water, and other activities that enable proper motor development for the learner. Besides this, studies show that proper aquatic skills are beneficial for decision-making, problem solving, and confidence in children and adults. Aquatic skills available to more advanced students include diving and water polo.

COMPETENCY 8.0 UNDERSTAND TECHNIQUES, SKILLS, STRATEGIES, RULES, ETIQUETTE, AND SAFETY PRACTICES FOR INDIVIDUAL AND DUAL SPORTS, RECREATIONAL ACTIVITIES, AND OUTDOOR PURSUITS

SKILL 8.1 Techniques, skill progressions, strategies, rules, etiquette, safety practices, and types and uses of equipment for individual and dual sports.

OVERVIEW

Badminton – Students in a badminton class will have to master the strokes as basic skills and should learn at least some of them by name (e.g. types of serves, net shot, net kills, drive, push, lift). Students should also know which strokes are appropriate from which areas of the court.

Handball – Skills that students will learn in a handball class will include catching and accurately throwing the ball, taking steps while bouncing it (similar to basketball's dribble), and quick analysis of the playing situation to determine who the best target is for a pass.

Strategy in handball centers on staying one step ahead of the opposing team. Keep them guessing and have multiple contingencies for given situations, so that game play doesn't become predictable (and easier to counter). Specific tactics can include types of shots that are harder for the opponent to hit, and shots that will put the ball out of play (when it is advantageous to do so).

Pickleball – Skills that students will learn in pickleball classes include manipulation of the ball with the racket and the variety of strokes.

Pickleball strategy is similar to tennis. Students should learn to vary their strokes to keep their opponents guessing, with the goal of reaching the frontcourt in a net volley position first. This places the students in the best position to win the point.

Table Tennis (Ping Pong) – Skills that students will study when learning table tennis include the variety of grips (e.g. penhold, shakehand, V-grip), and the various types of offensive and defensive strokes. Students will also learn to gauge the force needed to manipulate the ball properly.

Strategies for success in table tennis involve manipulating and minimizing the opponent's ability to return a shot – this includes learning to hit to the opponent's weak side, putting a spin on the ball so as to make its movement less predictable, and setting the opponent up to receive a shot that he cannot return.

Tennis – Skills that students will learn when studying tennis include the proper grips of the racket and stroke techniques, which they should know by name (e.g. flat serve, topspin serve, twist serve, forehand, backhand, volley, overhead).

Golf – The most fundamental skills for students to learn when studying golf include the correct way to execute a golf swing with proper posture and how to judge distance for shot selection correctly. Further, students should learn specific shots and their names (e.g. tee shot, fairway shot, bunker shot, putt).

Strategy in golf centers on properly gauging distances and required force to control the ball to the best extent possible.

Safety practices in golf, especially with students, involve ensuring that the course is clear and there are no students nearby when players are swinging. Instructors should also remind students that golf clubs are not toys, and that misuse can result in injury.

Equipment necessary for a golf class includes a proper set of clubs and golf balls (a golf course or open area for hitting balls is also necessary).

Archery – Skills that students study in archery classes include proper care for their equipment, properly stringing the bow, drawing, and shooting with accuracy (including compensating for distance, angle, and wind).

Safety practices in archery include respectful handling of the equipment (which is potentially dangerous) and ensuring that students only draw bows when pointed at a (non-living) target. Finally, instructors should keep students away from the path between firing students and their targets at all times.

Proper equipment for archery classes include a bow and arrows, which can vary greatly in technical complexity and cost, and a target.

Bowling – Skills that students will learn in bowling classes include learning to select a ball of comfortable weight and appropriate for the shot they need to make, properly controlling the ball so it hits the pins they are aiming for, and learning the dynamics of pin interaction to plan the proper angle of entry for the ball.

Safety practices in bowling include wearing proper footwear, handling the balls cautiously, and preventing horseplay (to avoid situations where a heavy bowling ball may drop inopportunely and cause injury).

Equipment needed for a bowling class includes proper footwear, a bowling ball, pins, and a lane.

COMBATIVE ACTIVITIES

Basic knowledge of wrestling includes knowledge of basic techniques (familiarity with pins, reversals, and positioning transitions), drills for practicing technique (e.g. students can drill shooting and sprawling, drill reversals from pinned positions, etc.), and terminology (naming the techniques, e.g. shoot, sprawl, half nelson, full nelson, etc.).

Basic knowledge of self-defense includes familiarity with basic striking techniques (punches and kicks), blocks and evasions, knowledge of major vital points on the body (eyes, nose, ears, jaw, throat, solar plexus, groin, knees, in-step), knowledge of basic escape techniques (from chokes, grabs and bear-hugs) and some situational training (to prevent 'freezing' in a real-life encounter). Martial arts (e.g. judo, karate) are common forms of self-defense that physical education instructors can teach to students.

In-class focus should be placed on strategies for conflict recognition (based on developing an understanding of threat factors, like individuals in a hostile frame of mind), avoidance (physically avoiding potentially dangerous situations), and diffusion (overview of the psychology of confrontations, evaluation of the motivations behind a hostile encounter, understanding of the way body language and eye contact can impact the situation).

Related safety issues include stressing the potential harm that can result from the techniques being practiced (stressing specific damage potential to musculoskeletal systems), emphasizing students' responsibility for the well-being of their training partners, maintaining discipline throughout the class (ensuring students remain focused on their training activities and alert to the educator's instructions), and ensuring that students are aware and observant of the limits to force that they may apply (no-striking zones, like above the neck and below the belt; limits on striking force, like semi-contact or no-contact sparring; familiarity with the concept of a tap-out indicating submission). Students should perform warm-up, cool-down, and stretching as with any physical training program.

APPLY APPROPRIATE STRATEGIES TO GAME AND SPORT SITUATIONS

Archery strategies for correcting errors in aiming and releasing:

- Shifting position.

- Relaxing both the arms and shoulders at the moment of release.

- Reaching point of aim before releasing string.

- Pointing aim to the right or left of direct line between the archer and the target's center.

- Aiming with the left eye.
- Sighting with both eyes.
- Using the proper arrow.

Bowling for spares strategies:

- Identifying the key pin and determining where to hit it to pick up remaining pins.
- Using the three basic alignments: center position for center pins, left position for left pins, and right position for right pins.
- Rolling the spare ball in the same manner as rolled for the first ball of frame.
- Concentrating harder for the spare ball because of the reduced opportunity for pin action and margin of error.

Badminton Strategies:

Strategies for Return of Service:

- Returning serves with shots that are straight ahead.
- Returning service so that opponent moves out of his/her home base position.
- Returning long serves with an overhead clear or drop shot to near corner.
- Returning short serves with underhand clear or a net drop to near corner.

Strategies for Serving:

- Serving long to the backcourt near centerline.
- Serving short when opponent is standing too deep in his/her receiving court to return the serve, or using a short serve can be used to eliminate a smash return if opponent has a powerful smash from the backcourt.

Badminton Strategies:

Strategies for Return of Service

- Returning serves with shots that are straight ahead.

- Returning service so that opponent must move out of his/her starting position.

- Returning long serves with an overhead clear or drop shot to near corner.

- Returning short serves with underhand clear or a net drop to near corner.

Strategies for Serving

- Serving long to the backcourt near centerline.

- Serving short when opponent is standing too deep in his/her receiving court to return the serve, or using a short serve to eliminate a smash return if opponent has a powerful smash from the backcourt.

Handball or Racquetball Strategies:

- Identifying opponent's strengths and weaknesses.

- Making opponent use less dominant hand or backhand shots if they are weaker.

- Frequently alternating fastballs and lobs to change the pace (changing the pace is particularly effective for serving).

- Maintaining position near middle of court (the well) that is close enough to play low balls and corner shots.

- Placing shots that keep opponent's position at a disadvantage to return cross-court and angle shots.

- Using high lob shots that go overhead but do not hit the back wall with enough force to rebound to drive an opponent out of position when he/she persistently plays close to the front wall.

Tennis Strategies:

- Lobbing – using a high, lob shot for defense giving the player more time to get back into position.

- Identifying opponent's weaknesses, attacking them, and recognizing and protecting one's own weaknesses.

- Outrunning and out-thinking an opponent.

- Using change of pace, lobs, spins, approaching the net, and deception at the correct time.

- Hitting cross-court (from corner to corner of the court) for maximum safety and opportunity to regain position.

- Directing the ball where the opponent is not.

SAFETY PRACTICES AND EQUIPMENT – NET/WALL SPORTS

In addition to the general safety procedures discussed in the previous skill, there are several specific safety considerations for net/wall sports. First, because most of these sports involve swinging a racket or paddle and hitting a ball with a great deal of force, monitoring the area of play is very important. Instructors must ensure that students only swing rackets and hit balls at appropriate times. Second, instructors and students must keep the playing area clear of stray balls and other obstacles to prevent injuries. Finally, some of the net/wall sports, such as handball, require use of protective eyewear. Good and proper footwear is essential in protecting the player from possible ankle injuries.

The following is a list of sport-specific equipment for net/wall sports:

- Badminton – rackets, nets, shuttlecocks
- Handball – a wall, handballs, protective eyewear
- Pickleball – wood paddle rackets, plastic balls, nets, a paved surface
- Table Tennis – paddles, balls, table, nets
- Tennis – court, nets, rackets, tennis balls
- Volleyball – nets, volleyballs

APPLY THE RULES OF PLAY TO VARIOUS GAME AND SPORT SITUATIONS

ARCHERY:

- Arrows that bounce off the target or go through the target count as 7 points.

- Arrows landing on lines between two rings receive the higher score of the two rings.

- Arrows hitting the petticoat receive no score.

BADMINTON:

- Intentionally balking opponent or making preliminary feints results in a fault (side in = loss of serve; side out = point awarded to side in).

- When a shuttlecock falls on a line, it is in play (i.e. a fair play).

- If the striking team hits shuttlecock before it crosses net it is a fault.

- Touching the net when the shuttlecock is in play is a fault.
- The same player hitting the shuttlecock twice is a fault.
- The shuttlecock going through the net is a fault.

BOWLING:

- No score for a pin knocked down by a pinsetter (human or mechanical).
- There is no score for the pins when any part of the foot, hand, or arm extends or crosses over the foul line (even after ball leaves the hand) or if any part of the body contacts division boards, walls, or uprights that are beyond the foul line.
- There is no count for pins displaced or knocked down by a ball leaving the lane before it reaches the pins.
- There is no count when balls rebound from the rear cushion.

RACQUETBALL/HANDBALL:

- A server stepping outside service area when serving faults.
- The server is out (relinquishes serve) if he/she steps outside of serving zone twice in succession while serving.
- Server is out if he/she fails to hit the ball rebounding off the floor during the serve.
- The opponent must have a chance to take a position or the referee must call for play before the server can serve the ball.
- The server re-serves the ball if the receiver is not behind the short line at the time of the serve.
- A served ball that hits the front line and does not land back of the short line is "short"; therefore, it is a fault. The ball is also short when it hits the front wall and two sidewalls before it lands on the floor back of the short line.
- A serve is a fault when the ball touches the ceiling from rebounding off the front wall.
- A fault occurs when any part of the foot steps over the outer edges of the service or the short line while serving.

- A hinder (dead ball) is called when a returned ball hits an opponent on its way to the front wall - even if the ball continues to the front wall.

- A hinder is any intentional or unintentional interference of an opponent's opportunity to return the ball.

TENNIS:

A player loses a point when:

- The ball bounces twice on her side of the net.

- The player returns the ball to any place outside of designated areas.

- The player stops or touches the ball in the air before it lands out-of-bounds.

- The player intentionally strikes the ball twice with the racket.

- The ball strikes any part of a player or racket after initial attempt to hit the ball.

- A player reaches over the net to hit the ball.

- A player throws his racket at the ball.

- The ball strikes any permanent fixture that is out-of-bounds (other than the net).

    o a ball touching the net and landing inside the boundary lines is in play (except on the serve, where a ball contacting the net results in a "let" – replay of the point)

- A player fails, on two consecutive attempts, to serve the ball into the designated area (i.e. double fault).

APPROPRIATE BEHAVIOR IN PHYSICAL EDUCATION ACTIVITIES

Appropriate Student Etiquette/Behaviors include: following the rules and accepting the consequences of unfair action, good sportsmanship, respecting the rights of other students, reporting own accidents and mishaps, not engaging in inappropriate behavior under peer pressure encouragement, cooperation, paying attention to instructions and demonstrations, moving to assigned places and remaining in own space, complying with directions, practicing as instructed to do so, properly using equipment, and not interfering with the practice of others.

Appropriate Content Etiquette/Behaviors include the teacher describing the performance of tasks and students engaging in the task, the teacher assisting students with task performance, and the teacher modifying and developing tasks.

Appropriate Management Etiquette/Behaviors include the teacher directing the management of equipment, students, and space prior to practicing tasks; students getting equipment and partners; the teacher requesting that students stop "fooling around."

DEFINE THE TERMINOLOGY OF VARIOUS TARGET SPORTS

Archery Terminology:

- Addressing the target – standing ready to shoot with a proper shooting stance.

- Anchor point – specific location on the archer's face to which index finger comes while holding and aiming.

- Archery golf (adaptation of golf to archery) – players shoot for holes, scoring according to the number of shots required to hit the target.

- Arm guard – a piece of leather or plastic worn on the inside of the forearm, protecting the arm from the bowstring.

- Arrow plate – a protective piece of hard material set into the bow where the arrow crosses it.

- Arrow rest – a small projection at the top of the bow handle where the arrow rests.

- Back – the side of the bow away from the shooter.

- Bow arm – the arm that holds the bow.

- Bow sight – a device attached to the bow through which the archer sights when aiming.

- Bow weight – designates the amount of effort needed to pull a bowstring a specific distance.

- Cant – shooting while holding the bow slightly turned or tilted.

- Cast – the distance a bow can shoot an arrow.

- Clout shooting – a type of shooting using a target 48 feet in diameter laid on the ground at a distance of 180 yards for men and 120 or 140 yards for women. Participants usually shoot 36 arrows per round.

- Cock/Index feather – the feather that is set at a right angle to the arrow nock; differently colored than the other two feathers.

- Creeping – letting the drawing hand move forward at the release.

- Crest – the archer's identifying marks located just below the fletchings.

- Draw – pulling the bowstring back into the anchor position.

- End – a specific number of arrows shot at one time or from one position before retrieval of arrows.

- Face – the part of the bow facing the shooter.

- Finger tab – a leather flap worn on the drawing hand protecting the fingers and providing a smooth release of the bowstring.

- Fletchings – the feathers of the arrow that give guidance to its flight.

- Flight shooting – shooting an arrow the farthest possible distance.

- Handle – the grip at the midsection of the bow.

- Hen feathers – the two feathers that are not set at right angles to the arrow nock.

- Instinctive shooting – aiming and shooting instinctively rather than using a bow sight or point-of-aim method.

- Limbs – upper and lower parts of the bow divided by the handle.

- Nock – the groove in the arrow's end where the string is placed.

- Nocking point – the point on the string where the arrow is placed.

- Notch – the grooves of the upper and lower tips of the limbs where the bowstring is fitted.

- Over bow – using too strong a bow that is too powerful to pull a bowstring the proper distance.

- Overdraw – drawing the bow so that the pile of the arrow is inside the bow.

- Petticoat – the part of the target face outside the white ring.

- Pile/point – the arrow's pointed, metal tip.

- Plucking – jerking the drawing hand laterally away from the face on the release causing the arrow's flight to veer to the left.

- Point-blank range – the distance from the target where the point of aim is right on the bull's eye.

- Point-of-aim – a method of aiming that aligns the pile of the arrow with the target.

- Quiver – a receptacle for carrying or holding arrows.

- Recurve bow – a bow that is curved on the ends.

- Release – the act of letting the bowstring slip off the fingertips.

- Round – the term used to indicate shooting a specified number of arrows at a designated distance or distances.

- Roving – an outdoor archery game that uses natural targets (trees, bushes, stumps, etc.) for competition.

- Serving – the thread wrapped around the bowstring at the nocking point.

- Shaft – the long, body part of the arrow.

- Spine – the rigidity and flexibility characteristics of an arrow.

- Tackle – archery equipment referred to in its entirety.

- Target face – the painted front of a target.

- Trajectory – the flight path of the arrow.

- Vane – an arrow's plastic feather.

Bowling Terminology:

- Anchor – the teammate who shoots last.

- Baby split – the 1-7 or 3-10 pin railroads.

- Backup – a reverse hook rotating to the right for a right-handed bowler.

- Bed posts – the 7-10 railroad.

- Blow – an error or missing a spare that is not split.

- Box – a frame.

- Brooklyn – a crossover ball striking the 1-2 pocket.
- Bucket – the 2-4-5-8 or 3-5-6-9 leaves.
- Cherry – chopping off the front pin on a spare.
- Double – two consecutive strikes.
- Double pinochle – the 7-6 and 4-10 split.
- Crossover – same as a Brooklyn.
- Dutch 200 (Dutchman) – a score of 200 made by alternating strikes and spares for the entire game.
- Error – same as a "blow."
- Foul – touching or going beyond the foul line in delivering the ball.
- Frame – the box where scores are entered.
- Gutter ball – a ball that falls into either gutter.
- Handicap – awarding an individual or team a bonus score or score adjustment that is based on averages.
- Head pin – the number one pin.
- Hook – a ball that breaks to the left for a right-handed bowler and breaks to the right for a left-handed bowler.
- Jersey side – same as a Brooklyn.
- Kegler – synonym for a bowler.
- Lane – a bowling alley.
- Leave – pin or pins left standing after a throw.
- Light hit – hitting the head pin lightly to the right or left side.
- Line – a complete game as recorded on the score sheet.
- Mark – getting a strike or spare.
- Open frame – a frame in which no mark is made, leaving at least one pin standing after rolling both balls in a frame.

- Pocket – space between the head pin and pins on either side.

- Railroad – synonym for a split.

- Sleeper – a pin hidden from view.

- Spare – knocking all pins down with two balls.

- Split – a leave, after throwing the first ball, in which the number one pin plus a second pin are down, and when seven pins remain standing.

- Spot – a bowler's point of aim on the alley.

- Striking out – obtaining three strikes in the last frame.

- Tap – a pin that remains standing after an apparently perfect hit.

- Turkey – three consecutive strikes.

TERMINOLOGY OF VARIOUS NET/WALL SPORTS

Badminton Terminology:

- Alley – the area on each side of the court used for doubles that is 1.5 feet wide.

- Around-the-head stroke – an overhead stroke used to hit a forehand-like overhead stroke that is on the backhand side of the body.

- Back alley – the area between the baseline and the doubles long service line.

- Backcourt – the back third of the court.

- Backhand – a stroke made on the non-racket side of the body.

- Baseline – the back boundary line of the court.

- Bird – another name for the shuttlecock/shuttle.

- Block – a soft shot used mainly to defend a smash; intercepting opponent's smash and returning it back over the net.

- Carry/Throw – a call when the shuttle remains on the racket during a stroke. It is legal if the racket follows the intended line of flight.

- Centerline – the mid-line separating the service courts.

- Clear – a high shot that goes over the opponent's head and lands close to the baseline.

- Combination alignment – partners playing both up-and-back and side-by-side during doubles games and/or volleys.

- Crosscourt – a diagonal shot hit into the opposite court.

- Defense – the team or player hitting the shuttle upwards.

- Double hit – an illegal shot where the player contacts the shuttle twice with the racket in one swing.

- Doubles service court – the short, wide area to which the server must serve in doubles play.

- Down the line shot – a straight-ahead shot (usually down the sideline).

- Drive – a hard, driven shot traveling parallel to the floor (clears net but does not have enough height for opponent to smash).

- Drop – a shot just clearing the net and then falling close to it.

- Face – the racket's string area.

- Fault – an infraction of the rules resulting in loss of serve or a point awarded to the server.

- First serve – a term used in doubles play to indicate that the server is the "first server" during an inning.

- Foot fault – Illegal movement/position of the feet by either the server or receiver.

- Forecourt – the front area of the court (between the net and the short service line).

- Forehand – a stroke made on the racket side of the body.

- Game point – the point, if won, that allows the server to win the game.

- Hand in – a term indicating that the server retains the serve.

- Hand out – the term used in doubles to denote that one player has lost the service.

- Home base – a center court position where a player can best play any shot hit by an opponent.

- Inning – the period a player or team holds service.

- Let – stopping the point because of some type of outside interference. Players replay the point.

- Lifting the shuttle – stroking the shuttle underhanded and hitting it upward.

- Long serve – a high, deep serve landing near the long service line in doubles or the back boundary line in singles.

- Love – the term used to indicate a zero score.

- Match – a series of games. Winning two out of three games wins the match.

- Match point – the point, if won by the server, which makes that person the winner of the match.

- Midcourt – the middle-third of the court (between short service line and long service line for doubles).

- Net shot – a shot taken near the net.

- Non-racket side – the opposite side of the hand holding the racket.

- Offense – the team or player that is stroking the shuttle downward.

- Overhead – a motion used to strike the shuttle when it is above the head.

- Racket foot or leg – the foot or leg on the same side as the hand holding the racket.

- Ready position – the position a player assumes to be ready to move in any direction.

- Receiver – the player to whom the shuttle is served.

- Second serve – in doubles, the term indicates that one partner has lost the serve, and the other partner is now serving.

- Server – the player putting the shuttle into play.

- Setting – choosing the amount of additional points to play when certain tie scores occur.

- Short-serve – a serve barely clearing the net and landing just beyond the short service line.

- Shuttlecock/Shuttle – the feathered, plastic or nylon object that players volley back and forth over the net.

- Side Alley – see alley.

- Smash – an overhead stroke hit downward with great velocity and angle.

- "T" – the intersection of the centerline and the short service line.

- Underhand – an upward stroke to hit the shuttle when it has fallen below shoulder level.

- Unsight – illegal position taken by the server's partner so the receiver cannot see the shuttle.

- Up-and-back – an offensive alignment used in doubles. The "up" player is responsible for the forecourt and the "back" player is responsible for both.

Racquetball/Handball Terminology:

- Ace – a serve that completely eludes the receiver.

- Back-wall shot – a shot made from a rebound off the back wall.

- Box – see service box.

- Ceiling shot – a shot that first strikes the ceiling, then the front wall.

- Crotch – the junction of any two playing surfaces, as between the floor and any wall.

- Crotch shot – a ball that simultaneously strikes the front wall and floor (not good).

- Cut throat – a three-man game in which the server plays against the other two players. Each player keeps an individual score.

- Drive shot – a power shot against the front wall rebounding in a fast, low, and straight line.

- Fault – an illegally served ball.

- Handout – retiring the server who fails to serve legally or when the serving team fails to return a ball that is in play.

- Hinder – interference or obstruction of the flight of the ball during play.

- Kill – a ball rebounded off the front wall so close to the floor that it is impossible to return.

- Passing shot – a shot placed out of an opponent's reach on either side.

- Rally – continuous play of the ball by opponents.

- Receiving line – the broken line parallel to the short line on a racquetball court.

- Run-around shot – a ball striking one sidewall, the rear wall, and the other sidewall.

- Safety zone – a five-foot area bounded by the back edge of the short line and receiving line that is only observed during the serve in racquetball.

- Screen – a hinder due to obstruction of the opponent's vision.

- Server – person in the "hand-in" position and eligible to serve.

- Service box – the service zone bounded by the sidewall and a parallel line 18 inches away; denotes where server's partner must stand in doubles during the serve.

- Service court – the area where the ball must land when it is returned from the front wall on the serve.

- Service line – the line that is parallel to and five feet in front of the short line.

- Service zone – the area where the ball must be served.

- Short line – the line on the floor parallel to front wall and equidistant from front and back wall. The serve must go over this line when returning from the front wall.

- Shoot – attempt kill shots.

- Side out – loss of serve.

- Thong – the strap on the bottom handle of the racquetball racquet that is worn around the player's wrist.

- Volley – returning the ball to the front wall before it bounces on the floor.

- Z-ball – defensive shot that strikes the front wall, a sidewall, and then the opposite sidewall.

Tennis Terminology:

- Ace – serving a ball untouched by the opponent's racket.

- Advantage (Ad) – a scoring term. The next point won after the score is "deuce."

- Alley – the 4.5-foot strip on either side of the singles court that enlarges the court for doubles.

- Approach shot – a shot hit inside the baseline while approaching the net.

- Backcourt – the area between the service line and the baseline.

- Backhand – strokes hit on the left side of a right-handed player.

- Backspin – spin placed on a ball that causes the ball to bounce back toward the hitter.

- Back swing – the beginning of all groundstrokes and service motion requiring a back swing to gather energy for the forward swing.

- Baseline – the end line of a tennis court.

- Break – winning a game in when the opponent serves.

- Center mark – a short mark bisecting the baseline.

- Center service line – the perpendicular line to the net dividing the two service courts in halves.

- Center strap – the strap at the center of the net anchored to the court to facilitate a constant 3-foot height for the net at its center.

- Center stripe – same as the center service line.

- Chip – a short chopping motion of the racket against the back and bottom side of the ball imparting backspin.

- Chop – placing backspin on the ball with a short, high-to-low forward swing.

- Cross-court – a shot hit diagonally from one corner of the court over the net into the opposite corner of the court.

- Cut off the angle – moving forward quickly against an opponent's cross-court shot, allowing the player to hit the ball near the center of the court rather than near the sidelines.

- Deep (depth) – a shot bouncing near the baseline on groundstrokes and near the service line on serves.

- Default – a player who forfeits his/her position in a tournament by not playing a scheduled match.

- Deuce – a term used when the game score is 40-40 or in the new scoring system, 3-3.

- Double fault – two consecutive out-of-bounds or in the net serves on the same point resulting in loss of the point.

- Doubles lines – the outside sidelines on a court used only for doubles.

- Down the line – a shot hit near a sideline traveling close to, and parallel to, the same line from which the shot was initially hit.

- Drive – an offensive shot hit with extra force.

- Drop shot – a groundstroke hit so that it drops just over the net with little or no forward bounce.

- Drop volley – a volley hit in such a manner that it drops just over the net with little or no forward bounce.

- Error – a mistake made by a player during competition.

- Flat shot – occurs when a player hits a ball so there is no rotation or spin when traveling through the air.

- Foot fault – illegal foot movement before service, penalized by losing that particular serve. Common foot faults are: stepping on or ahead of the baseline before contacting the ball and running along the baseline before serving.

- Forecourt – the area between the net and the service line.

- Forehand – the stroke hit on the right side of a right-handed player.

- Frame – the rim of the racket head plus the handle of the racket.

- Game – scoring term when a player wins 4 points before an opponent while holding a minimum 2-point lead.

- Grip – the portion of the racket that the player grasps in his hand.

- Groundstroke – any ball hit after it has bounced.

- Half volley – a ball hit inches away from the court's surface after the ball has bounced.

- Hold serve – winning your own serve. If you lose your own serve, your serve has been "broken."

- Let (ball) – a point replayed because of some kind of interference.

- Let serve – a serve that touches the net tape, falls into the proper square, and is played over.

- Linesman – a match official who calls balls "in" or "out."

- Lob – a ball hit with sufficient height to pass over the out-stretched arm of a net player.

- Lob volley – a shot hit high into the air from a volleying position.

- Love – scoring term that means zero points or games.

- Match – a contest between two or four opponents.

- Match point – the point immediately before the final point of a match.

- Midcourt – the area in front of the baseline or behind the service line of the playing court.

- Net ball – a ball that hits the net, falling on the same side as the hitter.

- No man's land – a general area within the baseline and proper net position area. When caught in that area, the player must volley or hit ground strokes near his/her feet.

- Offensive lob – a ball hit just above the racket reach of an opposing net player.

- Open face racket – a racket whose face is moving under the ball. A wide-open racket face is parallel to the court surface.

- Overhead – a shot hit from a position higher than the player's head.

- Over-hitting – hitting shots with too much force; over-hitting usually results in errors.

- Pace – the speed of the ball.

- Passing shot – a shot passing beyond the reach of the net player landing inbounds.

- Poach – to cross over into your partner's territory in doubles in an attempt to intercept the ball.

- Racket face – the racket's hitting surface.

- Racket head – the top portion of the racket frame that includes the strings.

- Rally – opponents hitting balls back and forth across the net.

- Receiver – the player about to return the opponent's serve.

- Server – the player initiating play.

- Service line – the line at the end of the service courts parallel to the net.

- Set – a scoring term meaning the first player to win six games with a minimum two-game lead.

- Set point – the point, if won, which will give the player the set.

- Sidespin – a ball hit rotating on a horizontal plane.

- Signals in doubles – signaling your partner that you are going to poach at the net.

- Singles line – the sideline closest to the center mark that runs the entire length of the court.

- Slice – motion of the racket head going around the side of the ball, producing a horizontal spin on ball.

- Tape – the band of cloth or plastic running across the top of the net.

- Telegraphing the play – indicating the direction of one's intended target before hitting the ball.

- Topspin – forward rotation of the ball.

- Touch – the ability to make delicate, soft shots from several positions on the court.

- Twist – a special rotation applied to the ball during the serve causing the ball to jump to the left (of right-handed server).

- Umpire – the official that calls lines.

- Under spin – a counterclockwise spin placed on the ball (i.e. backspin).

- Volley – hitting the ball in the air before it bounces on the court.

SKILL 8.2 Recreational activities and outdoor pursuits.

OUTDOOR EDUCATION

Techniques and skills include:

- **Walking and Hiking** – Instructors can take students on walking/hiking trips through nature reserves and national parks. Such trips can incorporate team-building activities and nature education.

- **Sail Training** – Students taught to sail should display competence in the maintenance and piloting of a boat, including cooperative activities necessary to a successful sailing endeavor (e.g. working together to get the boat into and out of the water, paddling in rhythm, turning the boat, etc.). Prior to the start of sail training, students should understand all safety procedures and acceptable forms of behavior on a boat (e.g. only standing when necessary, no pushing, following instructions, wearing a life jacket, etc.). Students must also demonstrate swimming competence (i.e. ability to tread water, swim a distance continuously, and put on a life jacket while in the water).

- **Rope Challenge Courses** – Good activity for team-building purposes. Challenges include personal physical challenges (climbing various structures), or group activities (e.g. requiring students to work together to coordinate the crossing of a course). Safety requirements include helmets, harnesses, spotters, trained supervisors, and strict adherence to all safety procedures and educator instructions.

Related safety education should emphasize the importance of planning and research. Students should consider in advance what the potential dangers of an activity might be and to prepare plans accordingly (students and instructors should also examine weather forecasts). Of course, educator supervision is required. First-aid equipment and properly trained educators must be present for outdoor education activities. Students should use proper safety gear when appropriate (e.g. helmets, harnesses, etc.). Parental consent is generally required for outdoor education activities.

Bicycling – In bicycling classes, students should learn proper bicycling form and how to gauge which gear is most appropriate for their current speed and level of inclination. Students should also become familiar with the proper way to maintain and care for their bicycles.

Bicycling strategy is similar to track events – learning to gauge the appropriate levels of energy expenditure relative to the length of the track and the fitness of the cyclist.

Safety practices while bicycling include seriousness in practice (no horseplay, which can result in injury) and attentiveness to the track so that students can avoid potentially dangerous bumps or cracks. Instructors should remind students not to race with each other, but rather to focus on their own physical activity.

Equipment required for bicycling with students includes proper gear (which includes clothing without loose appendages that can catch in bicycle gears), water for longer trips, and, of course, the bicycles themselves.

Cross-country skiing – Students in cross-country skiing classes will learn the proper form for cross-country skiing (e.g. herringbone, diagonal stride, double pole) and will greatly improve their fitness (as cross-country skiing is a very taxing activity on a very wide range of muscle groups).
Like most endurance activities, cross-country skiing strategy involves regulating the levels of energy expenditure relative to the length of the course and the fitness level of the athlete.

Safety practices in cross-country skiing include ensuring the availability of first aid and instructor attentiveness to the students (as it is easier to 'lose track' of a student who is having trouble). Instructors should also instruct students not to wander away from the group – a good solution is the implementation of a buddy system.

Equipment required for cross-country skiing trips includes appropriate dress (make sure students dress warmly), cross-country skis, and poles.

Canoeing – Students in canoeing classes will learn the various forms of paddling strokes, how to manage their weight, and how to work as a team to maneuver a canoe properly.

Strategies for effective canoeing include the clear delineation of members of a rowing team and the role that each individual serves. The 'captain' coordinates the efforts of the rowers on the canoe and should become familiar with the course and destination.

Safety practices for canoeing call for the instructor to ensure that the students are all able to swim and equipped with proper flotation equipment (e.g. lifejackets). First aid should be available and the instructor should see to it that he remains close enough to students in different canoes to be able to hear them and reach them if needed.

Equipment required for canoeing classes includes canoes, canoeing paddles, and proper flotation equipment. Instructors should advise students to have a change of clothes available in the event that they get wet.

Orienteering – Skills that students will acquire during orienteering activities include the ability to read a map, critical thinking stemming from practice identifying locations, navigation ability, and strategic thinking for selection of efficient movement patterns between several points.

Strategies for orienteering include ascertaining early the destination points and mapping an efficient course to pass through all of them.

Safety practices include ensuring the availability and accessibility of first aid, properly instructing the students in emergency procedures (e.g. blow the whistle and remain where you are), and selecting an area small enough so the instructor can hear the whistle from any position.

Equipment required for orienteering with students includes proper outdoor clothing and a whistle for use in emergency situations. Students will also need a map and possibly a compass.

Fishing – Students studying fishing will learn the correct technique for casting a line and will learn to identify spots where fish are most likely to congregate. Fishing also teaches patience to students.

Strategies for effective fishing with groups of students include deploying students in such a way that one will not interfere with another's fishing activities. Students should also learn about the habits of the fish that they are after, to allow them to tailor their approaches accordingly.

Safety practices for fishing call for instructors to remind students that their equipment does not consist of toys and they should not play with it. Students should definitely handle fishing rods and hooks carefully around other students.

Equipment required for fishing includes fishing rods, hooks, bait, gear (e.g. boots), and a bucket or other receptacle for the fish.

Inline skating – Skills that students in inline skating class will acquire include skating techniques (e.g. braking and stopping, skating backwards, skating downhill) and improved balance. Students should also learn to care for their skating equipment.

Strategies in inline skating focus on maintaining proper form during the activity.

Safety practices in inline skating include requiring students to wear appropriate protective gear and ensuring that first aid is available. Instructors should instruct students not to attempt stunts, especially without supervision.

Equipment required for inline skating includes skates and appropriate protective gear (e.g. helmets, kneepads, elbow pads).

Rock climbing – Students studying rock climbing will gain proficiency in climbing techniques (including body positioning and learning to find proper toeholds and handholds in the rock face) belaying, and managing the climbing and harness equipment.

Strategies in rock climbing require the climber to remain aware not only of the current 'next step' of the climbing process, but to also remain aware of the entire rock face, and to plan on a course that she can follow through to completion (so as to prevent climbing to a dead-end area).

Safety practices include explaining all safety practices so students understand, ensuring that students wear all safety gear (protective gear and harnesses) properly, and that all students have spotters monitoring their activities.

Equipment required for rock climbing activities includes proper attire, suitable footwear, protective equipment, and harnessing equipment.

Alpine skiing (downhill skiing) – The skills that students of alpine skiing will gain center on learning to control the direction and speed of their descent; novices will begin by learning the "snow plough" technique to turn, and will learn to point their skis inward to stop. More advanced technique will center on "carving", which allows the skis to turn without skidding or slowing down.

Alpine skiing strategy calls for awareness of the practitioner's current level of skill and avoiding over-reaching (i.e. attempting courses that are too advanced and thus dangerous). Instructors should teach students to be aware of the course ahead of them, allowing them to better plan their movements.

Safety practices in alpine skiing include proper inspection of the equipment to ensure that everything is in order and instructing the students in appropriate safety procedures. Most importantly, instructors should not allow students to attempt courses that are beyond their current skill levels.

Equipment required for alpine skiing includes appropriate dress that is adequately warm (hats, gloves, and goggles), skis, and poles.

Camping – Camping imparts a wide range of skills, from tent pitching to fire building to outdoor cooking.

Successful camping strategy focuses on planning and preparing the students (mentally, physically, and in terms of their equipment) for the camping experience.

Safety practices for camping include packing a first aid kit and emergency supplies (e.g. a map, compass, whistle), checking the weather before departure, avoiding areas of natural hazards, and putting out fires appropriately. Instructors should teach students to identify and avoid poisonous plants.

Camping equipment includes a tent, lean-to, or other shelter device, a sleeping bag and sleeping pad (or air mattress), a portable stove (where campfires are impractical or not allowed), a lantern or flashlight, a hatchet, axe or saw, ropes, and tarps.

SKILL 8.3   Techniques for assessing skills in outdoor activities.

SEE ALSO DOMAIN V., Skill 4.1

The trend in physical education assessment is to move increasingly away from norm- and criterion-referenced evaluations (i.e. measuring a student's achievements against the achievements of a normative group or against criteria that are arbitrarily set by either the educator or the governing educational body), and towards performance-based, or "authentic" evaluations. This creates difficulty for physical educators because it eliminates preset reference points.

The advantage of performance-based evaluations is they are equally fair to individuals with diverse backgrounds, special needs, and disabilities. In all cases, the instructor evaluates students based on their personal performance.

Portfolio construction is one way of assessing the performance of a student. The student chooses the achievements to add to the portfolio. This creates a tool that assesses current abilities and serves as a benchmark against which the instructor can measure future performance (thus evaluating progress over time, and not just a localized achievement).

Student self-assessment is often an important part of portfolios. The instructor should ask children questions like, "Where am I now? Where am I trying to go? What am I trying to achieve? How can I get from here to there?" This type of questioning involves the child more deeply in the learning process.

Goal Setting: Student's set reasonable, realistic and measurable goals that they would like to achieve in a certain amount of time. Daily progress is noted by the student in a physical education notebook. At the end of the time period if the goal has been achieved, then they can set a new one. If not, then the student can make adjustments as needed and re-create a new goal.

SKILL 8.4 Activities appropriate for various developmental levels and purposes.

Physical education instructors should employ a variety of instructional strategies, techniques, and teaching methods to promote student learning. Instructors must also tailor their methods to match the age and developmental level of their students.

STRATEGIES THAT PROMOTE COMPETENCE IN PHYSICAL ACTIVITIES

Instructors must employ a variety of techniques to promote competence in physical activities. Instructors should use verbal instruction, demonstration, practice, and assessment.

Applying techniques that allow students to measure their competence is a very useful strategy for physical education teachers to use. Examples would be mapping, checklist of skills broken down into parts where students would be able to check off a "step" once they have mastered that level of an activity of skill and rewards of stars and so forth by their names on a master, posted chart.

It is important that instructors tailor their techniques to fit the age and skill level of their students. For example, activities for a third grade class will be much simpler than activities for a high school class. In addition, older, more developed students are better able to handle competitive situations than are younger students. Younger and less talented students require a cooperative, stress-free environment to maximize learning.

STRATEGIES THAT PROMOTE POSITIVE ATTITUDES TOWARD FITNESS

One of the most important tasks for physical education instructors is to instill in their students an appreciation of and a positive attitude toward physical fitness. Creating a safe and cooperative learning environment is the best strategy for fostering positive attitudes. Allowing students to explore activities, plan fitness goals, improve personal fitness levels, and generally take responsibility for their own physical selves promotes a positive attitude toward lifelong fitness. Additionally, students need to be taught and have an understanding of the many benefits being physical fit provides. Providing opportunities for many different types of physical activities allows for students to, hopefully find a sport or activity that they enjoy and can continue throughout their lives.

STRATEGIES THAT INVOLVE STUDENTS WITH VARYING INTERESTS AND ABILITIES

A major challenge that physical education instructors face is planning a curriculum that appeals to students of different ability levels and with different interests. Instructors should provide students with a choice of activities to appeal to different interests. Instructors must use a creative approach to inspire students that may not have a natural interest in sports and fitness. Finally, instructors must tailor their lessons to accommodate students of varying abilities and developmental stages. Not all students will be able to perform the same skills and tasks.

COMPETENCY 9.0   **UNDERSTAND TECHNIQUES, SKILLS, STRATEGIES, RULES, ETIQUETTE, AND SAFETY PRACTICES FOR TEAM SPORTS**

SKILL 9.1   **Techniques, skill progressions, strategies, rules, etiquette, safety practices, equipment, and types of lead-up activities for team sports.**

TEAM PASSING SPORTS

Basketball – The fundamental skills of basketball include passing, dribbling, and shooting. As students' skills improve, they may begin to specialize in playing a specific position (point guard, shooting guard, small forward, power forward or center).

Touch/Flag Football – Skills that students will practice include running and passing – tackling is not relevant in touch or flag football situations. As students improve, they may begin to specialize in playing specific positions (e.g. quarterbacks or receivers). They may also become more involved in the study and implementation of strategy.

The main goal of offensive strategy in football is to move closer to the opposing team's end zone, to the point where the ball is close enough to score either a touchdown or a field goal. The aim of defensive strategies is to prevent this same movement towards the end zone by the opposition. Both offensive and defensive strategies make important use of concepts of time management and the possibility of "running out the clock". Formations are central to football strategy, both on offense and on defense, and students should become familiar with simple formations for both.

Lacrosse – Lacrosse players must master the skills of catching and throwing the ball with their sticks and cradling (the motion that allows players to run with the ball in their stick).

Lacrosse strategy has many parallels with other team sports like basketball, soccer, and field hockey. In all of these sports, the team of players has to maneuver to outflank and outsmart their opponents in order to score a goal.

Soccer – Soccer players must master the skills of running, accurate kicking, manipulation of the ball, and footwork that allows the student to maneuver when in motion.

The key to soccer strategy is for students to understand that the goal is to get the ball to the right person's feet – the one who has the most time and space (facing the least pressure) and is in the most advantageous position to score (or make a goal-scoring pass). Broadly, offensive strategy will spread the team out, to allow for coverage of more of the field. Defensive strategy will have the team compress to a compact unit that is able to cover the goal effectively.

Team Handball – Skills that students will learn in a handball class will include catching and accurately throwing the ball, taking steps while bouncing the ball (similar to basketball's dribble), and quick analysis of the playing situation to ascertain who the best target is for a pass.

Strategy in handball centers around staying one step ahead of the opposing team, keeping them guessing, and having multiple contingencies for given situations so that game play doesn't become predictable (and easier to counter). Specific tactics can include types of shots that are harder for the opponent to hit and shots that will put the ball out of play (when it is advantageous to do so).

Ultimate Frisbee – Skills that students must acquire to play ultimate Frisbee proficiently include catching the Frisbee, accurately throwing the Frisbee, and running. Instructors should also emphasize strategic thinking, as there is limited time to select a destination for and execute a throw.

The goal of offensive strategy in ultimate Frisbee is to create open lanes in the field that are free of defenders. Common offensive strategies include the 'vertical stack' and 'horizontal stack' (similar to a spread offense in football). Defensive strategy aims to gain control of the Frisbee and deflect passes made by the opposing team. A basic defensive principle is the 'force', which calls for the defense to cut off the handler's access to half of the field, thereby forcing the offensive player to throw the Frisbee to the other side of the field.

SAFETY PRACTICES AND EQUIPMENT – TEAM PASSING SPORTS

Important safety considerations for team passing sports include proper maintenance of facilities and playing fields, use of protective equipment, and proper enforcement of the rules of play. Enforcement of rules is particularly important to prevent participants from injuring other participants either intentionally or unintentionally through reckless play.

The following is a list of sport-specific equipment for team passing sports:

- Basketball – basketballs, goals, appropriate shoes
- Touch or Flag Football – footballs, flags and flag belts, cones to mark boundaries and end zones
- Lacrosse – lacrosse sticks and balls, protective pads, goals (nets)
- Soccer – soccer balls, goals, field markers, protective shin guards
- Team Handball – handballs and goals
- Ultimate Frisbee – Frisbees and an open playing field

APPLY APPROPRIATE STRATEGIES TO GAME AND SPORT SITUATIONS

Basketball Strategies:

Use a Zone Defense

- To prevent drive-ins for easy lay-up shots.
- When playing area is small.
- When team is in foul trouble.
- To keep an excellent rebounder near opponent's basket.
- When opponents' outside shooting is weak.
- When opponents have an advantage in height.
- When opponents have an exceptional offensive player, or when the best defenders cannot handle one-on-one defense.

Offensive Strategies Against Zone Defense

- Using quick, sharp passing to penetrate zone forcing opposing player out of assigned position.
- Overloading and mismatching.

Offensive Strategies for One-On-One Defense

- Using the "pick-and-roll" and the "give-and-go" to screen defensive players to open up offensive players for shot attempts.
- Teams may use free-lancing (spontaneous one-one-one offense), but more commonly they use "sets" of plays.

Soccer Strategies:

- **Heading** – using the head to pass, to shoot, or to clear the ball.
- **Tackling** – objective is to take possession of the ball from an opponent. Successful play requires knowledgeable utilization of space.

Volleyball Strategies:

- Using forearm passes (bumps, digs, or passes) to play balls below the waist, to play balls that are driven hard, to pass the serve, and to contact balls distant from a player.

RULES OF TEAM SPORTS

BASKETBALL:

- A player touching the floor on or outside the boundary line is out-of-bounds.

- The ball is out of bounds if it touches anything (a player, the floor, an object, or any person) that is on or outside the boundary line.

- An offensive player remaining in the three-second zone of the free-throw lane for more than three seconds is a violation.

- A ball firmly held by two opposing players results in a jump ball.

- A throw-in is awarded to the opposing team of the last player touching a ball that goes out-of-bounds.

SOCCER:

The following are direct free-kick offenses:

- Hand or arm contact with the ball

- Using hands to hold an opponent

- Pushing an opponent

- Striking/kicking/tripping or attempting to strike/kick/trip an opponent

- Goalie using the ball to strike an opponent

- Jumping at or charging an opponent

- Kneeing an opponent

- Any contact fouls

The following are indirect free-kick offenses:

- Same player playing the ball twice at the kickoff, on a throw-in, on a goal kick, on a free kick, or on a corner kick.

- The goalie delaying the game by holding the ball or carrying the ball more than four steps.

- Failure to notify the referee of substitutions/re-substitutions and that player then handling the ball in the penalty area.

TEACHER CERTIFICATION STUDY GUIDE

- Any person, who is not a player, entering playing field without a referee's permission.

- Unsportsmanlike actions or words in reference to a referee's decision.

- Dangerously lowering the head or raising the foot too high to make a play.

- A player resuming play after being ordered off the field.

- Offsides – an offensive player must have two defenders between him and the goal when a teammate passes the ball to him or else he is offsides.

- Attempting to kick the ball when the goalkeeper has possession or interference with the goalkeeper to hinder him/her from releasing the ball.

- Illegal charging.

- Leaving the playing field without referee's permission while the ball is in play.

SOFTBALL:

- Each team plays nine players in the field (sometimes 10 for slow pitch).

- Field positions are one pitcher, one catcher, four infielders, and three outfielders (four outfielders in ten player formats).

- The four bases are 60 feet apart.

- Any ball hit outside of the first or third base line is a foul ball (i.e. runners cannot advance and the pitch counts as a strike against the batter)

- If a batter receives three strikes (i.e. failed attempts at hitting the ball) in a single at bat he/she strikes out.

- The pitcher must start with both feet on the pitcher's rubber and can only take one step forward when delivering the underhand pitch.

- A base runner is out if:

    - A. The opposition tags him with the ball before he reaches a base.
    - B. The ball reaches first base before he does.
    - C. He runs outside of the base path to avoid a tag.
    - D. A batted ball strikes him in fair territory.

- A team must maintain the same batting order throughout the game.

- Runners cannot lead off and base stealing is illegal.

- Runners may overrun first base, but can be tagged out if off any other base.

VOLLEYBALL:

The following infractions by the receiving team result in a point awarded to the serving side and an infraction by serving team results in side-out:

- Illegal serves or serving out of turn.

- Illegal returns or catching or holding the ball.

- Dribbling or a player touching the ball twice in succession.

- Contact with the net (two opposing players making contact with the net at the same time results in a replay of the point).

- Touching the ball after it has been played three times without passing over the net.

- A player's foot completely touching the floor over the centerline.

- Reaching under the net and touching a player or the ball while the ball is in play.

- The players changing positions prior to the serve.

SAMPLE OFFICIATING SITUATIONS

NOTE: Since rules change yearly, acquiring new rulebooks every year is necessary for proper officiating.

Basketball situation: Actions of the spectators interfere with the progression of the game.

Ruling: An official may call a foul on the team whose supporters are interfering with the game.

Basketball situation: A1 is attempting a field goal and B1 fouls him. A1 continues with the field goal attempt and, before releasing the ball, crashes into B2 who has a legal position on the floor. A1 successfully completes the field goal.

Ruling: The ball was immediately dead when A1 fouled B2; therefore, field goal does not count. However, since B1 fouled A1 while attempting the field goal, A1 receives two free throws.

Basketball situation: The official in the frontcourt runs into a pass thrown from the backcourt by A1 and goes out-of-bounds.

Ruling: B receives a throw-in. The official is part of the court.

Basketball Situation: A1 catches the ball in mid-air and lands with the right foot first and then the left foot. A1 pivots on the left foot.

Ruling: A violation has occurred because A1 can only pivot on the foot that first lands on the floor, which was the right foot.

Soccer situation: The ball is alive when a substitute enters the playing field.

Ruling: A non-player foul. Referee can either penalize at location of the next dead ball or at the place of entry (usually when the team offended is at an advantage).

Soccer situation: B1 charges A1's goalie in A1's penalty area.

Ruling: Team A receives a direct free kick at the spot of foul. A flagrant charge awards team A a penalty-kick at the other end of the field, and B1 is disqualified.

Soccer situation: The goalie is out of position when a back on team B heads the ball out and falls into the net. A2 gets the ball, passes it to A1, and has only the goalie to beat.

Ruling: A1 is not offside because the B back left the field during legal play.

Volleyball situation: Team A's second volley hits an obstruction directly over the net, returns to A's playing area, and team A plays it again.

Ruling: Fair play and the next play is team A's third play.

Volleyball situation: The serving team has three front line players standing close together in front of the server at the spiking line.

Ruling: Illegal alignment is called for intentional screening.

Volleyball situation: RB and CB on the receiving team are overlapping when at the time of the serve, and the serve lands out-of-bounds.

Ruling: Serving team receives a point because of receiving team's illegal alignment.

Volleyball situation: LB on team B saves a spiked ball and it deflects off his/her shoulder.

Ruling: A legal hit.

TERMINOLOGY OF VARIOUS TEAM PASSING SPORTS

Basketball Terminology:

- Backcourt players (Guards) – players who set up a team's offensive pattern and bring the ball up the court.

- Backdoor – an offensive maneuver in which a player cuts toward the baseline to the basket, behind the defenders, and receives a ball for a field goal attempt.

- Baseline – the end line of the court.

- Blocking/Boxing out – a term used when a player is under the backboard to prevent an opposing player from achieving a good rebounding position.

- Charging – personal contact by a player with the ball against the body of a defensive opponent.

- Corner players (Forwards) – tall players that make up the sides of the offensive set-up who are responsible for the rebounding and shooting phases of the team's offense.

- Cut – a quick, offensive move by a player attempting to get free for a pass.

- Denial defense – aggressive individual defense to keep an offensive player from receiving a pass.

- Double foul – two opponents committing personal fouls against each other simultaneously.

- Dribble – ball movement by a player in control who throws or taps the ball in the air or onto the floor and then touches it. The dribble ends when the dribbler touches the ball with both hands concurrently, loses control, or permits it to come to rest while in contact with it.

- Drive – an aggressive move by a player with the ball toward the basket.

- Fake (Feint) – using a deceptive move with the ball pulling the defensive player out of position.

- Fast break – quickly moving the ball down court to score before the defense has a chance to set up.

- Field goal – a basket scored from the field.

- Freelance – no structure or set plays in the offense.

- Free throw – the right given a player to score one or two points by unhindered shots for a goal from within the free throw circle and behind the free throw line.

- Give-and-go – a maneuver when the offensive player passes to a teammate and then immediately cuts in toward the basket for a return pass.

- Held ball – occurs when two opponents have one or both hands firmly on the ball and neither can gain possession without undue roughness.

- Inside player (Center, Post, Pivot) – this player is usually the tallest team player who is situated near the basket, around the three-second lane area, and is responsible for rebounding and close-range shooting.

- Jump ball – a method of putting the ball into play by tossing it up between two opponents in the center circle to start the game or any overtime periods.

- Outlet pass – a term used that designates a direct pass from a rebounder to a teammate (the main objective is starting a fast break).

- Overtime period – an additional period of playing time when the score is tied at the end of the regulation game.

- Personal foul – a player foul that involves contact with an opponent while the ball is alive or after the ball is in possession of a player for a throw-in.

- Pick – a special type of screen where a player stands so the defensive player slides to make contact to free an offensive teammate for a shot or drive.

- Pivot – occurs when a player who is holding the ball steps once or more than once in any direction with the same foot while the other foot, called the pivot foot, remains at its point of contact with the floor. Also, another term for the inside player.

- Posting up – a player cutting to the three-second lane area, pausing, and anticipating a pass.

- Rebound – when the ball bounces off the backboard or basket.

- Restraining circles – three circles with a six-foot radius. One is located in the center of the court, and the others are located at each of the free-throw lines.

- Running time – not stopping the clock for fouls or violations.

- Screen – an offensive maneuver positioning a player between the defender and a teammate to free the teammate for an uncontested shot.

- Switching – defensive guards reversing their guarding assignments.

- Technical foul – a non-contact foul by a player, team, or coach for unsportsmanlike behavior or failing to abide by rules regarding submission of lineups, uniform numbering, and substitution procedures.

- Telegraphing a pass – a look or signal to indicate where the ball is going to be passed.

- Throw-in – a method of putting the ball in play from out-of-bounds.

- Traveling – illegal movement, in any direction, of a player in possession of the ball within bounds. Moving with the ball without dribbling.

- Violation – an infraction of the rules resulting in a throw-in from out-of-bounds.

Soccer Terminology:

- Center – passing from the outside of the field near the sideline into the center.

- Charge – illegal or legal body contact between opponents.

- Chip – lofting the ball into the air using the instep kick technique; contacting the ball very low causing it to loft quickly with backspin.

- Clear – attempting to move the ball out of danger by playing the ball a great distance.

- Corner kick – a direct free kick from the corner arc awarded to the attacking players when the defending team last played the ball over their own end line.

- Cross – a pass from the outside of the field near the end line to a position in front of the goal.

- Dead ball situation – the organized restarting of the game after stopping play.

- Direct free kick – a free kick whereby the kicker may score immediately from that initial contact.

- Dribble – the technique of a player self-propelling the ball with the foot in order to maintain control of the ball while moving from one spot to another.

- Drop ball – the method used to restart the game after temporary suspension of play when the ball is still in play.

- Goal area – the rectangular area in front of the goal where the ball is placed for a goal kick.

- Half volley – contacting the ball just as it hits the ground after being airborne.

- Head – playing the ball with the head.

- Indirect free kick – a free kick from which a player, other than the kicker, must contact the ball before the team can score a goal.

- Kickoff – the free kick starting play at the beginning of the game, after each period, or after a score.

- Obstruction – illegally using the body to shield an opponent from reaching the ball.

- One-touch – immediately passing or shooting a received ball without stopping it.

- Penalty area – the large rectangular area in front of the goal where the goalkeeper may use the hands to play the ball.

- Penalty kick – a direct free kick awarded in the penalty area against the defending team for a Direct Free Kick foul.

- Settle – taking a ball out of the air and settling it on the ground so that it is rolling and no longer bouncing.

- Square pass – a pass directed toward the side of a player.

- Tackle – a technique to take the ball away from the opponents.

- Through pass – a pass penetrating between and past the defenders.

- Throw-in – the technique to restart the game when the ball goes out of play over the sideline.

- Touchline – the side line of the field.

- Trap – the technique used for receiving the ball and bringing it under control.

- Two-touch- receiving – trapping and immediately re-passing the ball.

Volleyball Terminology:

- Attack – returning the ball across the net in an attempt to put the opponents at a disadvantage.

- Ball handling – executing any passing fundamental.

- Block – intercepting the ball just before or as it crosses the net.

- Bump – see forearm pass.

- Court coverage – a defensive player's court assignment.

- Dig – an emergency pass usually used to defend a hard-driven attack.

- Dink – a soft shot off the fingertips to lob the ball over a block.

- Double foul – infraction of rules by both teams during the same play.

- Drive – an attacking shot contacted in the center that attempts to hit the ball off the blocker's hands.

- Fault – any infraction of the rules.

- Forearm pass – a pass made off the forearms to play served balls, hard-driven spikes, or any low ball.

- Free ball – a ball returned by the opponent that is easily handled.

- Frontcourt – the playing area where it is legal to block or attack.

- Held ball – a ball that opponents simultaneously contact and momentarily hold above the net.

- Kill – an attack that the opposition cannot return.

- Lob – a soft attack contacted on the back bottom-quarter of the ball causing an upward trajectory.

- Overhand pass – a pass made by contacting the ball above the head with the fingers.

- Overlap – an illegal foot position when the ball is dead, with an adjacent player putting another out of position.

- Play over – replaying the rally because of a held ball or the official prematurely suspending play. The server re-serves with no point awarded.

- Point – a point is scored when the receiving team fails to return the ball to the opponents' court legally.

- Rotation – clockwise rotation of the players upon gaining the ball from the opponents.

- Serve – putting the ball in play over the net by striking it with the hand.

- Set – placing the ball near the net to facilitate attacking.

- Setter – the player assigned to set the ball.

- Side out – side is out when the serving team fails to win a point or plays the ball illegally.

- Spike – a ball hit with top spin and with a strong downward force into the opponents' court.

- Spiker – the player assigned to attack the ball.

- Spike-roll – an attack that first takes an upward trajectory using the spiking action (with or without jumping).

- Topspin (Overspin) – applying forward spin to the ball during the serve, spike, or spike roll.

SKILL 9.2 Techniques for assessing skills in team sports.

SEE DOMAIN V., Skill 4.1

SKILL 9.3 Activities appropriate for various levels and purposes.

See Domain III - Skill 8.4

One of the most challenging aspects of being a teacher is the ability to provide a curriculum that uses strategies and adaptations, meeting the needs of an always diverse population. Schools have made huge strides in meeting these needs through resource teachers that work specifically with student's of varying handicaps.

The law now requires that all teacher's and schools provide the "least restrictive environment" for all students. The student's this applies to in particular are those students that have IEP's, or Individualized Educational Plans. These students have varying handicaps. The determination of least restrictive environment for these students is made by annual meetings (or during the school year as needed) that includes, the resource teacher, all the classroom, including the P.E. teacher of the student and the parents. In the higher grades, such as high school, at the parent's discretion, the student may attend these meetings.

Specific strategies involve:

- Peer to peer activities. For example, if a student is unable to shoot a basketball correctly, instruct a peer student that does know how too, assist the student

- Groupings by skill levels.

- Station rotations where more diverse exposure to activities is allowed

- Bringing in the student's resource teacher to assist the student as needed

ADAPTING SELECTED ACTIVITIES:

Walking: adapt distance, distance over time, and number of steps in specified distance; provide handrails for support; change slope for incline walking; and change width of walking pathway.

Stair climbing: change pathway, pace of climbing, and number and height of steps.

Running: change distance over time, use an incline-changing slope (distance over time), and form a maze (distance over time).

Jumping: change distance and height of jump, change distance in a series and from a platform, change participants' arm positions.

Hopping: change distance for one and two hops (using preferred and non-preferred leg) and distance through obstacle course.

Galloping: change number of gallops over distance, change distance covered in number of gallops, and widen pathway.

Skipping: change number of errorless skips, change distance covered in number of skips, change number of skips in distance, and add music for skipping in rhythm.

Leaping: change distance and height of leaps.

Bouncing balls: change size of ball (larger), have participant use two hands, reduce number of dribbles, bounce ball higher, have participant stand stationary and perform bounces one at a time.

Catching: use larger balls and have participant catch balls thrown at chest level from a lower height of release, shorten catching distance, have participant stop and then catch ball (easier than moving and catching).

ADAPTING FOR PROBLEMS WITH STRENGTH, ENDURANCE, AND POWER ACTIVITIES:

1. Lower basketball goals or nets; increase size of target.

2. Decrease throwing distance between partners, serving distance, and distance between bases.

3. Reduce size or weight of projectiles or balls to be thrown.

4. Shorten length and/or reduce weight of bat or other striking apparatus.

5. Play games in lying or sitting positions to lower center of gravity.

6. Select a "slow ball" (one that will not get away too fast), deflate ball in case it gets away, or attach a string to the ball for recovery.

7. Reduce playing time and lower number of points to win.

8. Use more frequent rest periods.

9. Rotate often or use frequent substitution when needed.

10. Use mobilization alternatives, such as using scooter boards one inning/period and feet for one inning/period.

ADAPTING FOR BALANCE AND AGILITY PROBLEMS:

1. Use chairs, tables, or bars to help with stability.

2. Have participants learn to utilize eyes optimally for balance skills.

3. Teach various ways to fall and incorporate dramatics into fall activities.

4. Use carpeted surfaces.

5. Lower center of gravity.

6. Have participant extend arms or provide a lightweight pole.

7. Have participant keep as much of his/her body in contact with the surface.

8. Widen base of support (distance between feet).

9. Increase width of walking parameters.

ADAPTING FOR COORDINATION AND ACCURACY:

Throwing Activities: use beanbags, yarn or nerf balls, and/or smaller-sized balls.

Catching and Striking Activities: use larger, softer, and lighter balls; throw balls to mid-line; shorten distance; and reduce speed of balls.

Striking/Kicking Activities: enlarge striking surface, choke up on bats, begin with participant successfully striking stationary objects and then progress to striking with movement, and increase target size.

EXERCISE PHYSIOLOGY ADAPTATIONS:

Decrease the amount of weight, amount of reps/sets, pace, and/or distance of exercise; increase the amount of intervals; and combine together any of the previous modifications.

DOMAIN IV. COGNITIVE, SOCIAL, AND PERSONAL DEVELOPMENT

COMPETENCY 1.0 UNDERSTAND COGNITIVE, SOCIAL, AND PERSONAL DEVELOPMENT IN RELATION TO PHYSICAL EDUCATION

SKILL 1.1 Characteristics of cognitive, psychosocial, and emotional development during childhood and adolescence.

Effective physical education supports psychosocial, cognitive, and affective development.

Physical education through the Psychosocial Domain contributes greatly to students social development. Through cooperation involved in team sports, competition and the learning of handling both winning and losing, teamwork, team building and the overall sense of belongingness that a student feels when being a part of a team. Improved communication, respect for one another and sheer bonding are just a few of the social benefits of physical education.

Physical education in the Cognitive Domain contributes to academic achievement; is related to higher thought processes via motor activity; contributes to knowledge of exercise, health and disease; contributes to an understanding of the human body; contributes to an understanding of the role of physical activity and sport in the American cultures; and contributes to the knowledgeable consumption of goods and services.

Physical education in the Affective Domain contributes to self-actualization, self-esteem, and a healthy response to physical activity; contributes to an appreciation of beauty; contributes to directing one's life toward worthy goals; emphasizes humanism; affords individuals the chance to enjoy rich social experiences through play; assists cooperative play with others; teaches courtesy, fair play, and good sportsmanship; contributes to humanitarianism.

Teaching methods that facilitate cognitive learning include:

1. **Problem Solving** - The instructor presents the initial task and students come to an acceptable solution in unique and divergent ways.

2. **Conceptual Theory** - The instructor's focus is on acquisition of knowledge.

3. **Guided Inquiry** – Stages of instructions strategically guide students through a sequence of experiences.

Initially, performing skills will be variable, inconsistent, error-prone, "off-time," and awkward. Students' focus will be on remembering what to do. Instructors should emphasize clear information of the skill's biomechanics and correct errors in gross movement that effect significant parts of the skill. So students will not be overburdened with too much information, they should perform one or two elements at a time. Motivation results from supportive and encouraging comments. Peer to peer encouragement is also very useful and helpful.

Techniques to facilitate cognitive learning include:

1. **Transfer of learning** – Identifying similar movements of a previous learned skill present in a new skill.

2. **Planning for slightly longer instructions and demonstrations** as students memorize cues and skills.

3. **Using appropriate language** for the level of the students.

4. **Conceptual Thinking** - giving more capable students more responsibility for their learning.

Aids to facilitate cognitive learning include:

1. Frequent assessments of student performance

2. Movement activities incorporating principles of biomechanics

3. Laser discs, computers and software

4. Videorecordings of student performance

Teaching methods and techniques that facilitate affective development include:

1. **Fostering a positive learning environment** – Instructors should create a comfortable, positive learning environment by encouraging and praising effort and emphasizing respect for others.

2. **Grouping students appropriately** – Instructors should carefully group students to best achieve equality in ability, age, and personalities.

3. **Ensure all students achieve some level of success** – Instructors should design activities that allow students of all ability levels to achieve success and gain confidence.

Physical Education and the Psychosocial Domain

Physical education activities can promote positive social behaviors and traits in a number of different ways. Instructors can foster improved relations with adults and peers by making students active partners in the learning process and delegating responsibilities within the class environment to students. Giving students leadership positions (e.g. team captain) can give them a heightened understanding of the responsibilities and challenges facing educators.

Team-based physical activities like team sports promote collaboration and cooperation. In such activities, students learn to work together, both pooling their talents and minimizing the weaknesses of different team members, in order to achieve a common goal. The experience of functioning as a team can be very productive for development of loyalty between children, and seeing their peers in stressful situations that they can relate to can promote a more compassionate and considerate attitude among students. Similarly, the need to maximize the strengths of each student on a team (who can complement each other and compensate for weaknesses) is a powerful lesson about valuing and respecting diversity and individual differences. Varying students between leading and following positions in a team hierarchy are good ways to help students gain a comfort level being both followers and leaders.

Physical fitness activities incorporate group processes, group dynamics, and a wide range of cooperation and competition. Ranging from team sports (which are both competitive and cooperative in nature) to individual competitive sports (like racing), to cooperative team activities without a winner and loser (like a gymnastics team working together to create a human pyramid), there is a great deal of room for the development of mutual respect and support among the students, safe cooperative participation, and analytical, problem solving, teamwork, and leadership skills.

Teamwork situations are beneficial to students because they create opportunities for them to see classmates with whom they might not generally socialize, and with whom they may not even get along, in a new light. It also creates opportunities for students to develop reliance on each other and practice interdependence. Cooperation and competition can also offer opportunities for children to practice group work. These situations provide good opportunities to practice analytical thinking and problem solving in a practical setting.

The social skills and values gained from participation in physical activities include:

- The ability to make adjustments to both self and others by an integration of the individual to society and the environment.

- The ability to make judgments in a group situation.

- Learning to communicate with others and be cooperative.

- The development of the social phases of personality, attitudes, and values in order to become a functioning member of society such as being considerate.

- The development of a sense of belonging and acceptance by society.

- The development of positive personality traits.

- Learning for constructive use of leisure time.

- A development of attitude that reflects good moral character.

- Respect of school rules and property.

The above list represents a sample of the socio-cultural benefits of participating in physical activity with others. Physical activity serves as a very important part of the socialization process. Physical activity during the socialization process creates an opportunity for children to define personal comfort levels with different types of physical interaction, as well as to establish guidelines for what is (and is not) acceptable physical behavior as related to their relationship with other individuals.

SKILL 1.2 The influence of peers and others in determining social attitudes and behaviors.

Adolescents usually spend their spare time with peers. It is a time characterized by friendly relationships that mature and become deeper. At this stage, teenagers tend to distance themselves from their parents in a quest for more independence. This is a very crucial stage for teenagers as they have a tendency to acquire the attitudes and behaviors of their peers unconsciously. Parents must understand the critical stage their child is going through while still acting as a guiding force. For example, parents should encourage their child to be selective in choosing her friends. If she happens to spend time in the company of peers who spend most of their time studying, chances are they too will become studious. However, if her group of friends frequents bars and clubs and stays out late, she will be more likely to do the same. This can have a domino effect on the child and cause a lack of sleep and related physical and psychological ailments. If this behavior becomes habitual, she will later be prone to absenteeism and may develop a negative reputation. In order to prevent this negative situation, an appropriate inquiry for a parent, guardian, or teacher is to ask what kind of company the child is keeping. It is also beneficial for a parent to become familiar and friendly with their child's friends.

SKILL 1.3 The influence of expectations related to gender, physical appearance, and skill level on the development of self-image.

Historically, males have had greater expectations place on them in sports and physical activities. Since Title IX, however, the pressure of female athletes to succeed is just as great. In general, however, males are expected to outperform females, specifically in the male dominated sports such as, football and baseball.

A young man who is 6'10", a basketball coach, in all likelihood will immediately go to and put the pressure on him to play for the school team. The assumption being, that because of his height, no doubt he will be an outstanding basketball player. This may be true, however in many cases height does not determine the abilities of a basketball player. As a result, the 6'10" students self image will be affected due to his inability to be the athlete that many assuming he is because of his height.

A different type of example is a young student who really stands out during the volleyball section of physical education classes. It is clear to the instructor and the other students that she is at a much higher skill level than her peers. This in turn will have a positive influence on her self image.

Expectations based on gender, physical appearance and skill level are often time inaccurate and biased. This can have a negative effect on the students self image. Oppositely, students that have the physical appearance and do in fact posses a high skill level as opposed to their peers, can have their self image positively affected.

SKILL 1.4 Cause and effects of anxiety related to performance.

The ability to overcome pressure and anxiety is an important factor that will determine the performance of an athlete. Even experienced and famous athletes admit that they feel a considerable amount of stress and anxiety when faced with competition. In an Olympic festival, most of the consultations focus on stress or anxiety-related problems. However, a good athlete possesses the ability to control her anxiety, which enables her to perform the best that she can.

Early research defines anxiety as a feeling of tension and apprehension associated with arousal of the nervous system. A high state of anxiety is a person's response to a threatening situation.

In order to assess anxiety levels, there are subscales that professionals utilize. In fact, there are three independent subscales of the Competition State Anxiety Inventory-2 (CSAI-2) developed by Martens (et. al). The subscales are cognitive anxiety, somatic anxiety, and self-confidence. Cognitive anxiety occurs when an individual is afraid of failure or the inability to perform to the liking of his coach and/or teammates. He fears a negative outcome of the game due to his failure. Somatic anxiety refers to the psychological state in response to a stressful situation. The self-confidence subscale represents the high confidence level of a person, which prompts him to issue an achievement-oriented statement and to maintain a positive outlook.

Other sources of anxiety stem from the fear of a mediocre performance, possible negative remarks from a coach or trainer, losing, and the inability to perform at the peak level expected of an athlete.

SKILL 1.5 Stress management principles and strategies.

IDENTIFY COMMON SIGNS OF STRESS

Emotional signs of stress include: depression, lethargy, aggressiveness, irritability, anxiety, edginess, fearfulness, impulsiveness, chronic fatigue hyper excitability, inability to concentrate, frequent feelings of boredom, feeling overwhelmed, apathy, impatience, pessimism, sarcasm, humorlessness, confusion, helplessness, melancholy, alienation, isolation, numbness, purposelessness, isolation, numbness, self-consciousness or an inability to maintain an intimate relationship.

Behavioral signs of stress include: elevated use of substances (alcohol, drugs; tobacco), crying, yelling, insomnia or excessive sleep, excessive TV watching, school/job burnout, panic attacks, poor problems solving capability, avoidance of people, aberrant behavior, procrastination, accident proneness, restlessness, loss of memory, indecisiveness, aggressiveness, inflexibility, phobic responses, tardiness, disorganization and sexual problems.

Physical signs of stress include: pounding heart, stuttering, trembling/nervous tics, excessive perspiration, teeth grinding, gastrointestinal problems (constipation, indigestion, diarrhea, queasy stomach), dry mouth, aching lower back, migraine/tension headaches, stiff neck, asthma attacks, allergy attacks, skin problems, frequent colds or low grade fevers, muscle tension, hyperventilation, high blood pressure, amenorrhea, nightmares and cold intolerance.

IDENTIFY COMMON "STRESSORS" WHICH MAY AFFECT INDIVIDUALS

Common stressors that can affect individuals include the death of a spouse, death of a close family member or a close personal friend, divorce or separation from a significant other, divorce of parents, addition of a new family member, personal injury/illness, unintentional pregnancy, getting married, jail term, dysfunctional family and social ties, financial problems, fired from a job, moving, poor time management, overcrowding, expectations of others, workaholic personality, lack of self-control, self confidence, and self-efficacy, low self-esteem, lack of social support, general insecurity, change, heat/cold extremes, poor living conditions, unsafe work environment, one's occupation, retirement, academic/business readjustment, taking out a major loan, discrimination, being a victim of a crime, exposure to water borne or air borne chemicals and noise.

IDENTIFY BOTH POSITIVE AND NEGATIVE COPING STRATEGIES FOR INDIVIDUALS UNDER STRESS

Positive coping strategies to cope with stress include: using one's social support system, spiritual support, managing time, initiating direct action, re-examining priorities, active thinking, acceptance, meditation, imagery, biofeedback, progressive relaxation, deep breathing, massage, sauna, Jacuzzi, humor, recreation and diversions, and exercise.

Negative coping strategies to cope with stress include: using alcohol or other mind altering substances, smoking, excessive caffeine intake, poor eating habits, negative "self-talk," and expressing feelings of distress, anger, and other feelings in a destructive manner.

SKILL 1.6 Relationship between physical activity and the development of personal identity and psychological well being.

Physical activity has tremendous benefits to the overall healtha and well being of an individual. When the body physically feels good, looks good and function optimally, an individuals psychologically well being is absolutely going to be benefited in a positive way. Below are specifics of each.

Physiological benefits of physical activity include:

- improved cardio-respiratory fitness
- improved muscle strength
- improved muscle endurance
- improved flexibility
- more lean muscle mass and less body fat
- quicker rate of recovery
- improved ability of the body to utilize oxygen
- lower resting heart rate
- increased cardiac output
- improved venous return and peripheral circulation
- reduced risk of musculoskeletal injuries
- lower cholesterol levels
- increased bone mass
- cardiac hypertrophy and size and strength of blood vessels
- increased number of red cells
- improved blood-sugar regulation
- improved efficiency of thyroid gland
- improved energy regulation
- increased life expectancy

Psychological benefits of physical activity include:

- relief of stress
- improved mental health via better physical health
- reduced mental tension (relieves depression, improves sleeping patterns)
- better resistance to fatigue
- better quality of life
- more enjoyment of leisure
- better capability to handle some stressors
- opportunity for successful experiences
- improved self-concept and self confidence
- better ability to recognize and accept limitations
- improved appearance and sense of well-being
- better ability to meet challenges
- better sense of accomplishments

SKILL 1.7 Strategies for promoting creative expression through sport and dance.

SPORTS

Aesthetics – Human movement activities create an opportunity for individual participation in activities with intrinsic aesthetic qualities. A gymnastic technique or a perfectly executed swing of a baseball bat relies on both physical training and a level of intuitive action. This is an artistic form of expression that is readily accessible to students. Recognizing beauty in the activities and performances of others (in some cases from groups different from that of the viewing student) is a humanizing experience.

DANCE

Dancing requires many physical skills, but, just as importantly, it also calls on our mental and emotional states to convey messages. In dance whether in a full-length classical ballet, such as *The Nutcracker* or *Giselle*, or a peppy tap number, internal feelings are an integral part of any performance. In Romeo and Juliet, when Romeo thinks that Juliet is dead, his thoughts of suicide are clear. How do actors express seemingly intangible emotions on stage? Actors express emotions through movement; the highs, the lows, the hanging head, the slow gait, the arms thrown up in the air and, of course, the music. Dance requires expression of feelings of anger, sadness, joy, or happiness. The tempo of the music, the number of people turning in succession, costumes, and smiles can all express happiness. Conversely, all of these elements (except smiles) can convey sadness.

Dancing is also acting and, as such, it often requires a full spectrum of emotion. Dancers express feelings and moods as a result of emotion coming from the material. Dancers do not just arbitrarily "put on" feelings, rather they form from the inside and transform to the outside. One often may not realize that, though a dancer is far away on stage, spectators throughout the theatre can see his expression. When a dancer looks out into the audience, perhaps he ponders the arrival of a loved one. Perhaps as a dancer waits for the arrival of his lover, he laughs as he thinks of a funny moment that they shared together earlier. Dancing, like acting, transports us to another place; one where we can completely submerge ourselves in the expressions of the dancer and perhaps ourselves. Dancing conveys a message and the dancer's talent often determines the degree of success in conveying that message.

COMPETENCY 2.0 UNDERSTAND THE ROLE OF PHYSICAL EDUCATION IN THE DEVELOPMENT OF HIGHER-ORDER THNKING AND EVALUATION

SKILL 2.1 Techniques and activities for developing various skills in relation to physical activity and health-related lifestyle decisions.

Teaching methods that facilitate cognitive learning include:

1. **Problem Solving** - The instructor presents the initial task and students come to an acceptable solution in unique and divergent ways,

2. **Conceptual Theory** - The instructor's focus is on acquisition of knowledge,

3. **Guided Inquiry** - careful stages of instructions strategically guiding students through a sequence of experiences to help them reach their goals.

Initially, performing skills will be variable, inconsistent, error prone, "off-time," and awkward. Students' focus will be on remembering what to do. Instructors should direct corrections in gross movement at the significant elements of the skill, and emphasize clear information of the skill's biomechanics. So students will not be overburdened with too much information, one or two elements at a time should be performed. Motivation occurs with supportive and encouraging comments.

Techniques to facilitate cognitive learning include:

1. **Transfer of learning** - identifying similar movements of a previous learned skill and the new skill.

2. **Planning for slightly longer instructions and demonstrations** as students memorize cues and skills.

3. **Using appropriate language** for the level of the students.

4. **Conceptual Thinking** - giving those students' more responsibility for their learning who are capable of doing so.

Aids to facilitate cognitive learning include:

1. Assessing students' performance frequently.

2. Moving activities incorporating principles of biomechanics.

3. Using laser discs; computers and software.

4. Videotaping students' performance.

Teaching methods to facilitate psychomotor learning include:

1. **Task/Reciprocal** - The instructor programs task learning into the learning setting by utilizing stations.

2. **Command/Direct** - Task instruction is teacher-centered in which goals are clear, skills are explained and demonstrated, time is allocated for practice, and students' performance is frequently monitored.

3. **Contingency/Contract** - A task style of instruction that rewards completion of tasks.

Techniques that facilitate psychomotor learning include:

1. **Reflex movements** - Activities that create an automatic response to some stimuli. Responses encompass flexing, extending, stretching, and postural adjustment.

2. **Basic fundamental locomotor movements** - Activities that utilize instinctive patterns of movement established by combining reflex movements.

3. **Perceptual abilities** - Activities that involve interpreting auditory, visual, tactile stimuli in order to coordinate adjustments.

4. **Physical abilities** - Activities to develop physical characteristics of fitness providing students with the stamina necessary for highly advanced, skilled movement.

5. **Skilled movements** - Activities that involve instinctive, effective performance of complex movement including vertical and horizontal components.

6. **Nondiscursive communication** - Activities necessitating expression as part of the movement.

SKILL 2.2 Techniques and activities to promote critical evaluation of commercial products.

Exercise myths and gimmicks include:

- drinking beer/alcoholic beverages is a good way to replenish loss of body fluids after exercising.

- women should not exercise while menstruating or pregnant.

- physically fit people will not die from heart disease.

- you cannot be too flexible.

- spot reduction is effective.

- children are naturally active and do not need to exercise.

- muscle will turn into fat with the cessation of exercising.

- fat can turn into muscle.

- women will develop large muscles by weight training. You should exercise while sick regardless how ill you are.

- cardiac hypertrophy developed by exercising is harmful to health.

- exercise increases the appetite.

- exercise gets rid of sagging skin and wrinkles.

- yoga is a good way to develop fitness.

- losing cellulite requires special treatment.

- body wraps are a good way to lose weight.

COMPETENCY 3.0 UNDERSTAND THE ROLE OF PHYSICAL EDUCATION IN THE DEVELOPMENT OF POSITIVE PERSONAL AND SOCIAL BEHAVIORS AND TRAITS

SKILL 3.1 The role of physical education in fostering enjoyment of aesthetic and creative aspects of skilled performance and in respecting physical and performance limitations of self and others.

SEE ALSO DOMAIN IV., Skill 1.7

ENJOYMENT OF AESTHETIC AND CREATIVE ASPECTS OF SKILLED PERFORMANCE

Physical education instructors should instill in their students a respect for and appreciation of the aesthetic and creative aspects of skilled performances. Dance, gymnastics, and figure skating are examples of performance activities that have an obvious creative and expressive element. In addition, all sports require creativity and have aesthetic elements. For example, the ball control of an expert soccer player, the touch, control, and power of a professional tennis player, and the elegance and grace of a basketball player soaring for a slam-dunk are all aesthetically pleasing and awe inspiring to the trained eye. To truly appreciate the complexity and difficulty of skilled performances, one must have sufficient knowledge and understanding of the activity. Thus, the role of physical education is to introduce students to various physical activities so they can understand the aesthetic elements.

RESPECTING PHYSICAL AND PERFORMANCE LIMITATIONS

Physical education promotes respect of physical and performance limitations by providing students with an arena to interact with and observe other students in the course of physical activity. Such an environment promotes respect because students see that they are neither the best nor the worst at all physical activities. Thus, they learn to accept their limitations and the limitations of others. It is the role of the instructor to ensure that the physical education environment is indeed respectful. Instructors must act decisively to prevent bullying, teasing, and other disrespectful behavior.

SKILL 3.2 The potential socio-cultural benefits of participation in physical activities.

Physical fitness activities incorporate group processes, group dynamics, and a wide range of cooperation and competition. Additionally, mutual respect, safe cooperative participation, analytical skills, problem solving skills, teamwork and leadership skills are important during competitive or cooperative team sports, individual competitive sports and cooperative team activities.

Teamwork activities create an opportunity for students who do not normally interact or get along. Also, through teamwork, students begin to understand the value of diversity and the different skills an array of people can bring to a team. It also creates opportunities for students to develop reliance on each other and practice interdependence. Cooperation and competition can also offer opportunities for children to practice group work. These situations provide good opportunities to practice analytical thinking and problem solving in a practical setting.

The social skills and values gained from participation in physical activities are as follows:

- The ability to make adjustments to both self and others by an integration of the individual to society and the environment.

- The ability to make judgments in a group situation.

- Learning to communicate with others and cooperate.

- The development of the social phases of personality, attitudes, and values in order to become a functioning member of society such as being considerate.

- The development of a sense of belonging and acceptance by society.

- The development of positive personality traits.

- Learning for constructive use of leisure time.

- A development of attitude that reflects good moral character.

- Respect of school rules and property.

From an overall community and culture viewpoint, there are also sociological benefits of physical activity. They are listed below.

Sociological benefits of physical activity include:

- the opportunity to spend time with family and friends and make new friends

- the opportunity to be part of a team

- the opportunity to participate in competitive experiences

- the opportunity to experience the thrill of victory

- the opportunity to express your culture through sport and activity

SKILL 3.3 Ways in which physical education activities can promote positive personal and social behaviors and traits.

See Domain I Skill 3.2

POSITIVE AND NEGATIVE INFLUENCES OF PARTICIPATION IN PHYSICAL ACTIVITY ON PSYCHO-SOCIAL FACTORS

Physical activity can influence psychosocial development both positively and negatively. Thus, physical education instructors must create an environment that maximizes the benefits of physical activity and minimizes the potential negative aspects. A positive physical education experience can promote self-confidence, honesty, self-discipline, perseverance, and creativity.

Positive Individual Influences:

Reduces tension and depression; provides means of affiliation with others; provides exhilarating experiences; provides aesthetic experiences; creates positive body image; controls aggression, provides relaxation and a change of pace from long hours of work, study, or other stresses; provides challenge and sense of accomplishment; provides a way to be healthy and fit; improves self-esteem through skill mastery; provides creative experiences; creates positive addiction to exercise in contrast to negative addiction to substances.

Positive Group Influences:

Development of cooperation skills; acceptance of and respect for all persons regardless of race, creed or origin; assimilation of the group attitude; opportunity to develop a group relationships; development of a spirit of fairness; development of traits of good citizenship; development of leadership and following skills; development of self-discipline; additional avenues for social acquaintances; development of social poise and self-understanding; development of a social consciousness with an accompanying sense of values; and individual and social development.

Negative influences:

Ego-centered athletes; winning at all costs; false values; harmful pressures; loss of identity; role conflict; aggression and violence; compulsiveness; over-competitiveness; addiction to exercise, where commitment to exercise has a higher priority than commitments to family, interpersonal relationships, work, and medical advice; escape or avoidance of problems; exacerbation of anorexia nervosa; exercise deprivation effects; fatigue; overexertion; poor eating habits; self-centeredness; preoccupation with fitness, diet, and body image.

DOMAIN V. PROFESSIONAL KNOWLEDGE AND THE PHYSICAL EDUCATION PROGRAM

COMPETENCY 1.0 UNDERSTAND THE HISTORY AND PHILOSOPHIES OF PHYSICAL EDUCATION

SKILL 1.1 Significant events in the historical development of physical education.

Germany, Sweden and England greatly influenced the early development of Physical Education, particularly from the late 1700's to the mid 1800's. Turner Societies where introduced to the states by German immigrants. Turner Societies advocated a sort or system of gymnastics training that employed or utilized heavy equipment (e.g., horizontal and parallel bars, side horse) in their striving for fitness. In contrast, the Swedish preferred attaining and maintaining fitness through the use of light equipment. Their system of exercise to promote health was through systematic movements through the use of the light equipment (e.g., ropes, climbing and wands). The English brought to America, sports and games. The type of sports and games that the English brought emphasized moral development through participation in physical activities.

In 1823, the first school to include physical education as a requirement in its curriculum, The Round Hill School, a private school in Northhampton, Massachusetts. After this and continuing throughout the 1800's, the inclusion of physical education into schools across America became prominent. The "first American to design a program of exercise for American children" (Lumpkin, Angela. 1994. *Physical Education and Sport: A contemporary Introduction*, 3rd edition. St. Louis: Mosby. pg. 202.) was in 1824 by Catherine Beecher. Ms. Beecher was the founder of the Hartford Female Seminary. The curriculum of physical education that Ms. Beecher designed consisted of what we would refer to today as calisthenics. She was also an extremely active advocate for including physical education into the public schools curriculum. It took up until 1855, for this to happen, when Cincinnati, Ohio became the first city school system to offer physical education to its students in public schools.

California became the first state to pass a law, in 1866, that actually required two periods a day of exercise in its public schools. During this time, specifically between 1855 and 1900, Ms. Beecher, along with her contemporaries, Edward Hitchcock, Dudley Allen Sargent and Dio Lewis were the early leaders in physical education. Debates abounded as to whether it was best to use the system they had established in America or rather it would be better to use either the Germans, Swedes or English systems as a way of providing a national physical education program for America. These debates were referred to as the *Battle of Systems*.

Throughout the 1890's and during this great period of debate, John Dewey challenged the traditional education system. Mr. Dewey and his colleagues are responsible for expanding the education system based on the "three R's", to include physical education in America. It was also during this time in history that many higher education schools began to offer training for physical education teachers. Because of the strong emphasis on the sciences, including courses in physiology and anatomy, many professors of these students held medical degrees.

In 1983, Thomas Wood stated that "the great thought of physical education is not the education of the physical nature, but the relation of physical training to complete education, and then the effort to make the physical contribute its full share to the life of the individual." (National Education Association. 1893. *NEA Proceedings* 32:621. pg.621.) This was the beginning of a change in thinking in relation to the importance of physical education in regard to the overall education of the countries children. Many early twentieth century educational psychologists, including John Dewey, Edward Thorndike and Stanley Hall, supported Wood's line of thinking and the important role of children's play in furthering their ability to learn. As a result, in 1927, *The New Physical Education* was published by Wood and Rosalind Cassidy, who also was a strong advocate of education through the physical.

Charles McCloy, supported Wood's and Cassidy's line of thinking and published work, however he believed that physical education was more than just contributing to the overall well-being and learning of children. He held that physical education's primary objective was and is the development of skills as well as the maintenance of the body. It was an expanded view on Wood's and Cassidy's theories. The testing of motor skills was a significant part of McCloy's contribution to physical education. Additionally, his philosophy of testing motor skills paralleled with the scientific movement in education during this time period.

In the early 1920's many states passed legislation that required physical education in the schools. This trend continued until the 1950's when all states eventually required physical education in their schools. The curriculum of physical education changed as the events in the country occurred. For example, during World War II, the emphasis in physical education shifted from games to physical conditioning. In 1953, the President's Council on Physical Fitness was established when it was noted through the Kraus-Weber study that American children were far less fit than children in European countries. The council was established to assist the falling fitness levels of America's children and youth.

SKILL 1.2 **Past and present philosophies of physical education and their effects on the goals, scope, and practices of physical education programs.**

The various philosophies of education greatly influence the goals and values of physical education. Important educational philosophies related to physical education are Idealism, Realism, Pragmatism, Naturalism, Existentialism, Humanism, and Eclecticism.

Idealism – The **mind**, developed through the acquistion of knowledge, is of highest importance. Values exist independently of individuals. Fitness and strength activities contribute to the development of one's personality. Horace Mann, Wadsworth, Kant, Plato, and Descartes were Idealists.

Realism – The physical world is **real.** A realist believes in the laws of nature, the scientific method, and mind and body harmony. Religion and philosophy co-exist. Physical fitness results in greater productivity, physical drills are important to the learning process, athletic programs lead to desired social behavior, and play and recreation help life adjustment. Aristotle was a realist.

Pragmatism – **Experience** is key to life. Dynamic experience shapes individuals' truth. Education is child-centered. Physical Education thus takes the form of creating numerous physical activities and sports for children to experience and thus discover. \
Varied activities present more meaningful experiences. Activities are socializing. Problem-solving accomplishes learning. John Dewy and Charles Pierce were pragmatists.

Naturalism – This philosophy is materialistic. Things that actually exist are found only within the physical realm of nature. Nature is valuable. The individual is more important than society. Self-activities accomplish learning and activities are more than physical in nature. Naturalists promote play and discourage high levels of competition. Physical education takes a holistic approach.

Existentialism – The chief concern is **individualism.** Existentialists do not want the individual to conform to society. They promote freedom of choice and a variety of interests. Individuals need to have their own system of values. Playing develops creativity and the discovery of the "inner self." Sartre, Soren, and Kierkegaard were Existentialists.

Humanism and **Eclecticism** – The modern philosophies of physical education that most schools follow today. The Humanistic philosophy is based on development of individual talents and total fulfillment that encourages total involvement and participation in one's environment. Humanists encourage self-actualization and self-fulfillment. Curriculums based on the Humanistic approach are more student-centered. The Eclectic approach combines beliefs from different philosophies and does not resemble any single philosophy. When blended skillfully, the Eclectic approach affords a sound philosophy for an individual.

PHILOSOPHIES OF EDUCATION APPLIED TO PHYSICAL EDUCATION GOALS

Physical/Organic Development Goal (Realism philosophy) – activities build physical power by strengthening the body's systems, resulting in the ability to sustain adaptive effort, shorten recovery time, and develop resistance to fatigue. The core values are individual health, greater activity, and better performance by an adequately developed and properly functioning body.

Motor/Neuromuscular Development Goal (Realism philosophy) – develops body awareness producing movement that is proficient, graceful, and aesthetic and uses as little energy as possible. Students develop as many skills as possible so their interests are wide and varied to allow more enjoyment and better adjustment to group situations. Varied motor development skills affect health by influencing how leisure time is spent. Values include reducing energy expenditure, building confidence, bringing recognition, enhancing physical and mental health, making participation safer, and contributing to aesthetic sense.

Cognitive Development Goal (Idealism philosophy) – deals with acquiring knowledge and ability to think and interpret knowledge. Scientific principles explain time, space, and flow of movement. Learning physical activities requires thinking and coordination of movement and mastering and adapting to one's environment. Individuals also should acquire knowledge of rules, techniques, and strategies of activities. Cognitive values include healthy attitudes and habits such as body awareness, personal hygiene, disease prevention, exercise, proper nutrition, and knowledge of health service providers.

Social/Emotional/Affective Development Goal (Existentialism philosophy) – deals with helping individuals make adjustments – personal, group, and societal – by positively influencing human behavior. Performance defines success, and success develops self-confidence. Wholesome attitudes throughout the various growth stages promote the development of an appropriate Self-Concept, which is very important. Values include meeting basic social needs (sense of belonging, recognition, self-respect, and love) that produce a socially, well-adjusted individual.

SKILL 1.3 Current issues and trends that affect the field.

CURRENT TRENDS

National trends and philosophies greatly affect physical education curricula. National trends toward greater longevity, increased obesity, and sedentary lifestyles increase the need for a renewed emphasis on fitness and activity to prevent and reduce fitness related health problems. The philosophies of life-long learning and fitness are also an important aspect of physical education. Instructors should design curricula that encourage and motivate students to become active and take a life-long interest in the physical health of their bodies.

MAJOR TRENDS SINCE WWII INFLUENCING PHYSICAL EDUCATION

WWII - Selective Service examinations revealed the poor physical fitness condition of the country's youth. Thus, **physical education classes focused on physical conditioning.**

1942 - President Roosevelt established the **Division of Physical Fitness** run by John B. Kelly (who alerted Roosevelt about the poor fitness levels of youths). This division was dissolved and **placed under the Federal Security Agency [FSA]** with numerous organizations **promoting fitness**. Under the FSA, Frank Lloyd was Chief of the Physical Fitness Division, William Hughs was Chief Consultant, and Dorothy LaSalle was head of the work for women and children. **After WWII ended, the eagerness for fitness waned.**

1953 - **Kraus-Webber tests** - Of the 4,264 USA participants, 57% failed a general muscular fitness test. Only 8.7% of Europeans failed. Again, John Kelly alerted the President (Eisenhower) of the **need for a fitness movement.** Eisenhower ordered a **special conference** that was held in **June 1956.**

1956 - AAHPERD Fitness Conference established the President's Council on Youth Fitness and a President's Citizens Advisory Committee on the Fitness of American Youth.

Modern dance gave way to contemporary. Gymnastics had new equipment, including a higher balance beam, trampolines, and uneven parallel bars. The Swedish gymnastics boom was over, and ropes and ladders, wands, dumbbells, and Indian clubs were no longer fashionable. Core sports for boys were football, baseball, basketball, and track and field. Core sports for women were basketball and volleyball.

John Fitzgerald Kennedy changed the name of the President's Citizens Advisory Committee of Fitness of American Youth to the **President's Council on Physical Fitness.**

Lyndon Baines Johnson changed the name to **President's Council on Physical Fitness and Sports.**

1972 - **passage of Title IX** of the Educational Amendments Act to ensure girls and women receive the same rights as boys and men for educational programs - including physical education and athletics

1970 to Present Trends - Preventative medicine, wellness, physical fitness, and education that is more scholarly, more specialized, and more applicable to all segments of population such as the elderly, handicapped persons, and those out of organizations (Non-School sports): AAU - mid 20th century controlled amateur sports; Little League; North American Baseball Association.

International Amateur Sports: Olympic Governing Committee.

Intercollegiate: National Collegiate Athletic Association (NCAA scholarship in 1954); National Association of Intercollegiate Athletics (NAIA); National Junior College Athletic Association (NJCAA).

Interscholastic Sports: National Federation of State High School Athletic Associations.

Organizations for Girls' and Women's Sports: Athletic and Recreation Federation of College Women (ARFCW); the Women's Board of the U.S. Olympic Committee; National Section of Women's Athletics (NSWA - promoted intercollegiate sports such as US Field Hockey and Women's International Bowling and established special committees). The Women's Division of NAAF merged its interests in the NSWA of AAHPERD changing its name to National Section for Girls and Women's Sports (NSGWS). **Mel Lockes, chairperson of NSGWS in 1956, was against intercollegiate athletics for women.** In 1957, NSGWS changed its name to Division of Girls and Women's Sports (DGWS), still a division of AAHPER. A lack of funds hurt DGWS.

SKILL 1.4   Contributions of noteworthy physical educators.

See Domain V- Skill 1.1

Change is inevitable, especially during childhood and adolescence. Students' needs and interests often go hand in hand with the changes taking place within society. In order to remain relevant, schools and their programs must also evolve in with society. This especially includes the physical education curriculum.

W. G. Anderson, D. Siedentop, R.J. Brustad, and D.A. Zehrung are a few of the physical educators who have contributed to physical education understanding and advancement. Anderson (1989) stated that while there is much research on teaching physical education andresearch of the components lacking in a physical education curriculum. Siedentop posed questions about the ideal physical education curriculum and why students voluntarily take part in the subject. He also wondered what we could add to the curriculum at varying school levels to make the most impact on students. Anderson (1989) asserted that the physical education curriculum is an extremely large and exceedingly complicated study. He further demonstrated the difficulty in comprehending, recording, and explaining the number of events that happen within a semester physical education program by examining the teaching methods of a physical education instructor responsible for 40 students.

In hopes of continuing research about the physical education curriculum, many professional periodicals and journals feature the work of noteworthy physical educators. In 1992, T.J. Templin wrote the "Journal of Physical Education, Recreation, and Dance." Templin tried to address important physical education issues. One such issue was whether or not practitioners were concerned with physical education research and why they should be.

R.J. Brustad & D.A. Zehrung (1994) studied the consequences of everyday physical education instruction on physical fitness, motor skill development, and self-perceptions of children in the elementary grade levels. In the study, researchers gave more than 200 children a daily or an every-other day physical education schedule for a year. These students achieved vast improvements on the mile-run as well as the 50-yard dash. Children who did not receive daily physical education schedules showed no significant change. This study confirmed the theory that physical activity has a positive effect on a child's physical development.

COMPETENCY 2.0 UNDERSTAND THE STRUCTURE, GOALS, AND PURPOSES OF PHYSICAL EDUCATION PROGRAMS

SKILL 2.1 Structure, organization, goals, and purposes of physical education programs.

Physical education is a technique that helps in understanding, motivating and promoting the physical fitness and well-being of a body over an entire life span.

The primary aim of physical education, otherwise known as physical training, is to equip students with the knowledge, skills, capabilities, values, and enthusiasm necessary to the maintenance of a healthy lifestyle into adulthood, regardless of physical ability. Activities included in the program promote physical fitness, develop motor skills, instill knowledge and understanding of rules, concepts, and strategies, and teach students to work as part of a team or as individuals in a wide variety of play-based and competitive activities.

Physical education has come to occupy a very important role in most school programs. There are various curriculum models for physical education courses. Such curricula stress the meaning of human movement, physiology of exercise, sport sociology, aesthetic appreciation of movement, and the acquisition of skills. Modern curricula include all of these competencies.

The modern physical education curriculum provides students a basic experience in the following activities: aquatics, conditioning activities, gymnastics, individual/dual sports, team sports, and rhythm and dance. All states in the United States offer physical education to students in grades K through 12, and many states require the self-contained classroom teacher to implement a physical education program.

All curriculum models have the following characteristics: physical activity, by which students will become competent in a variety of, and proficient in a few, physical activities; human movement, in which students will understand and apply principles of human movement to the learning and development of motor skills; fitness; responsible behavior, wherein students will exhibit responsible personal and social behavior in physical activity settings; respect for differences; and benefits of physical activity, by which students will identify and understand how physical activity provides personal enjoyment, challenge, self-expression, and social interaction.

SKILL 2.2 Procedures and components of curriculum development and appropriate scope and sequence in the physical education curriculum.

Both long- and short-term planning are important aspects of effective curriculum design.

Physical education instructors must make short-term plans (e.g. one day, one week) that maximize learner participation and success.
For example, instructors should plan an appropriate variety of activities that will appeal to the varied interests and abilities of the students and promote some level of success for each student. In addition, appropriate rotations of students, planned before each class, allows for maximum participation and limits downtime.

Long-term planning (e.g. one month, one unit, or one semester) allows instructors to build a comprehensive, sequential curriculum that promotes the development of student skills, fitness, and knowledge over time. For example, an elementary instructor may plan a sequence of units starting with basic running and jumping skills and ending with the introduction of organized sports activities.

SKILL 2.3 Criteria and procedures for evaluating physical education programs.

Evaluation of physical education programs relies heavily on assessment of the progress of individual students. Instructors should compare assessment data to grade equivalency norms to determine where each child is relative to where he should be. However, the instructor should place the most emphasis on evaluating the child relative to past performance. Progress is more important than current achievement. A learning-disabled child might display below average levels of achievement despite having made a great deal of progress. On the other hand, a gifted child might be above grade equivalency norms despite stagnation.

STUDENT AND PROGRAM EVALUATIONS IN PHYSICAL EDUCATION

The **Cheffers Adaptation of the Flanders Interaction Analysis System** (CAFAIS) and the **Academic Learning Time in Physical Education** (ALT-PE) are *Systematic Analyses* that detect continuous and discrete behaviors, actions and interactions, and teaching characteristics. Relating the goals of a systematic analysis to the data obtained during the instructional process can indicate which of the following instructional strategies need changing:

- The ability of the teacher to question and the time engaged in questioning
- The cognitive response of students
- The time spent on task instruction (rate per minute)
- The number of times task instruction takes place (rate of occurrence)

Instructors can use the following **Systematic Observational Evaluations** to identify changes that they need to make in events, in duration, in groups, and in self-recording:

- **Event Recording** (rate-per-minute, rate of occurrence) – counts the number of attempts students have to try a skill and the number of positive teacher-student interactions.

- **Duration Recording** – measures amount of time teacher spends on instructions, time spent on managing student activities, and time spent managing the participation of students.

- **Group Time Sampling/Playcheck Recording** – counts the number of students participating in the activity.

- **Self-Recording** – students sign in their arrival time to class and how many completed tasks they accomplish.

Student assessments that can facilitate changes in instructional strategies include:

- **Formal assessments** such as win/loss records, written tests, skills tests, performance records, and reviewing videotaped performances.

- **Informal assessments** such as rating scales, observational performance descriptions, completion of skills checklist, and observational time utilization.

SKILL 2.4 Ways to adapt or modify physical education programs based on evaluation results

Adapting and modifying physical education programs are analogous to modifying individual fitness plans. Modification and adaptation involve identifying areas of strength and weakness from the assessment results and adjusting goals and activities to address the weaknesses. For example, if the students in a particular physical education program score poorly on cardiovascular fitness tests, the instructor should integrate more aerobic activities into the curriculum.

WAYS TO MODIFY PROGRAMS AND RECOMMEND CHANGES WHERE NEEDED.

Personal fitness program design requires careful self-assessment and problem-solving. After assessing an individual's fitness level, an instructor can prescribe a personal fitness program. Prescription of a fitness program begins with:

1. identifying the components of fitness that need changing (via assessment)

2. establishing short-term goals

3. developing a plan to meet the established goals

4. keeping records to monitor progress

5. evaluating progress of goals and making changes based on success or failure

For successful programs, formulating new goals changes the personal fitness program to accomplish those new goals.

For unsuccessful programs, changing the goals, particularly if the goals were too unrealistic, is appropriate for the individual to make progress and succeed. In addition, analyzing positive and negative reinforcements may identify barriers preventing an individual's success in his/her personal fitness program. Incorporating periodic, positive rewards for advancing can provide positive reinforcement and encouragement.

SKILL 2.5 Relationships between physical education and other areas of instruction.

Physical education is a key component of an interdisciplinary learning approach because it draws from many other curriculum areas. Instructors can relate concepts from the physical sciences, mathematics, natural sciences, social sciences, and kinesiology to physical education activities.

Physical science is a term for the branches of science that study non-living systems. However, the term "physical" creates an unintended, arbitrary distinction, since many branches of physical science also study biological phenomena. Topics in physical science such as movement of an object through space and the effect of gravity on moving objects are of great relevance to physical education. Physical sciences allow us to determine the limits of physical activities.

Mathematics is the search for fundamental truths in pattern, quantity, and change. Examples of mathematical applications in sport include measuring speed, momentum, and height of objects; measuring distances and weights; scorekeeping; and statistical computations.

Natural science is the study of living things. Content areas in the natural sciences of great importance to physical education include physiology, nutrition, anatomy, and biochemistry. For example, a key component of physical education is an understanding of proper nutrition and the affect of food on the body.

The social sciences are a group of academic disciplines that study the human aspects of the world. Social scientists engage in research and theorize about both aggregate and individual behaviors. For example, a basic understanding of psychology is essential to the discussion of human patterns of nutrition and attitudes toward exercise and fitness. In addition, sport psychology is a specialized social science that explores the mental aspects of athletic performance.

Finally, kinesiology encompasses human anatomy, physiology, neuroscience, biochemistry, biomechanics, exercise psychology, and sociology of sport. Kinesiologists also study the relationship between the quality of movement and overall human health. Kinesiology is an important part of physical therapy, occupational therapy, chiropractics, osteopathy, exercise physiology, kinesiotherapy, massage therapy, ergonomics, physical education, and athletic coaching. The purpose of these applications may be therapeutic, preventive, or high-performance. The application of kinesiology can also incorporate knowledge from other academic disciplines such as psychology, sociology, cultural studies, ecology, evolutionary biology, and anthropology. The study of kinesiology is often part of the physical education curriculum and illustrates the truly interdisciplinary nature of physical education.

SKILL 2.6   Ways to integrate physical education into the overall school curriculum.

See Domain IV – Skill 2.5

SKILL 2.7   Methods for communicating and maintaining positive relations with students, families, and community members.

SEE ALSO DOMAIN V., Skill 4.6

PROMOTING THE PHYSICAL EDUCATION PROGRAM

An effective strategy for promoting the physical education curriculum is to relate physical education to the purposes and goals of the entire educational process. By providing satisfying, successful, and enriching experiences that are properly taught, physical educators shape a physically, mentally, and socially fit society. Advocates should relate physical education to the total educational process through the cognitive, affective, and psychomotor domains.

COMPETENCY 3.0 UNDERSTAND INSTRUCTIONAL STRATEGIES IN PHYSICAL EDUCATION

SKILL 3.1 Instructional methods and their characteristics.

Common instructional methods that physical education instructors can use to facilitate learning include command style, practice style, reciprocal style, and inclusion style.

In the **command style**, the teacher makes all the decisions and controls all activities. The command style is particularly useful in teaching students a skill in a short period of time. Because command style allows very little student-teacher and student-student interaction, instructors should limit its use to initial demonstrations and explanations.

Practice style allows students to make decisions and move at their own skill level during the implementation phase of skill development. Practice style is particularly useful when students have achieved basic skill competency because it allows self-paced practice and individualized feedback.

Reciprocal style involves the interaction of pairs of students. Reciprocal style provides needed social interaction and allows students to learn from each other through observation. The instructor is also free to interact with the students.

Inclusion style gives all students the chance to participate in the same task regardless of skill level. Students make decisions on how best to go about practicing and developing their skills. They learn their strengths and weaknesses through trial and error. For example, when learning to throw objects at a target, students can choose the size and type of target and the distance between themselves and the target that best suits their ability level.

COMMUNICATION DELIVERY SYSTEMS

Three basic types of communication delivery systems relevant to physical education are written, verbal, and visual.

Written communication is particularly effective in communicating large amounts of information. In addition, instructors may choose to provide students with written instructions for classroom activities to eliminate the need for extended and repeated explanation.

Verbal communication is traditionally the foundation of teacher-student interaction. Verbal communication is an effective method of explaining skills and concepts. Physical education instructors should, however, attempt to limit verbal instructions and explanations to allow for maximum physical activity during class time.

Visual communication is an important, and often underutilized, method of communication in physical education. Visual demonstrations are often the most effective way to introduce athletic skills and activities.

SKILL 3.2   Appropriate instructional methods and activities for various objectives, situations, and developmental levels.

See Domain V – Skill 3.1

See Domain I – Skill 4.2

See Domain II – Skill 3.4

With a history that spans centuries and roots traceable to the ancient Greeks, physical education is a technique that helps in promoting the physical fitness and well-being of a body.

The primary aim of physical education, otherwise known as physical training, is to equip students with the knowledge, skills, capabilities, values, and enthusiasm necessary to the maintenance of a healthy lifestyle into adulthood, regardless of physical ability. Activities included in the program promote physical fitness, develop motor skills, instill knowledge and understanding of rules, concepts, and strategies, and teach students to work as part of a team or as individuals in a wide variety of play-based and competitive activities.

Physical education has come to occupy a very important role in most school programs. There are various curriculum models for physical education courses. Such curricula stress the meaning of human movement, physiology of exercise, sport sociology, aesthetic appreciation of movement, and the acquisition of skills. Modern curricula include all of these competencies.

The modern physical education curriculum provides students a basic experience in the following activities: aquatics, conditioning activities, gymnastics, individual/dual sports, team sports, and rhythm and dance. All states in the United States offer physical education to students in grades K through 12, and many states require the self-contained classroom teacher to implement a physical education program.

All curriculum models have the following characteristics: physical activity, by which students will become competent in a variety of, and proficient in a few, physical activities; human movement, in which students will understand and apply principles of human movement to the learning and development of motor skills; fitness; responsible behavior, wherein students will exhibit responsible personal and social behavior in physical activity settings; respect for differences; and benefits of physical activity, by which students will identify and understand how physical activity provides personal enjoyment, challenge, self-expression, and social interaction.

ACTIVITIES FOR VARIOUS OBJECTIVES, SITUATIONS, AND DEVELOPMENTAL LEVELS

The following is a list of physical activities that may reduce specific health risks, improve overall health, and develop skill-related components of physical activity. Some of these activities, such as walking and calisthenics, are more suitable to students at beginning developmental levels. Other physical activities, such as circuit training and rowing, are best suited for students at more advanced levels of development.

1. **Aerobic Dance**:
Health-related components of fitness = *cardio-respiratory, body composition.*

Skill-related components of fitness = *agility, coordination.*

2. **Bicycling**:
Health-related components of fitness = *cardio-respiratory, muscle strength, muscle endurance, body composition.*

Skill-related components of fitness = *balance.*

3. **Calisthenics**:
Health-related components of fitness = *cardio-respiratory, muscle strength, muscle endurance, flexibility, body composition.*

Skill-related components of fitness = *agility.*

4. **Circuit Training**:
Health-related components of fitness = *cardio-respiratory, muscle strength, muscle endurance, body composition.*

Skill-related components of fitness = *power.*

5. **Cross Country Skiing**:
Health-related component of fitness = *cardio-respiratory, muscle strength, muscle endurance, body composition.*

Skill-related components of fitness = *agility, coordination,; power.*

6. **Jogging/Running**:
Health-related components of fitness = *cardio-respiratory, body composition.*

7. **Rope Jumping**:
Health-related components of fitness = *cardio-respiratory, body composition.*

Skill-related components of fitness = *agility, coordination, reaction time, speed.*

8. **Rowing:**
Health-related components of fitness = *cardiorespiratory, muscle strength, muscle endurance, body composition.*

Skill-related components of fitness = *agility, coordination, power.*

9. **Skating:**
Health-related components of fitness = *cardiorespiratory, body composition.*

Skill-related components of fitness = *agility, balance, coordination, speed.*

10. **Swimming/Water Exercises**:
Health-related components of fitness = *cardiorespiratory, muscle strength, muscle endurance, flexibility, body composition.*

Skill related components of fitness = *agility, coordination.*

11. **Walking (brisk):**
Health-related components of fitness = *cardiorespiratory, body composition.*

SKILL 3.3 **Appropriate methods of instruction for students with special needs and students from diverse cultural and linguistic backgrounds.**

See Domain III – Skill 8.4
See Domain III – Skill 9.1

In general, teachers may need to modify instructional methods to accommodate students who have disabilities and participate in a physical education class. The physical educator should ensure that students with disabilities understand the purpose of the lesson before the activity begins. The teacher should design lesson plans that include alternate activities in the event that the originally planned activity does not work well for student with disabilities. Teachers should not place students with disabilities in activities where they have no chance of success. For example, teachers should avoid elimination games. The physical educator should praise minor displays of progress and achievement. The teacher should work with student(s) who have disabilities to set achievable goals, since goal attainment is a wonderful motivator.

Physical educators must have a strong, working knowledge of specific disabilities and how they affect a student's ability to learn. When working with students mentally retarded students, instructors should emphasize progressive gross motor movement. Teacher instruction should focus on demonstration rather than oral explanation. Instructors should reward the student's effort. Additionally, the practice period for handicapped students is short to alleviate boredom and aggravation. Instructors should also make modifications for the visually impaired student. Lesson planning for visually impaired student should focus on individual movement activities. The physical educator should use a whistle or loud verbal cues in class. If the visually impaired student has some residual eyesight, the teacher might have the student utilize a brightly colored ball against a contrasting backdrop. When working with hearing impaired students, the physical education teacher should use visual cues. The instructor or other students must read all written instructions aloud. During all stages of instruction, the hearing impaired student should be close to the teacher. If a student with an orthopedic disability is present in class, the teacher's lesson plans should focus on individual and dual sports to maximize the student's chance of success. Lastly, instructors may need to make modifications for students with emotional disabilities. Students with emotional disabilities can succeed in a stable, organized setting.

The teacher should praise individual student accomplishments. In order to avoid or minimize student behavior disruptions, the instructor should clearly identify and consistently enforce rules and expectations. Finally, when working with a student with any given disability, it is crucial that the physical education teacher follows the physician's instructions.

Instructors may also need to modify instructional methods to accommodate students from diverse cultural and linguistic backgrounds. When working with students from diverse cultural backgrounds, the physical educator should understand the cultural values and norms of the culture from which the students originate. When delivering instruction, the teacher should highlight information regarding participation in the activity. Often English is not the primary language for students from diverse cultural backgrounds. When working with students who utilize English as their second language, teachers should repeat instructions a number of times. The teacher should have knowledge of basic words relating to physical education in the language of the students present in class. The teacher should use precise English and avoid slang. During skill practice, the teacher could pair the student with others that might help them in their skill development. Finally, it is important that the teacher knows how to pronounce all students' names properly, especially the names of students from a diverse cultural background.

SKILL 3.4 Techniques for modifying rules, equipment, and setting to conform to the needs of students.

APPROPRIATE ACTIVITIES AND ADAPTATIONS FOR STUDENTS WITH LIMITATIONS

Appropriate activities are those activities in which handicapped students can successfully participate.

Adaptations include individualized instruction and modified rules, modified environments, and modified tasks. As needs warrant, instructors can move participants to less restrictive environments. Instructors can also initiate periodic assessments to advance a student's placement, review progress, and determine what the least restrictive environment is for each participant (including changing services to produce future optimum progress). However, the most appropriate placement depends on meeting the physical education needs, both educational and social, of the handicapped student.

FUNCTIONAL ADAPTATIONS

Instructors can provide blind students with auditory or tactile clues to help them find objects or to position their bodies in the activity area. Blind students also can learn the patterns of movement by manually mimicking the correct patterns or by verbal instructions.

Deaf students can read lips or learn signing to communicate and understand instructions.

Physically challenged students may have to use crutches to enable them to move.

Asthmatics can play goalie or similar positions requiring less cardio-respiratory demands.

Simplifying rules can accommodate a retarded participant's limited comprehension.

ADAPTING SELECTED ACTIVITIES

Walking: adapt distance, distance over time, and number of steps in specified distance; provide handrails for support; change slope for incline walking; and change width of walking pathway.

Stair climbing: change pathway, pace of climbing, and number and height of steps.

Running: change distance over time, use an incline-changing slope (distance over time), and form a maze (distance over time).

Jumping: change distance and height of jump, change distance in a series and from a platform, change participants' arm positions.

Hopping: change distance for one and two hops (using preferred and non-preferred leg) and distance through obstacle course.

Galloping: change number of gallops over distance, change distance covered in number of gallops, and widen pathway.

Skipping: change number of errorless skips, change distance covered in number of skips, change number of skips in distance, and add music for skipping in rhythm.

Leaping: change distance and height of leaps.

Bouncing balls: change size of ball (larger), have participant use two hands, reduce number of dribbles, bounce ball higher, have participant stand stationary and perform bounces one at a time.

Catching: use larger balls and have participant catch balls thrown at chest level from a lower height of release, shorten catching distance, have participant stop and then catch ball (easier than moving and catching).

ADAPTING FOR PROBLEMS WITH STRENGTH, ENDURANCE, AND POWER ACTIVITIES

10. Lower basketball goals or nets; increase size of target.

11. Decrease throwing distance between partners, serving distance, and distance between bases.

12. Reduce size or weight of projectiles or balls.

13. Shorten length and/or reduce weight of bat or other striking apparatus.

14. Play games in lying or sitting positions to lower center of gravity.

15. Select a "slow ball" (one that will not get away too fast), deflate ball in case it gets away, or attach a string to the ball for recovery.

16. Reduce playing time and lower number of points to win.

17. Use more frequent rest periods.

18. Rotate often or use frequent substitution when needed.

19. Use mobilization alternatives, such as using scooter boards one inning/period and feet for one inning/period.

ADAPTING FOR BALANCE AND AGILITY PROBLEMS

10. Verify if balance problem is due to medication (you may have to consult physician).

11. Use chairs, tables, or bars to help with stability.

12. Have participants learn to utilize eyes optimally for balance skills.

13. Teach various ways to fall and incorporate dramatics into fall activities.

14. Use carpeted surfaces.

15. Lower center of gravity.

16. Have participant extend arms or provide a lightweight pole.

17. Have participant keep as much of his/her body in contact with the surface.

18. Widen base of support (distance between feet).

19. Increase width of walking parameters.

ADAPTING FOR COORDINATION AND ACCURACY

Throwing Activities: use beanbags, yarn or nerf balls, and/or smaller-sized balls.

Catching and Striking Activities: use larger, softer, and lighter balls; throw balls to mid-line; shorten distance; and reduce speed of balls.

Striking/Kicking Activities: enlarge striking surface, choke up on bats, begin with participant successfully striking stationary objects and then progress to striking with movement, and increase target size.

EXERCISE PHYSIOLOGY ADAPTATIONS

Decrease the amount of weight, amount of reps/sets, pace, and/or distance of exercise; increase the amount of intervals; and combine together any of the previous modifications.

MODIFICATIONS OF THE LEARNING ENVIRONMENT THAT ENHANCE PARTICIPATION IN PHYSICAL EDUCATION.

Participation in physical education activities often leads to future participation in sports. There are three options for maximizing participation in physical education: activity modification, multi-activity designs, and homogeneous or heterogeneous grouping.

Activity modification is the first option to achieve maximum participation by simply modifying the type of equipment used or the activity rules. However, keep activity as close to the original as possible (i.e. substitute a yarn ball for a birdie for badminton).

Multi-activity designs permit greater diversification of equipment and more efficient use of available facilities (keeps all students involved).

Homogeneous and heterogeneous grouping for the purpose of individualized instruction, enhancing self-concepts, equalizing competition, and promoting cooperation among classmates.

Furthermore, plan activities that encourage the greatest amount of participation by utilizing all available facilities and equipment, involving students in planning class work/activities, and being flexible. Instructors can also use tangible rewards and praise.

SKILL 3.5   Strategies for consulting and collaborating with teachers and other school personnel.

Consultation and collaboration with an institution's personnel can often help identify necessary changes and the best methods of implementing the changes. If concerned persons did not participate in the process of change, a state of educational stagnation would occur. The method of communication can make a difference when dealing with a challenging issue. An open discussion arena is an effective strategy that can satisfy many objectives with appropriate adaptations.

First, interested parties must identify a problem. Second, they must develop and define a clear objective to remedy the problem. Also, personnel should send communications to the appropriate authorities. After doing so, information will cascade down to all concerned people. If a motive is clear and if it is for the good of all, people will respond and give their fair share in order to meet the objective. The people who share in the accomplishment of the objective will share a sense of achievement. Consequently, if another project that requires similar cooperation arises, these individuals will be ready to step in and make the change.

Additionally, physical educators need to attend all meetings that involve any of their students that other teachers also have in class.

COMPETENCY 4.0 UNDERSTAND PHYSICAL EDUCATION ASSESSMENT METHODS AND INSTRUMENTS

SKILL 4.1 Types, characteristics, advantages, and limitations of various assessment methods and instruments.

Evaluations determine the value of a particular activity. Instructors should integrate the continuous process of evaluation into the teaching-learning experience. The goal of an evaluation should not be limited to the school setting and the students' experiences. Rather, we should also think of it in terms of a community's progress. Measurements for evaluation provide other valuable services that instructors can use to classify students, determine students' status for grading, and aid in the diagnosis of students' weaknesses in relation to fitness skill development.

A renowned guide for educators includes the following three principles:

- Students should accept evaluations as an integral part of the teaching process.
- Instructors should use evaluations to assist students in achieving terminal competencies (psychomotor, cognitive, and affective).
- Instructors should base evaluations on the status of the individual student.

The Office of Instructional Services enumerates achievement standards for children in elementary school. An individualized, well-executed physical education program should enable a student to:

- Walk 500 yards without stopping.
- Run 30 yards dash in six seconds or less.
- Jump a standing broad jump a distance of approximately their height plus three inches.
- Bounce a ball to 2/4 or 4/4 music count.

Portfolio assessments are evaluations of the learning that happens in a natural setting. They can capitalize on student work, enhance both teacher and student involvement in evaluation, and satisfy the accountability needed to prompt school reform. Portfolio assessment includes active diaries, attitude inventories, entry-level skill test, and teacher/peer rating forms.

Interactive health CD-ROMs allow students and instructors to enter personal fitness data and evaluation results and receive immediate feedback and suggestions for improvement.

TYPES OF EVALUATION

Summative evaluation strategies involve assigning the student a letter or number grade, which can reflect both the student's performance and progress. Examples include:

- Performance evaluations – the instructor assigns a letter or number grade based on the student's performance on a task or set of tasks (e.g. push-ups and sit-ups, time to run one mile, etc.).
    - Appropriate for unbiased, objective assessment of performance, ability, and current level of competency.

- Progress evaluations – the instructor assigns a letter or number grade based on the student's improvement in the ability to perform a task or set of tasks.
    - Appropriate for assessment of effectiveness of physical education program in promoting improvement.

- Effort evaluations – the instructor assigns a letter or number grade based on the student's effort in working towards training goals.
    - Appropriate for assigning class grades, as instructors should reward effort and participation rather than natural ability.

- Behavior evaluations – the instructor assigns a letter or number grade based on the student's behavior in and attitude towards training and the training environment.
    - Appropriate for assigning class grades and maintaining an orderly, disciplined classroom.

Formative evaluation strategies do not provide a letter or number grade to the student, but rather focus on a textual analysis of the student's performance and progress. Examples include a written analysis of the student's performance, progress, effort, attitude, and behavior.

BASIC STATISTICAL APPLICATIONS

Statistical applications for physical education assessment purposes allow us to evaluate where the score of a given assessment stands in comparison to other assessments and compare different assessments of the same student's abilities (in other fields – tracking intra-individual differences, or in the same field over time – tracking the student's progress).

Central tendency and variability determine where a range of scores cluster on the assessment scale and whether they are all highly localized around one point on the scale, or spread out over a range.

Standard scores and norms allow us to evaluate where assessment results stand in relation to the 'normal' expected achievement level.

Correlations allow us to evaluate the frequency at which two assessment trends appear in conjunction. Note that correlation does not imply causation.

SKILL 4.2   Sources of standards of physical fitness.

The imperatives of the health and fitness concerns have resulted in the enactment of standards for physical education. These standards represent the essential skills and knowledge that all students need to maintain a physically active and healthy lifestyle.

FEDERAL STANDARDS FOR PHYSICAL EDUCATION

The goal of physical education is to impart the knowledge, skills, and confidence necessary for students to enjoy a life of healthful physical activity. There are six standards for physical education:

- **Standard 1:** Demonstrates competency in motor skills and movement patterns needed to perform a variety of physical activities.

- **Standard 2:** Demonstrates understanding of movement concepts, principles, strategies, and tactics as they apply to the learning and performance of physical activities.

- **Standard 3:** Participates regularly in physical activity.

- **Standard 4:** Achieves and maintains a health-enhancing level of physical fitness.

- **Standard 5:** Exhibits responsible personal and social behavior that respects self and others in physical activity settings.

- **Standard 6:** Values physical activity for health, enjoyment, challenge, self-expression, and/or social interaction.

(Source: National Association for Sport & Physical Education)

A comprehensive physical education curriculum emphasizes the importance of physical activity and nutrition to lifelong wellness. In addition, physical education should introduce students to various activities that promote healthy living. Finally, physical education should provide students with strategies to maintain proper nutrition and activity and design personal fitness programs.

ADAPTED PHYSICAL EDUCATION NATIONAL STANDARDS

Physical education standards adapted for disabled students include:

STANDARD 1 HUMAN DEVELOPMENT: Sets the foundation of proposed goals and activities for individuals with disabilities, which is grounded in a basic understanding of human development and its applications to those with various needs.

STANDARD 2 MOTOR BEHAVIOR: Sets the standard on teaching individuals with disabilities, which requires knowledge of typical physical and motor development as well as understanding the influence of developmental delays on these processes.

STANDARD 3 EXERCISE SCIENCE: The focus of this standard is on the principles that address the physiological and biomechanical applications encountered when working with diverse populations.

STANDARD 4 MEASUREMENT AND EVALUATION: Sets the standards on the measurements in gauging motor performance which is, to a large extent, based on a good grasp of motor development and the acquisition of motor skills covered in other standards.

STANDARD 5 HISTORY AND PHILOSOPHY: This standard sets the basic knowledge base of educators on legal and philosophical factors involved in current day practices in adapted physical education (APE). This standard also covers a review of history and philosophy related to special and general education.

STANDARD 6 UNIQUE ATTRIBUTES OF LEARNERS: This standard refers to information based on the disability areas found in the Individuals with Disabilities Education Act (IDEA).

STANDARD 7 CURRICULUM THEORY AND DEVELOPMENT: Sets the standards on knowledge of certain curriculum theory and development concepts, such as selecting goals based on relevant and appropriate assessment.

STANDARD 8 ASSESSMENT: This seeks to establish the parameters and conduct of assessment, which goes beyond data gathering to include measurements for the purpose of making decisions about special services and program components for individuals with disabilities.

STANDARD 9 INSTRUCTIONAL DESIGN AND PLANNING: Administration must develop standards on instructional design and planning before an APE teacher can provide services to meet legal mandates, educational goals, and, most importantly, the unique needs of individuals with disabilities.

STANDARD 10 TEACHING: This standard integrates many of the principles addressed earlier in covering areas such as human development, motor behavior, and exercise science. This will ensure that schools meet other standards to effectively provide quality physical education to individuals with disabilities.

STANDARD 11 CONSULTATION AND STAFF DEVELOPMENT: This standard sets the key competencies that an adapted physical educator should know in relation to consultation and staff development.

STANDARD 12 STUDENT AND PROGRAM EVALUATION: Sets the standards on how to conduct program evaluation, integrating the entire range of educational services.

STANDARD 13 CONTINUING EDUCATION: This standard sets the parameters on ways teachers of APE can remain current in their field.

STANDARD 14 ETHICS: This standard ensures that teachers of APE not only understand the importance of sound ethical practices, but also adhere to and advance such practices.

STANDARD 15 COMMUNICATION: This standard includes setting the quality of information on how to communicate with families and other professionals effectively. The standard encourages a team approach to enhance service delivery to individuals with disabilities.

SKILL 4.3 Techniques for selecting, constructing, adapting, and implementing formal and informal assessments.

Physical educators should construct assessments that evaluate all three domains of physical education: psychomotor, cognitive, and affective. Teachers should divide assessments in the psychomotor domain into two groups: skill-related fitness and sport-specific skills. The physical education teacher can objectively measure skill-related fitness utilizing assessments specifically designed to evaluate each component. Speed, agility, coordination, balance, and reaction time are the components of skill-related fitness. Teachers may choose to use standardized tests developed to assess each of these components. Most of these tests also include normative data. Similarly, many standardized tests are also available as an objective assessment of sport-specific skills. Many of these tests also include normative data.

Teachers should thoroughly evaluate an assessment before choosing to utilize it, as some of the existing tests are quite complicated and burdensome to implement. If a teacher chooses not to use an existing assessment, adaptation of an existing assessment is always an option. To adapt an existing assessment, the physical educator can evaluate the assessment and determine which components of the assessment are reasonable to implement and provide a valid assessment of the specified skill. The teacher would delete the remaining components from the assessment prior to implementation. In addition to the option of deleting segments of the existing assessment, the teacher might choose to make general modifications to the overall assessment. The physical educator can measure both skill-related fitness and sport-specific skills subjectively through informal assessments. Examples of informal assessments include student interviews, student self-evaluation, and checklists.

In addition to psychomotor skills, the physical educator also assesses development of the cognitive domain. Evaluation of the cognitive domain includes formal written assessments. When constructing a written assessment, the physical educator should design the assessment at an age appropriate level, include all written instructions on the test, and arrange similarly formatted questions together. Sample types of written test questions include matching, multiple choice, true-false, fill-in-the-blank, short answer, and essay. When possible, the physical educator should administer written assessments in a classroom setting, rather than on the gymnasium floor. Assessment of both the psychomotor and cognitive domains will occur at the end of each unit of instruction.

Finally, the physical educator should assess development in the affective domain. Informal assessment of the affective domain might include checklists similar to the informal checklists utilized to assess development in the psychomotor domain. Utilizing these affective checklists clarifies behavioral expectations. Additionally, standardized attitude scales are also available to physical educators. Instructors should measure development in the affective domain at various intervals throughout the school year.

SKILL 4.4 Appropriate assessment methods for various objectives and situations.

SEE ALSO DOMAIN V., Skill 4.1

ASSESSMENT IN THE AFFECTIVE DOMAIN

The affective domain includes interests, appreciations, attitudes, values, and adjustments inherent in the acquisition of physical activities. To measure in the affective domain, the teacher can observe the student and keep a record of those observations. Alternatively, the instructor can use opinion polls or surveys. To measure the social progress of an individual, use a sociogram. It plots the associations an individual student has with his peers.

The following is a list of appropriate tools for the assessment of affective development.

SOCIAL MEASURES (behavior, leadership, acceptance, and personality/character):

- **Harrocks Prosocial Behavior Inventory** (HPBBI) – measures prosocial play behavior of 5th and 6th graders in recreational play.
- **Adams Prosocial Inventory** – measures high school students' prosocial behaviors in physical education classes.
- **Nelson Leadership Questionnaire** – determines leaders as perceived by instructors, coaches, classmates, and teammates.
- **Cowell Personal Distance Scale** – measures congruity of a student within a group and his/her yearly development.
- **Blanchard Behavior Rating Scale** – measures student personality and character.

ATTITUDE MEASURES (predisposition to certain actions):

- **McKethan Student Attitude Inventory-Instructional Processes in Secondary Physical Education** (SAI-IPSPE) – measures attitudes of students toward instructional processes (e.g. teacher's verbal behavior, nature of activities, patterns of class organization, and regulations and policies in conceptual physical education environment).
- **Toulmin Elementary Physical Education Attitude Scale** (TEPEAS) – measures attitudes of the physical education program of elementary school students.
- **Feelings About Physical Activity** – measures commitment to activity.
- **Children's Attitudes Toward Physical Activity -Revised** (CATPA) – measures significance students place on physical activity.
- **Willis Sports Attitudes Inventory - Form C** - measures motives of competition in sports (achievement, power, success, avoiding failure).
- **Sport Orientation Questionnaire - Form B** - measures behaviors of achievement and competition during exercising and sports.
- **McMahan Sportsmanship Questionnaire** – measures high school students' attitudes toward sportsmanship.
- **Physical Estimation and Attraction Scale** – measures motivation and interest.

SELF-CONCEPT MEASURES (self-perception):

- **Cratly Adaptation of Piers-Harris Self-Concept and Scale** – measures/estimates students' own feelings about their appearance and skill performance abilities.
- **Merkley Measure of Actual Physical Self** – measures perception of physical self-relating to exercise and activity.
- **Nelson-Allen Movement Satisfaction** – measures satisfaction of movement.
- **Tanner Movement Satisfaction Scale** – measures students' own level of satisfaction/dissatisfaction with their own movement.

STRESS AND ANXIETY MEASURES:

- **Stress Inventory** (Miller and Allen) – measures level of stress according to stress indicators.
- **Sport Competition Anxiety Tests** – measures anxiety toward competition via one's perception of the competition as threatening or non-threatening.

ASSESSMENT IN THE COGNITIVE DOMAIN

1. **Standardized Tests** – scientifically constructed test with established validity and reliability.
2. **Teacher-made Tests** – developed personally by the teacher.
3. **Essay Tests/Written Assignments** – tests the ability to organize information presented logically in written paragraphs.
4. **Objective Tests** – true/false, multiple choice, matching, diagrams, completion, or short written response.
5. **Norm-Referenced Tests** – compares individual's score to the scores of others.
6. **Criterion-Referenced Tests** – Interpreting a score by comparing it to a predetermined standard.

SKILL 4.5 The use of technology for analysis of student fitness and performance.

The best sources for identifying current technological resources for accessing information on physical activity and health are the Internet and local district technology workshops. District workshops are an extremely valuable resource in obtaining additional knowledge of how to use technology to obtain more information on each teachers specific subject matter, including physical education.

Internet resources form an important part of current technology, which helps in accessing information on physical activity and health. There are internet sources, which also enable educators, students, performers, parents, and athletes to stay aware of up-to-date information and programs about physical activity and health.

Numerous websites also exist that allow educators as well as performers to know about the developments in the physical education training systems. Use of technological resources also helps students to grasp more knowledge about physical activity and health-related issues.

Some organizations such as the NASPE also provide information on physical fitness and health. For example, NASPE invites school districts nationwide to post their school wellness policy on the NASPE Forum.

Research also shows there are different types of devices that athletes can use to monitor physical activity and health. Such devices include virtual bicycles, rowing machines, and tread mills. Such technology helps plan and implement workouts and view workout results.

Instructors can use technology in a variety of ways to instruct the performers or athletes to improve or learn. We can summarize the uses of technology under the following headings:

• Actual use of technology, in which the teacher and the students use the technology in a "hands-on" setting. For example, students use a video or digital camera in physical education to analyze their skills.

• Utilizing technology products, such as the use of products during instruction and learning. Products may include gathering information or resources from the Internet, imaging results for analyzing a motor skill, etc.

• The teacher can use the technology to present information or to provide examples and illustrations.

Some of the offered examples currently available in technology mediated instruction as include: (1) audio technologies such as: radio, telephone, voice mail, and audiocassettes, (2) video technologies such as: television, teleconferencing, compressed video, and prerecorded videocassettes, (3) and information technologies such as: stand alone work stations, CD ROM prepackaged multimedia, e-mail, chat rooms and bulletin boards, and the World Wide Web.

SKILL 4.6 The development of exercises prescriptions based of assessment results.

Physical fitness assessments are an important tool for physical education instructors and students. Instructors must be careful not to overemphasize fitness assessments, as students that score poorly may become discouraged and students that perform well may become complacent. When used correctly, however, the results of fitness assessments are valuable tools in the development of exercise prescriptions. For example, an instructor can use the results of a multi-faceted fitness assessment to determine the fitness strengths and weaknesses of each student and the areas that each student needs to improve.

Simple exercises to improve aerobic endurance include walking, jogging, and bicycling. Exercises to improve muscular strength and endurance include push-ups, pull-ups, sit-ups, and weight lifting. Exercises to improve flexibility are stretches for various parts of the body. The exercises that help improve aerobic endurance, muscular strength, and muscular endurance also help improve body composition.

SKILL 4.7 Appropriate interpretation and communication of assessment results.

COMMUNICATING ASSESSMENT RESULTS

An important element of a successful physical education program is proper communication of assessment results. Instructors should communicate assessment data should differently to students, parents, and school board members.

- **Assessment data communicated to students** should be encouraging, and should be limited to a textual analysis of the child's progress and effort (it is not helpful or encouraging to remind a child that he is below grade level norms, especially if he has worked hard and made progress). The ultimate purpose of assessment data communicated to a child is to encourage further hard work.

- **Assessment data communicated to parents** should also be encouraging and should focus on the child's progress and effort. That said, it is also important that a parent receive an accurate picture of the child's status relative to grade level norms, especially if the child is in need of remedial assistance.

- **Assessment data communicated to school board members** is generally more summative in nature (a letter or number grade). Since school board members will generally see evaluations of entire classes at a time without knowing the individual children, it is not important for them to receive an encouraging picture of an individual child's progress. It is more important for them to see both current achievement levels and rates of progress to properly assess curriculum design, lesson planning, and program evaluation.

COMPETENCY 5.0 UNDERSTAND THE MANAGEMENT OF PHYSICAL EDUCATION ENVIRONMENTS AND PROGRAMS

SKILL 5.1 Techniques for organizing and managing physical education classes and environments and benefits and limitations of various management and discipline practices.

Historically, there is a belief that physical education teachers and instructors do not have to face the problems of maintaining discipline. However, physical education, just like all other disciplines, requires proper management and discipline practices. The problem of management is inherent in the discipline of physical education. The central question remains whether various management and discipline practices will be beneficial or harmful to students.

Many students treat physical education classes as a chance for rest and enjoyment, which makes maintaining disciplinary practices difficult. A common disciplinary goal is to create classroom rules and stick to them as well as to construct a creative environment by preparing activities for students.

Management and discipline practices are always valuable to physical education instructors. However, instructors must remember to deal with each student as an individual while taking into account their capabilities. Although implementing strict management practices might benefit the majority of the class and help in bringing decorum to the discipline, it might have negative effects too.

Curriculum design, group participation, cooperative work, fitness activities, and learning practices work well and instill exciting learning experiences for most. However, there are individuals who are left out and need special care.

Professional management and disciplinary practices infuse professionalism, strictness, and decorum to any physical education setting. However, too many management practices may make the physical education setting boring and even unproductive for students.

CLASSROOM MANAGEMENT

Proper organization of classroom procedures and information presentation is essential to classroom management and the fostering of a positive learning environment.

Instructors should establish and communicate procedures and rules to maintain an orderly classroom. Organizational strategies that enhance classroom management include grouping of students, pre-planning of classroom activities, and rotation of students through various activities.

Organizational strategies that enhance information presentation include balancing instructional delivery methods, planning a variety of activities to appeal to students with different learning profiles, and planning a proper progression of information delivery to promote continual learning. Clustering, prioritizing, and categorizing are three common approaches to the organization of information. Adequate supervision and behavioral management in the classroom is essential to student learning. Instructors must establish and communicate procedures, rules, and consequences of misbehavior to promote order in the classroom. Physical education instructors face unique behavioral management challenges because activities often take place in large, disperse environments. Techniques to consider when planning supervision and behavioral management include grouping students to achieve maximum compatibility, removing misbehaving students from activities, and establishing an orderly system to handle class procedures (e.g., activity time, instruction time, rotations, clean up, and dismissal).

SKILL 5.2   Logistics related to the availability and use of facilities, supplies, and other resources.

The management of facilities, supplies, and other resources is an important part of the physical educator's job. Instructors must plan the availability, use, and safety of facilities. In addition, instructors must develop procedures for transporting, distributing, and collecting equipment. Finally, instructors must develop lesson plans that maximize the use of time and keep students active.

Facility management is the first task physical educators must consider. Instructors must ensure, through communication with other school personnel, that the required facilities are available when needed. In addition, instructors must inspect facilities prior to use to ensure the safety of the students. Instructors should carefully note uneven surfaces, holes, obstructions, and obstacles. Instructors may also have to modify rules or game procedures as the facility dimensions dictate.

Equipment management is another important responsibility of physical educators. Instructors must develop procedures for transporting equipment to and from the playing field or gymnasium. One way to simplify equipment transportation is to use a shopping cart, which many grocery stores will donate, to carry equipment. Instructors can also designate students as equipment managers to help carry and distribute equipment. Equipment distribution and collection is another important concern for physical educators. Spreading equipment throughout the playing area can speed the distribution process. Instructors should also establish a protocol for equipment return and set up areas for collection. Finally, instructors should develop signals, either verbal or visual, that direct students to stop the activity and either hold or put down the equipment.

One final physical educators' concern is class time management. One effective strategy for maximizing participation and the use of class time and equipment is to use stations. Stations allow students to rotate through a series of different activities in small groups. Instructors should use stations only for activities that the students are familiar with and are able to complete without constant supervision.

SKILL 5.3　Financial issues related to physical education programs.

Physical education programs are mandatory in almost all school districts. Thus, lawmakers believe physical education is fundamental to the physical and intellectual development of students.

Considering their imperative role in molding and shaping the personality of children and novices in physical education, state and district budgets are the main source of funding. Title V, Part D, Subpart 10 of the Elementary and Secondary Education Act of 1965, as amended by the No Child Left Behind Act of 2001 authorizes the funding of physical education programs. The federal government gives other grants, such as the PEP grants, that allow schools to provide a more comprehensive, integrated approach to physical activity.

Grants offered by the State include the 'National School Lunch Program' and the 'Child and Adult Care Food Program.' These specific grants offer education on nutrition and physical training.

There are other groups, such as the Health, Mental Health, Environmental Health, and Physical Education (HMHEHPE) group, which help in providing financial assistance for physical education programs. The aforementioned group offers the 'Carol M. White Physical Education Program' (Discretionary Grants).

Such programs help institutions by providing funds for the initiation, expansion, and enhancement of physical education and training for students from kindergarten through high school.

SKILL 5.4　Care and maintenance procedures for facilities and equipment.

Facilities and equipment are basic components of every physical education program. However, such facilities and equipments require regular service in order to maintain longevity and safety features.

Schools, clubs, gyms, and other centers have facilities, such as sport and other exercise equipment, which need to be taken care of regularly in order to prolong their lives and to avoid injuries to users. Instructors and maintenance staff must inspect fields and equipments carefully and on a consistent basis.

To enable students to exercise and improve free of risks, outdated, worn-out, or defective physical education machines, the equipment should always be serviced. In order to avoid serious problems, faulty equipment should always be removed. This helps to guarantee the student's safety.

Outdoor facilities should also have a system by which authorities and other officials in charge can inform participants to take shelter in case of dangerous and threatening weather conditions.

All authorities, such as schools, public authorities, and governments of different countries, should undertake adequate responsibility to use safe and proper installations, equipment, and other physical education facilities.

Although the safety of the students depends to a great extent upon the children themselves, we can hardly ignore the role of proper facilities and equipment.

School officials and instructors should base **equipment selection** on the following: (a) quality and safety (b) goals of physical education and athletics (c) participants interests, age, sex, skills, and limitations (d) and (e) trends in athletic equipment and uniforms. Knowledgeable personnel should select equipment, keeping in mind continuous service and replacement considerations (i.e. what's best in year of selection may not be best the following year). One final consideration is the possibility of reconditioning versus the purchase new equipment.

Additional Guidelines for Selection of Equipment
- follow purchasing policies
- relate purchasing to program, budget, and finances
- consider maintenance
- abide by legal regulations
- recognize administrative considerations (good working relationships at all personnel levels)
- determine best value for money spent
- ensure that participants have own equipment and supplies when necessary
- purchase from reputable manufacturers and distributors
- follow competitive purchasing regulations
- use school forms with clearly identified brand, trademark, and catalog specifications

Equipment Maintenance Procedures
- inspect supplies and equipment upon arrival
- label supplies and equipment with organization's identification
- have policies for issuing and returning supplies and equipment
- keep equipment in perfect operating condition
- store properly
- properly clean and care for equipment (including garments).

Facility Selection Considerations
- bond issues for construction
- availability to girls, women, minorities, and the handicapped
- energy costs and conservation
- community involvement
- convertibility (movable walls/partitions)
- environment must be safe, attractive, clean, comfortable, practical, and adaptable to individual needs
- compliance with public health codes
- effective disease control.

Facility Maintenance Procedures
- custodial staff, participants, and the physical education and athletic staffs must work together to properly maintain facility
- for pool's, water temperature, hydrogen ion concentration, and chlorine need daily monitoring
- gymnasium play areas must be free from dust and dirt
- showers and drying areas need daily cleaning and disinfecting
- participants' clothing should meet health standards to prevent odor and bacterial growth
- outdoor playing fields must be clear of rocks and free of holes and uneven surfaces
- disinfect and clean drinking fountains, sinks, urinals, and toilets daily
- air out and sanitize lockers frequently.

SKILL 5.5 Procedures for maintaining a safe physical education environment.

EMERGENCY ACTION PLANS

The first step in establishing a safe physical education environment is creating an Emergency Action Plan (EAP). The formation of a well-planned EAP can make a significant difference in the outcome of an injury situation.

Components of an Emergency Action Plan
To ensure the safety of students during physical activity, an EAP should be easily comprehensible yet detailed enough to facilitate prompt, thorough action.

Communication
Instructors should communicate rules and expectations clearly to students. This information should include pre-participation guidelines, emergency procedures, and proper game etiquette. Instructors should collect emergency information sheets from students at the start of each school year. First-aid kits, facility maps, and incident report forms should also be readily available. Open communication between students and teachers is essential. Creating a positive environment within the classroom allows students to feel comfortable enough to approach an adult/teacher if she feels she has sustained a potential injury.

Teacher Education
At the start of each school year, every student should undergo a pre-participation physical examination. This allows a teacher to recognize the "high-risk" students before activity commences. The teacher should also take note of any student that requires any form of medication or special care. When a teacher is aware of his/her students' conditions, the learning environment is a lot safer.

Facilities and Equipment
It is the responsibility of the teacher and school district to provide a safe environment, playing area, and equipment for students. Instructors and maintenance staff should regularly inspect school facilities to confirm that the equipment and location is adequate and safe for student use.

First Aid Equipment
It is essential to have a properly stocked first aid kit in an easily reachable location. Instructors may need to include asthma inhalers and special care items to meet the specific needs of certain students. Instructors should clearly mark these special care items to avoid a potentially harmful mix-up.

Implementing the Emergency Plan

The main thing to keep in mind when implementing an EAP is to remain calm. Maintaining a sufficient level of control and activating appropriate medical assistance will facilitate the process and will leave less room for error.

COMPETENCY 6.0 UNDERSTAND PRINCIPLES AND PROCEDURES OF INJURY PREVENTION AND EMERGENCY FIRST-AID ASSISTANCE

SKILL 6.1 Types and characteristics of injuries common in physical activities and injury care and prevention.

SEE DOMAIN II., SKILL 1.7 and DOMAIN V., SKILL 5.4

SKILL 6.2 Purposes and procedures for CPR.

CPR BASICS

Cardiopulmonary resuscitation (CPR) is a first-aid technique used to keep victims of cardiac arrest alive. It is also prevents brain damage while the individual is unconscious and more advanced medical help is on the way. CPR keeps blood flowing through the body and in and out of the lungs.

CPR Steps

- Step 1 – Call 911
- Step 2 – Tilt head, lift chin, check breathing
- Step 3 – Give two breaths
- Step 4 – Position hands in the center of chest
- Step 5 – Firmly push down two inches on the chest 15 times

Continue with two breaths and 15 pumps until help arrives. The American Heart Association and the American Red Cross both offer classes to train individuals in CPR.

SKILL 6.3 First-aid procedures related to the control of emergency situations and immediate treatment tips.

INJURY TREATMENT AND FIRST AID

Immediate treatment tips

When a student endures a physical injury, the first priority is to avoid further damage. Following an injury the teacher should look for the obvious cause of the accident (i.e., ill-fitting equipment, improper sliding technique, a missed step while running). The next step is to reduce swelling. The primary means of accomplishing this is a sequence of treatments (rest, ice, compression, elevation) known as **R.I.C.E.** It is vital to implement this procedure following an injury since swelling causes pain and a loss of motion.

Steps for the immediate treatment of an injury

1. Stop the activity immediately

2. Wrap the injured part in a compression bandage (i.e., an ACE bandage).

3. Apply ice to the injured part (crushed ice or frozen vegetables are ideal) for no more than 15 minutes at a time. You should allow the area to warm periodically.

4. Elevate the injured part.

5. For a proper diagnosis, send the injured student to the school's nurse or, for more serious injuries, to a physician.

Treating specific illnesses

Diabetes
Most children with diabetes suffer from Type 1 (insulin-dependent or juvenile) diabetes. Type 1 diabetes limits the pancreas' ability to produce insulin, a hormone vital to life. Without insulin, the body cannot use the sugar found in blood. In order to stay alive, an individual suffering from Type 1 diabetes must take one or more injections of insulin daily.

Diabetics control their disease by keeping the level of sugar (glucose) in the blood as close to normal as possible. The means to achieve diabetes control include proper nutrition, exercise, and insulin. Most children with diabetes self-monitor blood glucose levels to track their condition and respond to changes. Some rules of thumb to keep in mind when dealing with a diabetic child are:

- Food makes the glucose level rise
- Exercise and insulin make the glucose level fall
- Hypoglycemia occurs when the blood sugar level is low
- Hyperglycemia occurs when the blood sugar level is high

Low Blood Sugar (Hypoglycemia)
This is the diabetic emergency most likely to occur. Low blood sugar may result from eating too little, engaging in too much physical activity without eating, or by injecting too much insulin. **Symptoms include:**
- Headache
- Sweating
- Shakiness
- Pale, moist skin
- Fatigue/Weakness
- Loss of coordination

Treatment:
Provide sugar immediately. You may give the student ½ cup of fruit juice, non-diet soda, or two to four glucose tablets. The child should feel better within the next 10 minutes. If so, the child should eat some additional food (e.g. half a peanut butter, meat, or cheese sandwich). If the child's status does not improve, treat the reaction again.

High Blood Sugar (Hyperglycemia)
Hyperglycemia can result from eating too much, engaging in too little physical activity, not injecting enough insulin, or illness. You can confirm high blood sugar levels by testing with a glucose meter.

Symptoms:
- Increased thirst
- Weakness/Fatigue
- Blurred vision
- Frequent urination
- Loss of appetite

Treatment:
If hyperglycemia occurs, the instructor should contact the student's parent or guardian immediately.

Dehydration
Dehydration occurs when a person loses more fluids than he/she takes in. The amount of water present in the body subsequently drops below the level needed for normal body functions. The two main causes of dehydration are gastrointestinal illness (vomiting, diarrhea) and sports. It is essential to replace fluids lost by sweating to prevent dehydration, especially on a hot day.

Symptoms:
- Thirst
- Dizziness
- Dry mouth
- Producing less/darker urine

Prevention/Treatment:
- Drink lots of fluids. Water is usually the best choice.
- Dress appropriately (i.e., loose-fitting clothes and a hat).
- If you begin to feel thirsty/dizzy, take a break and sit in the shade.
- Drink fluids prior to physical activity and then in 20-minute intervals after activity commences.
- Play sports or train in the early morning or late afternoon. You will avoid the hottest part of the day.

SKILL 6.4 Safety precautions in administering emergency care procedures.

Statistics show that students suffer injuries in sports activities, sometimes due to a lack of appropriate medical facilities and negligence.

The root cause of such situations is a significant lack of medical assistance or personnel. To avoid such situations, schools should formulate an emergency action plan (EAP). School personnel should follow the EAP guidelines during an emergency to keep danger from progressing.

Communication, conducting a pre-participation physical examination (PPE), and maintaining first aid and emergency medical supplies, constitute the core of an EAP. Communication among all concerned parties is the first pre-requisite, especially when someone suffers a serious injury.

Before conducting sporting events, it is necessary to conduct the pre-participation test, which can determine the fitness level of each student.

After an injury has occurred, it is important not to panic while administering care and treatment. Medical assistance is a must in the case of a serious injury. Also, school personnel must treat the injured student by using a first aid kit. The first aid kit should include items and supplies that will treat a range of potential injuries. Instructors should tailor the first aid kit's contents based on the type of sport the students are playing.

Some basic items that should be a part of first aid kit include a CPR mask, latex gloves, bandages, compression wraps, tape, and scissors.

Physical education and slight injuries go hand-in-hand. It is important not to neglect injuries and to take precautions, such as keeping everything that one might need in an emergency situation on hand.

COMPETENCY 7.0 UNDERSTAND LEGAL AND ETHICAL ISSUES RELATED TO PHYSICAL EDUCATION PROGRAMS

SKILL 7.1 Legal requirements and responsibilities associated with teaching physical education.

LEGAL AND ETHICAL RESPONSIBILITIES

There are many issues related to the legal responsibilities of the professional physical educator. Failing to foresee potential hazardous conditions and to take practical steps to avoid these situations can result in litigation. In general, teachers must follow the standard of care expected of any physical education practitioner with a similar level of education and training. Liability refers to a legal responsibility. Often in litigious situations, the term liability refers to negligence, or breach of duty. Negligence refers to actions that do not meet the minimum standard of care. In successful litigation, the defense proves the existence of the following: duty, breach of duty, injury, and proximate cause. When determining liability, courts will determine whether the injury was foreseeable.

To avoid legal action, professional physical educators must meet their legal responsibilities in several areas: equipment and facilities, instruction, supervision, and general safety. Regular inspection of the instructional area identifies potential hazards. When physical educators find hazards, they should submit written notification to the principal immediately. Students should also receive proper instruction of equipment use prior to the first use. In an instructional setting, the physical educator protects students from unreasonable harm. Students receive appropriate training before and during activity. Supervision of all activities in a school setting is mandatory. An unsupervised student in the school at any time or on the school grounds during the school day is unacceptable. The approach to overall safety should be proactive.

Physical educators participate in safety in-service programs each year. The teacher or another school medical professional reviews the student's medical records prior to allowing participation in physical education. Physical education practitioners teach the safety rules for each activity at the beginning of each unit. When a student sustains an injury in physical education class, the school nurse or other medical professional evaluates the student. The physical educator completes and files an accident report the same day that the accident occurred.

An Emergency Action Plan (EAP) should be in place for the physical education department at each school. The EAP identifies the following: emergency care procedures and the individual responsible for rendering care, the individual responsible for parental notification, the individual responsible for activating the emergency medical system (EMS), the policy for transportation of injured students, and a copy of a blank student accident report. To reduce the financial consequences of litigation, each teacher should purchase and maintain personal professional liability insurance. Teachers should not rely on school district legal liability insurance for personal financial protection.

In addition to legal responsibilities, the physical educator also has ethical responsibilities. Teachers are responsible for helping each student to realize his or her abilities. Physical educators are accountable for the welfare of each student entrusted to their care. Teachers should maintain a professional relationship with their students. Teachers should maintain confidentiality. Physical educators should follow national, state, and district or school curricular standards. Teachers should establish and maintain a classroom routine that promotes student achievement. Finally, the physical education teacher is responsible for promoting healthful living within the school community.

ESTABLISHMENT OF CURRICULUM FRAMEWORKS AND STUDENT PERFORMANCE STANDARDS

A curriculum framework is a set of broad guidelines that aids educational personnel in producing specific instructional plans for a given subject or study area. The legislative intent was to promote a degree of **uniformity and instructional consistency** in curriculum offerings.

Intended outcomes of the selected curriculum frameworks dictate student achievement standards. The legislature developed student performance standards for 40 physical education courses and 15 dance courses.

STATE LEGISLATION

State governments (Department of Education) are primarily responsible for education. Departments of education establish policies for course curriculum, number of class days and class time, and amount of credits required for graduation.

IMPACT OF EDUCATION REFORMS AND FEDERAL LEGISLATION

Enrollment went up and there was renewed administrative, parental, and student support. Additional impacts include: coeducational classes, separate teams for boys and girls and men and women (otherwise the school must create a coeducational team), equal opportunities for both sexes (for facilities, equipment and supplies, practice and games, medical and training services, academic tutoring and coaching, travel and per diem allowances, and dining and housing facilities), and equitable expenditure of funds for both sexes.

The Department of Health and Human Services recommended legislative changes - including those for education. **Title IX** prohibits sex discrimination in educational programs and **PL 94-142** requires schools to provide educational services for handicapped students. In 1990, Congress passed the **Individuals with Disabilities Education Act** (IDEA) that amended earlier laws. IDEA specifies physical education as a required educational service. In addition, IDEA defines physical education as the development of physical fitness, motor skills, and skills in group and individual games and dance, aquatics, and lifetime sports.

Title IX takes precedence over all conflicting state and local laws and conference regulations. Federal aid (even aid not related to physical education or athletics) must comply with Title IX. Finally, Title IX prohibits discrimination in personnel standards and scholarships selection.

Finally, Congress enacted the Physical Education for Progress (PEP) Act in 2000. The PEP program provides funds that the Department of Education uses to award grants to help initiate, expand, and develop physical education programs for Kindergarten through 12th grade students.

SKILL 7.2   Issues related to pool safety.

Water safety issues include student familiarity with appropriate medical responses to life-threatening situations. Students should recognize signs that someone needs medical attention (e.g. not moving, not breathing, etc.) and have knowledge of the proper response (e.g. who to contact and where to find them). With older children, the instructor can introduce rudimentary first aid. The instructor must also ensure that students are aware and observant of safety rules (e.g. no running near the water, no chewing gum while swimming, no swimming without a lifeguard, no roughhousing near or in the water, etc.).

SKILL 7.3   Issues related to supervision, safety, liability, and negligence.

LIABILITY CONCERNS IN PHYSICAL EDUCATION

Historically, common-law rules stated that individuals could not sue government agencies without consent of the agencies. However, federal and state courts have begun to allow individuals to sue both federal and state governments. Thus, public schools and school districts are now subject to liability lawsuits.

Compulsory elements of the school curriculum, such as physical education, prompt courts to decide based on what is in the best interests of the public.

Although school districts still have immunity in many states, teachers do not have such immunity. Whether employed by private person or a municipal corporation every employee owes a duty not to injure another by a negligent act of commission.

The following is a list of common legal terms and conditions applicable to physical education.

1. Tort – a legal wrong resulting in a direct or indirect injury; includes omissions and acts intended or unintended to cause harm.

2. Negligence – failing to fulfill a legal duty according to common reasoning; includes instruction and facility maintenance; instructors must consider sex, size, and skill of participants when planning activities and grouping students.

3. In Loco Parentis – acting in the place of the parent in relation to a child.

4. Sports Product Liability – liability of the manufacturer to the person using the manufacturer's product who sustains injury/damage from using the product.

5. Violence and legal liability (intentional injury in sports contests) – harmful, illegal contact of one person by another (referred to as battery).

6. Physical education classes held off campus and legal liability – primary concern is providing due care, which is the responsibility of management and staff members of sponsoring organization; failing to observe "due care" can result in findings of negligence.

7. Attractive Nuisance – an object that results in physical injury that the responsible party should have foreseen.

ACTIONS THAT CAN AVOID LAWSUITS

1. Knowing the health status of each person in the program.

2. Considering the ability and skill level of participants when planning new activities.

3. Grouping students to equalize competitive levels.

4. Using safe equipment and facilities.

5. Properly organizing and supervising classes.

6. Never leaving a class.

7. Knowing first aid (Do not diagnose or prescribe).

8. Keeping accident records.

9. Giving instruction prior to dangerous activities.

10. Being sure that injured students get medical attention and examination.

11. Getting exculpatory agreements (parental consent forms).

12. Having a planned, written disposition for students who suffer injuries or become ill.

13. Providing a detailed accident report if one occurs.

14. Join your district's union. This will make you a member of the NEA and provide up to 1 million dollars in liability as well as providing legal counsel should you run into a legal situation involving a student.

SKILL 7.4 State and federal laws and guidelines regarding gender equity, special education, religious issues, and other aspects of students' rights.

SEE ALSO DOMAIN V., Skill 7.1

Physical education and training has been and remains a priority in many schools, clubs, and other institutions and organizations. Physical education has been described as a fundamental right of every person, regardless of sex, religion, or creed.

Recognizing the aforementioned fact, Federal and State governments have formulated certain laws to protect the rights of all students. The Federal law that protects every student's right to physical education is the Individuals with Disabilities Education Act (IDEA). This act extends support to special education and other programs. Enacted in 1975, it includes all children and youth with disabilities. Under this act, all eligible school-aged children and youth with disabilities are entitled to receive a free, appropriate education (FAPE) in the least restrictive environment.

Federal and state governments have also enacted laws addressing gender equity in physical education and athletics. Research reveals that Title IX, a Federal law, protects the rights of girls and women against unwarranted discrimination in physical education by different schools, clubs, and other organizations. Title IX is a Federal law that prohibits high schools and colleges that receive federal funds from discriminating based on gender. Girls and women most often invoke Title IX to ensure equal opportunities for high school and college athletics.

Considering their vital role in the lives of children, many organizations offer opportunities for disabled people as well as children who require extra care, instruction, and accommodations to be a part of physical education classes.

SKILL 7.5 The application of ethical issues and guidelines in various physical education situations.

Physical education involves cooperation, dedication and respect between the instructor and students. Dedication and mutual respect help create a professional and friendly physical education atmosphere.

However, to attain such an ambience, it is mandatory to observe certain basic codes of ethics in the physical education setting.

The United Nations Universal Declaration of Human Rights 1948, article 1, stresses the freedom and equality of human beings. Humans have advanced reasoning skills and. Therefore, possess the essential ability to treat each other with respect and understanding.

The IDEA Health & Fitness Association also prescribes a code of ethics for physical education instructors, which includes being attentive to the interests of the student, maintaining a professional code of conduct, and being truthful and using fairness in all relationships and decisions.

The application of ethical standards in the physical education setting is an absolute must for creating a healthy, safe, and professional setting. Instructors must take utmost care to create, follow, and maintain such ethical standards in a physical education setting.

ANNOTATED LIST OF RESOURCES FOR PHYSICAL EDUCATION

This list identifies resources that may help candidates prepare to take the Physical Education examination. While not a substitute for coursework or other types of teacher preparation, these resources may enhance a candidate's knowledge of the content covered on the examination. The references listed do not represent a comprehensive listing of all potential resources. Candidates need not read all of the materials listed below, and passage of the examination will not require familiarity with these specific resources. When available, we have provided a brief summary for the reference cited. We have organized the resources alphabetically and by content domain in subtest order.

GROWTH, MOTOR DEVELOPMENT, AND MOTOR LEARNING

Colvin, A. Vonnie; Nancy J.; and Walker, Pamela. (2000). *Teaching the Nutes and Bolts of Physical Education: Building Basic Movement Skills.* Champaign, IL: Human Kinetics.
> Provides foundational content knowledge in locomotor and manipulative skills. Topics include rolling, throwing, catching, passing, dribbling, striking, kicking, and punting.

Fronske, H. (2001). *Teaching Cues for Sports Skills* (2nd edition). San Francisco, CA: Pearson/Cummings.
> Designed to provide verbal and alternate teaching cues and point out common errors in a variety of sports.

Graham, George. (1992). *Teaching Children Physical Education: Becoming a Master Teacher.* Champaign, IL: Human Kinetics.
> Includes the skills and techniques that successful teachers use to make their classes more interesting and developmentally appropriate. A reference for K-5 teachers and physical education department chairs and administrators.

Lawson, H.A. (1984). *Invitation to Physical Education.* Champaign IL: Human Kinetics.
> Shows students and practitioners how to apply basic business management principles to a variety of health promotion programs.

Pangrazi, Robert. (2004). *Dynamic Physical Education for Elementary School Children* (14th edition). San Francisco, CA: Pearson/Cummings.
> Provides step-by-step techniques for teaching physical education while navigating through today's challenging educational terrain.

Powers, S.K., and Howley, E.T. (2003). *Exercise Physiology* (5th edition). New York, NY: McGraw Hill.
> Explains theory of exercise science and physical education with application and performance models to increase understanding of classroom learning.

Schmidt, R.A., and Lee, T.D. (1999). *Motor Control Learning: A Behavioral Emphasis* (3rd Edition). Champaign: IL: Human Kinetics.
> Addresses many factors that affect the quality of movement behaviors and the ease with which students can learn them.

Sherrill, C. (1998). *Adapted Physical Activity, Recreation and Sport: Cross-disciplinary and Lifespan* (5th edition). Dubuque, IA: WCB McGraw Hill.
> Emphasizes attitude change, inclusion, and psychosocial perspectives for understanding individual differences.

Siedentop, D. (1994). *Sport Education.* Champaign, IL: Human Kinetics.
> Shows how sport can help students learn fair play, leadership skills, and self-responsibility, in addition to becoming competent players. Also shows physical educators how to implement effective sport education programs to achieve these goals.

Summers, J.J. (1992). *Approaches to the Study of Motor Control and Learning.* Amsterdam: Elsevier Science.
> Provides analysis of research with particular emphasis on the methods and paradigms employed and the future direction of their work.

Thomas, Katherine, et al. (2003). *Physical Education Methods for Elementary Teachers.* Champaign, IL: Human Kinetics.
> Takes a research approach and offers a user-friendly technique to applicable teaching modalities for physical education for grades K-12.

Winnick, J.P. (2000). *Adapted Physical Education and Sport* (3rd edition). Champaign, IL: Human Kinetics.
> Provides a thorough introduction for students preparing to work with individuals with disabilities in a variety of settings.

THE SCIENCE OF HUMAN MOVEMENT

Birrell, S., and Cole, C.L. (1994). *Women, Sport, and Culture.* Champaign, IL: Human Kinetics.
> The text is a collection of essays that examine the relationship between sport and gender.

Grantham, W.C.; Patton, R.W.; Winick, M.L.; and York, T.D. (1998). *Health Fitness Management.* Champaign, IL: Human Kinetics.
> Brings conventional business management principles and operational guidelines to the unconventional business of health and fitness.

Hall, S. (2003). *Basic Biomechanics.* Boston, MA: McGraw-Hill.

Hamill, J., and Knutzen, K. (1995). *Biomechanical Basis of Human Movement.* Hagerstown, MD: Lippincott, Williams & Wilkins.
> Integrates aspects of functional anatomy, physics, calculus, and physiology into a comprehensive discussion of human movement.

Hopper, Chris; Fisher, Bruce; and Muniz, Kathy. (1997). *Health-Related Fitness: Grades 1-2, 3-4, 5-6.* Champaign, IL: Human Kinetics.
> These three books provide a wealth of health and fitness information and are an excellent resource for classroom teachers with limited backgrounds in physical education.

Lawson, H.A. (1984). *Invitation to Physical Education.* Champaign, IL: Human Kinetics.
> Shows students and practitioners how to apply basic business management principles to a variety of health promotion programs.

Sample Test

1. Which of the following countries did not greatly influence the early development of P.E. in the States :

   A. Germany

   B. England

   C. Norway

   D. Sweden

2. What was the first state in the U.S. to require P.E. in its public schools?

   A. Florida

   B. Massachusetts

   C. New York

   D. California

3. President Eisenhower was alerted to the poor fitness levels of American youths. How was the poor physical conditioning of youths discovered in the Eisenhower Administration?

   A. By WWII Selective Service Examination

   B. By organizations promoting physical fitness

   C. By the Federal Security Agency

   D. By the Kraus-Webber Tests

4. In 1956, the AAHPER Fitness Conferences established:

   A. The President's Council on Youth Fitness

   B. The President's Citizens' Advisory Committee

   C. The President's Council on Physical Fitness

   D. A and B

5. The physical education philosophy based on experience is:

   A. Naturalism

   B. Pragmatism

   C. Idealism

   D. Existentialism

6. Idealism believes in:

   A. The laws of nature

   B. Experience is the key

   C. Practice, practice, practice

   D. The mind is developed through acquisition of knowledge

7. The Round Hill School (a private school) in Massachusetts was the first school to require P.E. in its curriculum. What year was this?

   A. 1792

   B. 1823

   C. 1902

   D. 1806

8. Social skills and values developed by activity include all of the following except:

   A. Winning at all costs

   B. Making judgments in groups

   C. Communicating and cooperating

   D. Respecting rules and property

9. Physical Education is a key component of an interdisciplinary learning approach because :

   A. It is usually held outside

   B. It does not involve other subject areas

   C. It allows for students to burn off energy

   D. It draws from many other curriculum areas

10. Developmentally, by what age has walking become automatic?

    A. Age 4

    B. Age 3

    C. Age 2

    D. Age 1

11. Which of the following psycho-social influences is not negative?

    A. Avoidance of problems

    B. Adherence to exercise

    C. Ego-centeredness

    D. Role conflict

12. Which professional organization protects amateur sports from corruption?

    A. AIWA

    B. AAHPERD

    C. NCAA

    D. AAU

13. Which professional organization works with legislatures?

    A. AIWA

    B. AAHPERD

    C. ACSM

    D. AAU

14. Research in physical education is published in all of the following periodicals except the:

    A. School PE Update

    B. Research Quarterly

    C. Journal of Physical Education

    D. YMCA Magazine

15. Which of the following is a sign of a possible body awareness problem:

    A. Can only do 10 sit-ups at a time

    B. Is overweight

    C. Runs looking ahead and not down

    D. Moves awkwardly or stiffly

16. The affective domain of physical education contributes to all of the following except:

    A. Knowledge of exercise, health, and disease

    B. Self-actualization

    C. An appreciation of beauty

    D. Good sportsmanship

17. A physical education instructor anticipates and prevents potential injuries, watches for hidden injuries, and takes an injury evaluation of the entire class. Which of the following strategies to prevent injuries is the teacher demonstrating?

    A. Maintaining hiring standards

    B. Proper use of equipment

    C. Proper procedures for emergencies

    D. Participant screening

18. Which of the following is not a consideration for the selection of a facility?

    A. Community involvement

    B. Custodial staff

    C. Availability to women, minorities, and the handicapped

    D. Bond issues

19. Which of the following is not a class-management technique?

    A. Explaining procedures for roll call, excuses, and tardiness

    B. Explaining routines for changing and showering

    C. Explaining conditioning

    D. Promoting individual self-discipline

20. Long-term planning is essential for effective class management. Identify the management techniques not essential to long-term planning.

    A. Parental observation

    B. Progress evaluation

    C. Precise activity planning

    D. Having the field lined already

21. Although Mary is a paraplegic, she wants to participate in some capacity in the physical education class. What federal legislative act entitles her to do so?

    A. PE 94-142

    B. Title IX

    C. PL 94-142

    D. Title XI

22. A legal wrong resulting in a direct or an indirect injury is:

    A. Negligence

    B. A Tort

    C. In loco parentis

    D. Legal liability

23. All of the following actions help avoid lawsuits except:

    A. Ensuring equipment and facilities are safe

    B. Getting exculpatory agreements

    C. Knowing each students' health status

    D. Grouping students with unequal competitive levels

24. Which of the following actions does not promote safety?

    A. Allowing students to wear the current style of shoes

    B. Presenting organized activities

    C. Inspecting equipment and facilities

    D. Instructing skill and activities properly

25. An instructor notices that class participation is much lower than expected. By making changes in equipment and rules, the instructor applied which of the following concepts to enhance participation?

    A. Homogeneous grouping

    B. Heterogeneous grouping

    C. Multi-activity designs

    D. Activity modification

26. Using tactile clues is a functional adaptation that can assist which type of students?

   A. Deaf students

   B. Blind students

   C. Asthmatic students

   D. Physically challenged students

27. Which of the following is not a skill assessment test to evaluate student performance?

   A. Harrocks Volley

   B. Rodgers Strength Test

   C. Iowa Brace Test

   D. AAHPERD Youth Fitness Test

28. All of the following are methods to evaluate the affective domain except:

   A. Adams Prosocial Inventory

   B. Crowell Personal Distance Scale

   C. Blanchard Behavior Rating Scale

   D. McCloy's Prosocial Behavior Scale

29. Educators can evaluate the cognitive domain by all of the following methods except:

   A. Norm-Referenced Tests

   B. Criterion Referenced Tests

   C. Standardized Tests

   D. Willis Sports Inventory Tests

30. Coordinated movements that project a person over an obstacle is:

   A. Jumping

   B. Vaulting

   C. Leaping

   D. Hopping

31. Using the same foot to take off from a surface and land is which locomotor skill?

   A. Jumping

   B. Vaulting

   C. Leaping

   D. Hopping

32. Which nonlocomotor skill entails movement around a joint where two body parts meet?

    A. Twisting

    B. Swaying

    C. Bending

    D. Stretching

33. A sharp change of direction from one's original line of movement is which nonlocomotor skill?

    A. Twisting

    B. Dodging

    C. Swaying

    D. Swinging

34. Which manipulative skill uses the hands to stop the momentum of an object?

    A. Trapping

    B. Catching

    C. Striking

    D. Rolling

35. Playing "Simon Says" and having students touch different body parts applies which movement concept?

    A. Spatial Awareness

    B. Effort Awareness

    C. Body Awareness

    D. Motion Awareness

36. Which movement concept involves students making decisions about an object's positional changes in space?

    A. Spatial Awareness

    B. Effort Awareness

    C. Body Awareness

    D. Motion Awareness

37. Applying the mechanical principles of balance, time, and force describes which movement concept?

    A. Spatial Awareness

    B. Effort Awareness

    C. Body Awareness

    D. Motion Awareness

38. Having students move on their hands and knees, move on lines, and/or hold shapes while moving develops which quality of movement?

   A. Balance

   B. Time

   C. Force

   D. Inertia

39. Students that paddle balls against a wall or jump over objects with various heights are demonstrating which quality of movement?

   A. Balance

   B. Time

   C. Force

   D. Inertia

40. Having students move in a specific pattern while measuring how long they take to do so develops which quality of movement?

   A. Balance

   B. Time

   C. Force

   D. Inertia

41. There are two sequential phases to the development of spatial awareness. What is the order of these phases?

   A. Locating more than one object in relation to each object; the location of objects in relation to one's own body in space.

   B. The location of objects in relation to one's own body in space; locating more than one object in relation to one's own body.

   C. Locating more than one object independent of one's body; the location of objects in relation to one's own body.

   D. The location of objects in relation to one's own body in space; locating more than one object in relation to each object and independent of one's own body.

42. Equilibrium is maintained as long as:

   A. Body segments are moved independently.

   B. The center of gravity is over the base of support

   C. Force is applied to the base of support.

   D. The center of gravity is lowered.

43. Which of the following does not enhance equilibrium?

    A. Shifting the center of gravity away from the direction of movement.

    B. Increasing the base of support.

    C. Lowering the base of support.

    D. Increasing the base of support and lowering the center of support.

44. All of the following affect force except:

    A. Magnitude

    B. Energy

    C. Motion

    D. Mass

45. For a movement to occur, applied force must overcome inertia of an object and any other resisting forces. What concept of force does this describe?

    A. Potential energy

    B. Magnitude

    C. Kinetic energy

    D. Absorption

46. The energy of an object to do work while recoiling is which type of potential energy?

    A. Absorption

    B. Kinetic

    C. Elastic

    D. Torque

47. Gradually decelerating a moving mass by utilization of smaller forces over a long period of time is:

    A. Stability

    B. Equilibrium

    C. Angular force

    D. Force absorption

48. The tendency of a body/object to remain in its present state of motion unless some force acts to change it is which mechanical principle of motion?

    A. Acceleration

    B. Inertia

    C. Action/Reaction

    D. Linear motion

49. The movement response of a system depends not only on the net external force, but also on the resistance to movement change. Which mechanical principle of motion does this definition describe?

    A. Acceleration

    B. Inertia

    C. Action/Reaction

    D. Air Resistance

50. Which of the following mechanical principles of motion states that every motion has a similar, contrasting response?

    A. Acceleration

    B. Inertia

    C. Action/Reaction

    D. Centripetal force

51. What is the proper order of sequential development for the acquisition of locomotor skills?

    A. Creep, crawl, walk, jump, run, slide, gallop, hop, leap, skip; step-hop.

    B. Crawl, walk, creep, slide, walk, run, hop, leap, gallop, skip; step-hop.

    C. Creep, crawl, walk, slide, run, hop, leap, skip, gallop, jump; step-hop.

    D. Crawl, creep, walk, run, jump, hop, gallop, slide, leap, skip; step-hop.

52. Having students pretend they are playing basketball or trying to catch a bus develops which locomotor skill?

    A. Galloping

    B. Running

    C. Leaping

    D. Skipping

53. Having students play Fox and Hound develops:

    A. Galloping

    B. Hopping

    C. Stepping-hopping

    D. Skipping

54. Having students take off and land with both feet together develops which locomotor skill?

    A. Hopping

    B. Jumping

    C. Leaping

    D. Skipping

55. What is the proper sequential order of development for the acquisition of nonlocomotor skills?

    A. Stretch, sit, bend, turn, swing, twist, shake, rock & sway, dodge; fall.

    B. Bend, stretch, turn, twist, swing, sit, rock & sway, shake, dodge; fall.

    C. Stretch, bend, sit, shake, turn, rock & sway, swing, twist, dodge; fall.

    D. Bend, stretch, sit, turn, twist, swing, sway, rock & sway, dodge; fall.

56. Activities such as pretending to pick fruit off a tree or reaching for a star develop which non-locomotor skill?

    A. Bending

    B. Stretching

    C. Turning

    D. Twisting

57. Picking up coins, tying shoes, and petting animals develop this nonlocomotor skill.

    A. Bending

    B. Stretching

    C. Turning

    D. Twisting

58. Having students collapse in their own space or lower themselves as though they are a raindrop or snowflake develops this nonlocomotor skill.

    A. Dodging

    B. Shaking

    C. Swinging

    D. Falling

59. Which is the proper sequential order of development for the acquisition of manipulative skills?

   A. Striking, throwing, bouncing, catching, trapping, kicking, ball rolling; volleying.

   B. Striking, throwing, kicking, ball rolling, volleying, bouncing, catching; trapping.

   C. Striking, throwing, catching, trapping, kicking, ball rolling, bouncing; volleying.

   D. Striking, throwing, kicking, ball rolling, bouncing; volleying.

60. Having students hit a large balloon with both hands develops this manipulative skill.

   A. Bouncing

   B. Striking

   C. Volleying

   D. Trapping

61. Progressively decreasing the size of a target that balls are projected at develops which manipulative skill.

   A. Throwing

   B. Trapping

   C. Volleying

   D. Kicking

62. Hitting a stationary object while in a fixed position, then incorporating movement, develops this manipulative skill.

   A. Bouncing

   B. Trapping

   C. Throwing

   D. Striking

63. A subjective, observational approach to identifying errors in the form, style, or mechanics of a skill is accomplished by:

   A. Product assessment

   B. Process assessment

   C. Standardized norm-referenced tests

   D. Criterion-referenced tests

64. What type of assessment objectively measures skill performance?

   A. Process assessment
   B. Product assessment
   C. Texas PE Test
   D. Iowa Brace Test

65. Process assessment does not identify which of the following errors in skill performance.

   A. Style
   B. Form
   C. End result
   D. Mechanics

66. Determining poor performance of a skill using process assessment can best be accomplished by:

   A. Observing how fast a skill is performed.
   B. Observing how many skills are performed.
   C. Observing how far or how high a skill is performed.
   D. Observing several attributes comprising the entire performance of a skill.

67. Which of the following principles is not a factor to assess to correct errors in performance for process assessment?

   A. Inertia
   B. Action/Reaction
   C. Force
   D. Acceleration

68. Which of the following methods measures fundamental skills using product assessment?

   A. Criterion-referenced tests
   B. Standardized norm-referenced tests
   C. Both A and B
   D. Neither A nor B

69. Product assessment measures all of the following except:

   A. How the student performs the mechanics of a skill.
   B. How many times the student performs a skill.
   C. How fast the student performs a skill.
   D. How far or high the student performs a skill.

70. **Instructors can evaluate skill level of achievement in archery by:**

    A. Giving students a written exam on terminology.

    B. Having students demonstrate the correct tension of arrow feathers.

    C. Totaling a student's score obtained on the target's face.

    D. Time how long a student takes to shoot all arrows.

71. **Instructors can determine skill level achievement in golf by:**

    A. The number of "birdies" that a student makes.

    B. The number of "bogies" a student makes.

    C. The score obtained after several rounds

    D. The total score achieved throughout the school year.

72. **Instructors can determine skill level achievement in swimming by:**

    A. How long a student can float

    B. How many strokes it takes a student to swim a specified distance.

    C. How long a student can stay under the water without moving.

    D. How many times a student can dive in five minutes.

73. **Instructors can assess skill level achievement in bowling by:**

    A. Calculating a student's average score.

    B. Calculating how many gutter-balls the student threw.

    C. Calculating how many strikes the student threw.

    D. Calculating how many spares the student threw.

74. Although they are still hitting the target, the score of some students practicing archery has decreased as the distance between them and the target has increased. Which of the following adjustments will improve their scores?

   A. Increasing the velocity of their arrows.

   B. Increasing the students' base of support.

   C. Increasing the weight of the arrows.

   D. Increasing the parabolic path of the arrows.

75. Some students practicing basketball are having difficulty with "free throws," even though the shots make it to and over the hoop. What adjustment will improve their "free throws?"

   A. Increasing the height of release (i.e. jump shot).

   B. Increasing the vertical path of the ball.

   C. Increasing the velocity of the release.

   D. Increasing the base of support.

76. An archery student's arrow bounced off the red part of the target face. What is the correct ruling?

   A. No score.

   B. Re-shoot arrow.

   C. 7 points awarded.

   D. Shot receives same score as highest arrow shot that did not bounce off the target.

77. A student playing badminton believed that the shuttlecock was going to land out-of-bounds. The shuttlecock landed on the line. What is the correct ruling?

   A. The shuttlecock is out-of-bounds.

   B. The shuttlecock is in-bounds.

   C. The point is replayed.

   D. That player is charged with a feint.

78. A mechanical pinsetter accidentally knocked down the only bowling pin left standing for a spare attempt after clearing all the other pins knocked down by the first ball thrown. What is the correct ruling?

   A. Foul

   B. Spare

   C. Frame is replayed

   D. No count for that pin

79. The ball served in racquetball hits the front line and lands in front of the short line. What is the ruling?

   A. Fault

   B. Reserve

   C. Out-of-bounds

   D. Fair ball

80. Two opposing soccer players are trying to gain control of the ball when one player "knees" the other. What is the ruling?

   A. Direct free kick

   B. Indirect free kick

   C. Fair play

   D. Ejection from the game

81. Two students are playing badminton. When receiving the shuttlecock, one student consistently stands too deep in the receiving court. What strategy should the server use to serve the shuttlecock?

   A. Smash serve

   B. Clear serve

   C. Overhead serve

   D. Short serve

82. A basketball team has an outstanding rebounder. In order to keep this player near the opponent's basket, which strategy should the coach implement?

   A. Pick-and-Roll

   B. Give-and-Go

   C. Zone defense

   D. Free-lancing

83. When a defensive tennis player needs more time to return to his position, what strategy should he apply?

   A. Drop shot

   B. Dink shot

   C. Lob shot

   D. Down-the-line shot

84. An overhead badminton stroke used to hit a fore-hand-like overhead stroke that is on the backhand side of the body is a(n):

   A. Around-the-head-shot

   B. Down-the-line shot

   C. Lifting the shuttle

   D. Under hand shuttle

85. A maneuver when an offensive player passes to a teammate and then immediately cuts in toward the basket for a return pass is:

   A. Charging

   B. Pick

   C. Give-and-go

   D. Switching

86. A bowling pin that remains standing after an apparently perfect hit is a:

   A. Tap

   B. Turkey

   C. Blow

   D. Leave

87. A soccer pass from the outside of the field near the end line to a position in front of the goal is a:

   A. Chip

   B. Settle

   C. Through

   D. Cross

88. A volleyball that opponents simultaneously contact and momentarily hold above the net is a(n):

   A. Double fault

   B. Play over

   C. Overlap

   D. Held ball

89. Volleyball player LB on team A digs a spiked ball. The ball deflects off LB's shoulder. What is the ruling?

   A. Fault

   B. Legal hit

   C. Double foul

   D. Play over

90. A teacher who modifies and develops tasks for a class is demonstrating knowledge of which appropriate behavior in physical education activities.

    A. Appropriate management behavior

    B. Appropriate student behavior

    C. Appropriate administration behavior

    D. Appropriate content behavior

91. To enhance skill and strategy performance for striking or throwing objects, for catching or collecting objects, and for carrying and propelling objects, students must first learn techniques for:

    A. Offense

    B. Defense

    C. Controlling objects

    D. Continuous play of objects

92. Which of the following is not a type of tournament?

    A. Spiderweb

    B. Pyramid

    C. Spiral

    D. Round Robin

93. Which of the following is not a type of meet?

    A. Extramural

    B. Intramural

    C. Interscholastic

    D. Ladder

94. An instructor used a similar movement from a skill learned in a different activity to teach a skill for a new activity. The technique used to facilitate cognitive learning was:

    A. Conceptual thinking

    B. Transfer of learning

    C. Longer instruction

    D. Appropriate language

95. A teacher rewards students for completing tasks. Which method is the teacher using to facilitate psychomotor learning?

    A. Task/Reciprocal

    B. Command/Direct

    C. Contingency/Contract

    D. Physical/Reflex

96. All of the following are Systematic Observational Evaluations except:

    A. Reflective Recording

    B. Event Recording

    C. Duration Recording

    D. Self Recording

97. The ability for a muscle(s) to repeatedly contract over a period of time is:

    A. Cardiovascular endurance

    B. Muscle endurance

    C. Muscle strength

    D. Muscle force

98. The ability to change rapidly the direction of the body is:

    A. Coordination

    B. Reaction time

    C. Speed

    D. Agility

99. Students are performing the vertical jump. What component of fitness does this activity assess?

    A. Muscle strength

    B. Balance

    C. Power

    D. Muscle endurance

100. Students are performing trunk extensions. What component of fitness does this activity assess?

    A. Balance

    B. Flexibility

    C. Body Composition

    D. Coordination

101. Working at a level that is above normal is which exercise training principle?

    A. Intensity

    B. Progression

    C. Specificity

    D. Overload

102. Students on a running program to improve cardio-respiratory fitness apply which exercise principle.

   A. Aerobic

   B. Progression

   C. Specificity

   D. Overload

103. Adding more reps to a weightlifting set applies which exercise principle.

   A. Anaerobic

   B. Progression

   C. Overload

   D. Specificity

104. Which of the following does not modify overload?

   A. Frequency

   B. Perceived exertion

   C. Time

   D. Intensity

105. Using the Karvonen Formula, compute the 60% - 80% THR for a 16-year old student with a RHR of 60.

   A. 122-163 beats per minute

   B. 130-168 beats per minute

   C. 142-170 beats per minute

   D. 146-175 beats per minute

106. Using Cooper's Formula, compute the THR for a 15 year old student.

   A. 120- 153 beats per minute

   B. 123-164 beats per minute

   C. 135-169 beats per minute

   D. 147-176 beats per minute

107. Prior to activity, students perform a 5-10 minute warm-up. Which is not recommended as part of the warm-up?

   A. Using the muscles that will be utilized in the following activity.

   B. Using a gradual aerobic warm-up.

   C. Using a gradual anaerobic warm-up.

   D. Stretching the major muscle groups to be used in the activity.

108. **Which is not a benefit of warming up?**

   A. Releasing hydrogen from myoglobin.

   B. Reducing the risk of musculoskeletal injuries.

   C. Raising the body's core temperature in preparation for activity.

   D. Stretching the major muscle groups to be used in the activity.

109. **Which is not a benefit of cooling down?**

   A. Preventing dizziness.

   B. Redistributing circulation.

   C. Removing lactic acid.

   D. Removing myoglobin.

110. **Activities to specifically develop cardiovascular fitness must be:**

   A. Performed without developing an oxygen debt

   B. Performed twice daily.

   C. Performed every day.

   D. Performed for a minimum of 10 minutes.

111. **Overloading for muscle strength includes all of the following except:**

   A. Raising heart rate to an intense level.

   B. Lifting weights every other day.

   C. Lifting with high resistance and low reps.

   D. Lifting 60% to 90% of assessed muscle strength.

112. **Which of the following applies the concept of progression?**

   A. Beginning a stretching program every day.

   B. Beginning a stretching program with 3 sets of reps.

   C. Beginning a stretching program with ballistic stretching.

   D. Beginning a stretching program holding stretches for 15 seconds and work up to holding stretches for 60 seconds.

113. **Which of following overload principles does not apply to improving body composition?**

    A. Aerobic exercise three times per week.

    B. Aerobic exercise at a low intensity.

    C. Aerobic exercise for about an hour.

    D. Aerobic exercise in intervals of high intensity.

114. **Which of the following principles of progression applies to improving muscle endurance?**

    A. Lifting weights every day.

    B. Lifting weights at 20% to 30% of assessed muscle strength.

    C. Lifting weights with low resistance and low reps.

    D. Lifting weights starting at 60% of assessed muscle strength.

115. **Aerobic dance develops or improves each of the following skills or health components except...**

    A. Cardio-respiratory function

    B. Body composition

    C. Coordination

    D. Flexibility

116. **Rowing develops which health or skill related component of fitness?**

    A. Muscle endurance

    B. Flexibility

    C. Balance

    D. Reaction time

117. **Calisthenics develops all of the following health and skill related components of fitness except:**

    A. Muscle strength

    B. Body composition

    C. Power

    D. Agility

118. Which health or skill related components of fitness is developed by rope jumping?

   A. Muscle Force

   B. Coordination

   C. Flexibility

   D. Muscle strength

119. Swimming does not improve which health or skill related component of fitness?

   A. Cardio-respiratory function

   B. Flexibility

   C. Muscle strength

   D. Foot Speed

120. Data from a cardio-respiratory assessment can identify and predict all of the following except:

   A. Functional aerobic capacity

   B. Natural over-fatness

   C. Running ability

   D. Motivation

121. Data from assessing _____ identifies an individual's potential of developing musculoskeletal problems and an individual's potential of performing activities of daily living.

   A. Flexibility

   B. Muscle endurance

   C. Muscle strength

   D. Motor performance

122. A 17-year-old male student performed 20 sit-ups, ran a mile in 8 minutes, and has a body fat composition of 17%. Which is the best interpretation of his fitness level?

   A. Average muscular endurance, good cardiovascular endurance; appropriate body fat composition.

   B. Low muscular endurance, average cardiovascular endurance; high body fat composition.

   C. Low muscular endurance, average cardiovascular endurance; appropriate body fat composition.

   D. Low muscular endurance, low cardiovascular endurance; appropriate body fat composition.

123. Based on the information given in the previous question, what changes would you recommend to improve this person's level of fitness?

    A. Muscle endurance training and cardiovascular endurance training.

    B. Muscle endurance training, cardiovascular endurance training, and reduction of caloric intake.

    C. Muscle strength training and cardio-vascular endurance training.

    D. No changes necessary.

124. An obese student's fitness assessments were poor for every component of fitness. Which would you recommend first?

    A. A jogging program.

    B. A weight lifting program.

    C. A walking program.

    D. A stretching program.

125. Which of the following body types is the most capable of motor performance involving endurance?

    A. Endomorph

    B. Ectomorph

    C. Mesomorph

    D. Metamorph

126. Which is not a sign of stress?

    A. Irritability

    B. Assertiveness

    C. Insomnia

    D. Stomach problems

127. Which is not a common negative stressor?

    A. Loss of significant other

    B. Personal illness or injury.

    C. Moving to a new state.

    D. Landing a new job.

128. Which of the following is a negative coping strategy for dealing with stress?

    A. Recreational diversions

    B. Active thinking

    C. Alcohol use

    D. Imagery

129. The most important nutrient the body requires, without which life can only be sustained for a few days, is:

   A. Vitamins

   B. Minerals

   C. Water

   D. Carbohydrates

130. With regard to protein content, foods from animal sources are usually:

   A. Complete

   B. Essential

   C. Nonessential

   D. Incidental

131. Fats with room for two or more hydrogen atoms per molecule-fatty acid chain are:

   A. Monounsaturated

   B. Polyunsaturated

   C. Hydrosaturated

   D. Saturated

132. An adequate diet to meet nutritional needs consists of:

   A. No more than 30% caloric intake from fats, no more than 50 % caloric intake from proteins, and at least 20% caloric intake from carbohydrates.

   B. No more than 30% caloric intake from fats, no more than 40% caloric intake from proteins, and at least 30% caloric intake from carbohydrates.

   C. No more than 30% caloric intake from fats, no more than 15% caloric intake from proteins, and at least 55% caloric intake from carbohydrates.

   D. No more than 30 % caloric intake from fats, no more than 30% caloric intake from proteins, and at least 40% caloric intake from carbohydrates.

133. Maintaining body weight is best accomplished by:

   A. Dieting

   B. Aerobic exercise

   C. Lifting weights

   D. Equalizing caloric intake relative to output

134. Most high-protein diets:

   A. Are high in cholesterol

   B. Are high in saturated fats

   C. Require vitamin and mineral supplements

   D. All of the above

135. Which one of the following statements about low-calorie diets is false?

   A. Most people who "diet only" regain the weight they lose.

   B. They are the way most people try to lose weight.

   C. They make weight control easier.

   D. They lead to excess worry about weight, food, and eating.

136. Physiological benefits of exercise include all of the following except:

   A. Reducing mental tension

   B. Improving muscle strength

   C. Cardiac hypertrophy

   D. Quicker recovery rate

137. Psychological benefits of exercise include all of the following except:

   A. Improved sleeping patterns

   B. Improved energy regulation

   C. Improved appearance

   D. Improved quality of life

138. Which of the following conditions is not associated with a lack of physical activity?

   A. Atherosclerosis

   B. Longer life expectancy

   C. Osteoporosis

   D. Certain cancers

139. Which of the following pieces of exercise equipment best applies the physiological principles?

   A. Rolling machine

   B. Electrical muscle stimulator

   C. Stationary Bicycle

   D. Motor-driven rowing machine

Answer Key

1.	C	36.	A	71.	C	106.	B
2.	D	37.	B	72.	B	107.	C
3.	D	38.	A	73.	A	108.	A
4.	D	39.	C	74.	D	109.	D
5.	B	40.	B	75.	B	110.	A
6.	D	41.	D	76.	C	111.	A
7.	B	42.	B	77.	B	112.	D
8.	A	43.	A	78.	D	113.	A
9.	D	44.	D	79.	A	114.	B
10.	B	45.	B	80.	A	115.	D
11.	B	46.	C	81.	D	116.	A
12.	D	47.	D	82.	C	117.	C
13.	B	48.	B	83.	C	118.	B
14.	A	49.	A	84.	A	119.	D
15.	D	50.	C	85.	C	120.	B
16.	A	51.	D	86.	A	121.	A
17.	D	52.	B	87.	D	122.	C
18.	A	53.	A	88.	D	123.	A
19.	C	54.	B	89.	B	124.	C
20.	A	55.	C	90.	D	125.	B
21.	C	56.	B	91.	C	126.	B
22.	B	57.	A	92.	C	127.	D
23.	D	58.	D	93.	D	128.	C
24.	A	59.	B	94.	B	129.	C
25.	D	60.	C	95.	C	130.	A
26.	B	61.	A	96.	A	131.	B
27.	A	62.	D	97.	B	132.	C
28.	D	63.	B	98.	D	133.	D
29.	D	64.	B	99.	C	134.	D
30.	B	65.	C	100.	B	135.	C
31.	D	66.	D	101.	D	136.	A
32.	C	67.	C	102.	C	137.	B
33.	B	68.	C	103.	B	138.	B
34.	B	69.	A	104.	B	139.	C
35.	C	70.	C	105.	D		

Rationales with Sample Questions

1. Which of the following countries did not greatly influence the early development of P.E. in the States :

A. Germany

B. England

C. Norway

D. Sweden

(C) Norway did not greatly influence the early development of P.E.

2. What was the first state in the U.S. to require P.E. in its public schools?

A. Florida

B. Massachusetts

C. New York

D. California

(D) In 1866, California became the first state to require physical education in its public schools.

3. President Eisenhower was alerted to the poor fitness levels of American youths. How was the poor physical conditioning of youths discovered in the Eisenhower Administration?

A. By WWII Selective Service Examination
B. By organizations promoting physical fitness
C. By the Federal Security Agency
D. By the Kraus-Webber Tests

(D.) This is one of the programs that President Dwight Eisenhower implemented during his presidency. Using a test devised by Drs. Hans Kraus and Sonja Weber of New York Presbyterian Hospital, Bonnie began testing children in Europe, Central America, and the United States. The Kraus-Weber test involved six simple movements and took 90 seconds to administer. It compared US children to European children in the realms of strength and flexibility. The fitness emphasis in schools started by Kraus-Weber declined in the 1970s and early 1980s. The President's Council on Physical Fitness and Sports was one result of the Kraus-Weber test results.

TEACHER CERTIFICATION STUDY GUIDE

4. In 1956, the AAHPER Fitness Conferences established:

   A. The President's Council on Youth Fitness
   B. The President's Citizens' Advisory Committee
   C. The President's Council on Physical Fitness
   D. A and B

(D., A., and B.) The **President's Council on Youth Fitness** was founded on July 16, 1956 to encourage American children to be healthy and active after a study indicated that American youths were less physically fit than European children. President Eisenhower created the President's Council on Youth Fitness with cabinet-level status. The Executive Order specified "one" objective. The first Council identified itself as a "catalytic agent" concentrating on creating public awareness. A President's Citizens-Advisory Committee on Fitness of American Youth was confirmed to give advice to the Council.

5. The physical education philosophy based on experience is:

   A. Naturalism
   B. Pragmatism
   C. Idealism
   D. Existentialism

(B.) Pragmatism, as a school of philosophy, is a collection of different ways of thinking. Given the diversity of thinkers and the variety of schools of thought that have adopted this term over the years, the term pragmatism has become almost meaningless in the absence of further qualification. Most of the thinkers who describe themselves as pragmatists indicate some connection with practical consequences or real effects as vital components of both meaning and truth.

6 Idealism believes in:

   A. The laws of nature

   B. Experience is the key

   C. Practice, practice, practice

   D. The mind is developed through acquisition of knowledge

(D.) Idealism believes the mind is developed through acquiring knowledge. The more a person knows, the more their mind will be developed.

7. The Round Hill School (a private school) in Massachusetts was the first school to require P.E. in its curriculum. What year was this?

   A. 1792

   B. 1823

   C. 1902

   D. 1806

(B.) The Round Hill School in Massachusetts was the first school to offer P.E. in its curriculum in the United States. This occurred in 1823.

8. Social skills and values developed by activity include all of the following except:
   A. Winning at all costs
   B. Making judgments in groups
   C. Communicating and cooperating
   D. Respecting rules and property

(A.) Winning at all costs is not a desirable social skill. Instructors and coaches should emphasize fair play and effort over winning. Answers B, C, and D are all positive skills and values developed in physical activity settings.

9. Physical Education is a key component of an interdisciplinary learning approach because :

   A. It is usually held outside

   B. It does not involve other subject areas

   C. It allows for students to burn off energy

   D. It draws from many other curriculum areas

(D.) P.E. draws from the sciences and mathmatics and other areas of the school curriculum

10. Developmentally, children should be walking automatically by age

   A. 4
   B. 3
   C. 2
   D. 1

(B.) Children should be walking automatically by age three.

11. Which of the following psycho-social influences is not negative?

   A. Avoidance of problems
   B. Adherence to exercise
   C. Ego-centeredness
   D. Role conflict

(B.) The ability of an individual to adhere to an exercise routine due to her/his excitement, accolades, etc. is not a negative psycho-social influence. Adherence to an exercise routine is healthy and positive.

12. Which professional organization protects amateur sports from corruption?

   A. AIWA
   B. AAHPERD
   C. NCAA
   D. AAU

(D.) The Amateur Athletic Union (AAU) is one of the largest non-profit, volunteer sports organizations in the United States. A multi-sport organization, the AAU dedicates itself exclusively to the promotion and development of amateur sports and physical fitness programs. Answer C may be a tempting choice, but the NCAA deals only with college athletics.

13. Which professional organization works with legislatures?

   A. AIWA
   B. AAHPERD
   C. ACSM
   D. AAU

(B.) AAHPERD, or American Alliance for Health, Physical Education, Recreation and Dance, is an alliance of 6 national associations. AAHPERD is the largest organization of professionals supporting and assisting those involved in physical education, leisure, fitness, dance, health promotion, and education, as well as all other specialties related to achieving a healthy lifestyle. AAHPERD is an alliance designed to provide members with a comprehensive and coordinated array of resources, support, and programs to help practitioners improve their skills and in turn, further the health and well-being of the American public.

14. Research in physical education is published in all of the following periodicals except the:

   A. School PE Update
   B. Research Quarterly
   C. Journal of Physical Education
   D. YMCA Magazine

(A.) Each school has a PE Update that publishes their own periodicals about physical activities. It aims at helping the students to catch-up on what is happening around them. The school produces this update to encourage their students to become more interested in all of the physical activities that they offer. School PE Updates, however, do not include research findings.

15. Which of the following is a sign of a possible body awareness problem:

   A. Can only do 10 sit-ups at a time

   B. Is overweight

   C. Runs looking ahead and not down

   D. Moves awkwardly or stiffly

(D) A student that moves stiffly or awkwardly is exhibiting signs of a possible body awareness problem. Individual attention and at home activities should be addressed..

16. The affective domain of physical education contributes to all of the following except:

   A. Knowledge of exercise, health, and disease
   B. Self-actualization
   C. An appreciation of beauty
   D. Good sportsmanship

(A.) The affective domain encompasses emotions, thoughts, and feelings related to physical education. Knowledge of exercise, health, and disease is part of the cognitive domain.

17. A physical education instructor anticipates and prevents potential injuries, watches for hidden injuries, and takes an injury evaluation of the entire class. Which of the following strategies to prevent injuries is the teacher demonstrating?

   A. Maintaining hiring standards
   B. Proper use of equipment
   C. Proper procedures for emergencies
   D. Participant screening

(D.) In order for the instructor to know each student's physical status, she takes an injury evaluation. Such surveys are one way to know the physical status of an individual. It chronicles past injuries, tattoos, activities, and diseases the individual may have or had. It helps the instructor to know the limitations of each individual. Participant screening covers all forms of surveying and anticipation of injuries.

18. Which of the following is not a consideration for the selection of a facility?

   A. Community involvement
   B. Custodial staff
   C. Availability to women, minorities, and the handicapped
   D. Bond issues

(A.) While community involvement positively impacts the communities where individuals live and work, it is not a major consideration in facility selection. Factors that are more important are staffing, accessibility, and financial considerations.

19. Which of the following is not a class-management technique?

   A. Explaining procedures for roll call, excuses, and tardiness
   B. Explaining routines for changing and showering
   C. Explaining conditioning
   D. Promoting individual self-discipline

(C.) Explaining conditioning is not a class management technique. It is an instructional lesson.

20. **Long-term planning is essential for effective class management. Identify the management techniques not essential to long-term planning.**
    - A. Parental observation
    - B. Progress evaluation
    - C. Precise activity planning
    - D. Arrangements for line markings

(A.) While it is important that a child have support from his/her parents, parental observation is not an essential consideration in long-term planning. Progress evaluation, precise activity planning, and arranging line markings are all essential management techniques for long-term planning.

21. **Although Mary is a paraplegic, she wants to participate in some capacity in the physical education class. What federal legislative act entitles her to do so?**
    - A. PE 94-142
    - B. Title IX
    - C. PL 94-142
    - D. Title XI

(C.) It is the purpose of Act PL 94-142 to assure that all handicapped children have available to them, within the time periods specified in section 612(2), (B.), a free, appropriate public education that emphasizes special education and related services designed to meet their unique needs, to assure that the rights of handicapped children and their parents/guardians are protected, to assist states and localities to provide for the education of all handicapped children, and to assess and assure the effectiveness of efforts to educate handicapped children.

22. **A legal wrong resulting in a direct or an indirect injury is:**
    - A. Negligence
    - B. A Tort
    - C. In loco parentis
    - D. Legal liability

(B.) A tort is damage, injury, or a wrongful act done willfully, negligently, or in circumstances involving strict liability, but not involving breach of contract, for which the injured party can bring a civil suit.

23. All of the following actions help avoid lawsuits except:

   A. Ensuring equipment and facilities are safe
   B. Getting exculpatory agreements
   C. Knowing each students' health status
   D. Grouping students with unequal competitive levels

(D.) Grouping students with unequal competitive levels is not an action that can help avoid lawsuits. Such a practice could lead to injury because of the inequality in skill, size, and strength.

24. Which of the following actions does not promote safety?

   A. Allowing students to wear the current style of shoes
   B. Presenting organized activities
   C. Inspecting equipment and facilities
   D. Instructing skill and activities properly

(A.) Shoes are very important in physical education and the emphasis on current shoe styles does not promote safety because they focus more on the look of the clothing, rather than functionality.

25. An instructor notices that class participation is much lower than expected. By making changes in equipment and rules, the instructor applied which of the following concepts to enhance participation?

   A. Homogeneous grouping
   B. Heterogeneous grouping
   C. Multi-activity designs
   D. Activity modification

(D.) Activity modification involves changing rules and equipment to fit the needs of students of different ability levels and physical development levels. Activity modification can encourage participation by making games and activities more enjoyable and allowing for more student success.

26. Using tactile clues is a functional adaptation that can assist which type of students?

   A. Deaf students
   B. Blind students
   C. Asthmatic students
   D. Physically challenged students

(B.) Blind people use tactile clues to identify colors. Instructors should use tactile clues to help students see or hear targets by adding color, making them larger, or moving them closer. It will help cooperation in a creative way.

27. Which of the following is not a skill assessment test to evaluate student performance?

　　A. Harrocks Volley
　　B. Rodgers Strength Test
　　C. Iowa Brace Test
　　D. AAHPERD Youth Fitness Test

(A.) Harrocks Volley is a volleyball code for a popular player named James.

28. All of the following are methods to evaluate the affective domain except:

　　A. Adams Prosocial Inventory
　　B. Crowell Personal Distance Scale
　　C. Blanchard Behavior Rating Scale
　　D. McCloy's Prosocial Behavior Scale

(D.) McCloy's Prosocial Behavior scale provided one of the earliest discussions on the influence of participation in sports and on the development of socially desirable character traits. Not surprisingly, large voids still exist in the knowledge about athletes' moral reasoning. One area that has thus far received little attention by social psychologists is the relationship between sport involvement, moral development, and aggression.

29. Educators can evaluate the cognitive domain by all of the following methods except:

　　A. Norm-Referenced Tests
　　B. Criterion Referenced Tests
　　C. Standardized Tests
　　D. Willis Sports Inventory Tests

(D.) The Willis Sports Inventory Test is the tally of all wins and losses of the popular basketball player, Willis.

30. Coordinated movements that project a person over an obstacle is:

　　A. Jumping
　　B. Vaulting
　　C. Leaping
　　D. Hopping

(B.) Vaulting is the art of acrobatics on horseback. Vaulting is an internationally recognized, competitive sport that is growing in popularity. At the most basic level vaulting enhances riding skills. At any skill-level, this ancient dance between horse and rider deepens the sense of balance, timing, and poise for the rider, as well as a sensitivity to and respect for the horse-rider relationship. Participants can vault in competition individually or on a team of 8 people with up to 3 people on the horse at once.

31. Using the same foot to take off from a surface and land is which locomotor skill?

A. Jumping
B. Vaulting
C. Leaping
D. Hopping

(D.) Hopping is a move with light, bounding skips or leaps. Basically, it is the ability to jump on one foot.

32. Which nonlocomotor skill entails movement around a joint where two body parts meet?

A. Twisting
B. Swaying
C. Bending
D. Stretching

(C.) Bending is a deviation from a straight-line position. It is also means to assume a curved, crooked, or angular form or direction, to incline the body, to make a concession, yield, to apply oneself closely, or to concentrate (e.g., *she bent to her task*).

33. A sharp change of direction from one's original line of movement is which nonlocomotor skill?

A. Twisting
B. Dodging
C. Swaying
D. Swinging

(B.) Dodging is the ability to avoid something by moving or shifting quickly aside.

34. Which manipulative skill uses the hands to stop the momentum of an object?

A. Trapping
B. Catching
C. Striking
D. Rolling

(B.) The ability to use the hands to catch an object is a manipulative skill. Catching stops the momentum of an object. A successful catch harnesses the force of the oncoming object to stop the object's momentum.

35. Playing "Simon Says" and having students touch different body parts applies which movement concept?

   A. Spatial Awareness
   B. Effort Awareness
   C. Body Awareness
   D. Motion Awareness

(C.) Body Awareness is a method that integrates European traditions of movement and biomedical knowledge with the East Asian traditions of movement (e.g. Tai chi and Zen meditation).

36. Which movement concept involves students making decisions about an object's positional changes in space?

   A. Spatial Awareness
   B. Effort Awareness
   C. Body Awareness
   D. Motion Awareness

(A.) Spatial awareness is an organized awareness of objects in the space around us. It is also an awareness of our body's position in space. Without this awareness, we would not be able to pick food up from our plates and put it in our mouths. We would have trouble reading, because we could not see the letters in their correct relation to each other and to the page. Athletes would not have the precise awareness of the position of other players on the field and the movement of the ball, which is necessary to play sports effectively.

37. Applying the mechanical principles of balance, time, and force describes which movement concept?

   A. Spatial Awareness
   B. Effort Awareness
   C. Body Awareness
   D. Motion Awareness

(B.) Effort Awareness is the knowledge of balance, time, and force and how they relate to athletic movements and activities.

38. Having students move on their hands and knees, move on lines, and/or hold shapes while moving develops which quality of movement?

   A. Balance
   B. Time
   C. Force
   D. Inertia

(A.) Balance is one of the physiological senses. It allows humans and animals to walk without falling. Some animals are better at this than humans. For example, a cat (as a quadruped using its inner ear and tail) can walk on a thin fence. All forms of equilibrioception are essentially the detection of acceleration.

39. Students that paddle balls against a wall or jump over objects with various heights are demonstrating which quality of movement?

   A. Balance
   B. Time
   C. Force
   D. Inertia

(C.) Force is the capacity to do work or create physical change, energy, strength, or active power. It is a classical **force** that causes a free body with mass to accelerate. A net (or resultant) force that causes such acceleration may be the non-zero additive sum of many different forces acting on a body.

40. Having students move in a specific pattern while measuring how long they take to do so develops which quality of movement?

   A. Balance
   B. Time
   C. Force
   D. Inertia

(B.) Time is a sequential arrangement of all events or the interval between two events in such a sequence. We can discuss the concept of time on several different levels: physical, psychological, philosophical, scientific, and biological. Time is the non-spatial continuum in which events occur, in apparently irreversible succession, from the past through the present to the future.

41. There are two sequential phases to the development of spatial awareness. What is the order of these phases?

A. Locating more than one object to each object; the location of objects in relation to one's own body in space.
B. The location of objects in relation to ones' own body in space; locating more than one object in relation to one's own body.
C. Locating more than one object independent of one's body; the location of objects in relation to one's own body.
D. The location of objects in relation to one's own body in space; locating more than one object in relation to each object and independent of one's own body.

(D.) The order of the two sequential phases to develop spatial awareness are as follows: the location of objects in relation to one's own body in space, and locating more than one object in relation to each object and independent of one's own body.

42. Equilibrium is maintained as long as:

A. Body segments are moved independently.
B. The center of gravity is over the base of support
C. Force is applied to the base of support.
D. The center of gravity is lowered.

(B.) Equilibrium is a condition in which all acting influences are canceled by others, resulting in a stable, balanced, or unchanging system. It allows humans and animals to walk without falling. An object maintains equilibrium as long as its center of gravity is over its base of support.

43. Which of the following does not enhance equilibrium?

A. Shifting the center of gravity away from the direction of movement.
B. Increasing the base of support.
C. Lowering the base of support.
D. Increasing the base of support and lowering the center of support.

(A.) Equilibrium is a state of balance. When a body or a system is in equilibrium, there is no net tendency toward change. In mechanics, equilibrium has to do with the forces acting on a body. When no force acts to make a body move in a line, the body is in translational equilibrium. When no force acts to make the body turn, the body is in rotational equilibrium. A body in equilibrium while at rest is in static equilibrium. Increasing the base of support, lowering the base of support, and increasing the base of support and lowering the center of support all enhance equilibrium by balancing forces.

TEACHER CERTIFICATION STUDY GUIDE

44. All of the following affect force except:

   A. Magnitude
   B. Energy
   C. Motion
   D. Mass

(D.) Mass is a property of a physical object that quantifies the amount of matter and energy it contains. Unlike weight, the mass of something stays the same regardless of location. Every object has a unified body of matter with no specific shape.

45. For a movement to occur, applied force must overcome inertia of an object and any other resisting forces. What concept of force does this describe?

   A. Potential energy
   B. Magnitude
   C. Kinetic energy
   D. Absorption

(B.) Speaking of magnitude in a purely relative way states that nothing is large and nothing small. If everything in the universe increased in bulk one thousand diameters, nothing would be any larger than it was before. However, if one thing remained unchanged, all of the others would be larger than they had been. To a person familiar with the relativity of magnitude and distance, the spaces and masses of the astronomer would be no more impressive than those of the microscopist would. To the contrary, the visible universe may be a small part of an atom, with its component ions floating in the life-fluid (luminiferous ether) of some animal.

46. The energy of an object to do work while recoiling is which type of potential energy?

   A. Absorption
   B. Kinetic
   C. Elastic
   D. Torque

(C.) In materials science, the word elastomer refers to a material that is very elastic (like rubber). We often use the word elastic colloquially to refer to an elastomeric material such as rubber or cloth/rubber combinations. It is capable of withstanding stress without injury. Elastic potential energy describes the energy inherent in flexible objects.

PHYSICAL EDUCATION

47. Gradually decelerating a moving mass by utilization of smaller forces over a long period of time is:

   A. Stability
   B. Equilibrium
   C. Angular force
   D. Force absorption

(D.) Force absorption is the gradual deceleration of a moving mass by utilization of smaller forces over a long period of time.

48. The tendency of a body/object to remain in its present state of motion unless some force acts to change it is which mechanical principle of motion?

   A. Acceleration
   B. Inertia
   C. Action/Reaction
   D. Linear motion

(B.) Inertia (ĭnûr'shə) is a term used in physics that describes the resistance of a body to any alteration in its state of motion. Inertia is a property common to all matter. Galileo first observed this property and Newton later restated it. Newton's first law of motion is sometimes called the law of inertia. Newton's second law of motion states that the external force required to affect the motion of a body is proportional to that acceleration. The constant of proportionality is the mass, which is the numerical value of the inertia. The greater the inertia of a body, the less acceleration is needed for a given, applied force.

TEACHER CERTIFICATION STUDY GUIDE

49. The movement response of a system depends not only on the net external force, but also on the resistance to movement change. Which mechanical principle of motion does this definition describe?

    A. Acceleration
    B. Inertia
    C. Action/Reaction
    D. Air Resistance

(A.) Acceleration is the change in the velocity of a body with respect to time. Since velocity is a vector quantity involving both magnitude and direction, acceleration is also a vector. In order to produce acceleration, a force must on a body. The magnitude of the force (F) must be directly proportional to both the mass of the body (m) and the desired acceleration (a), according to Newton's second law of motion (F=ma). The exact nature of the acceleration depends on the relative directions of the original velocity and force. A force acting in the same direction as the velocity changes only the speed of the body. An appropriate force, acting always at right angles to the velocity, changes the direction of the velocity but not the speed.

50. Which of the following mechanical principles of motion states that every motion has a similar, contrasting response?

    A. Acceleration
    B. Inertia
    C. Action/Reaction
    D. Centripetal force

(C.) The principle of action/reaction is an assertion about the nature of motion from which we can determine the trajectory of an object subject to forces. The path of an object yields a stationary value for a quantity called the **action**. Thus, instead of thinking about an object accelerating in response to applied forces, one might think of them as picking out the path with a stationary action.

51. What is the proper order of sequential development for the acquisition of locomotor skills?

   A. Creep, crawl, walk, jump, run, slide, gallop, hop, leap, skip; step-hop.
   B. Crawl, walk, creep, slide, walk, run, hop, leap, gallop, skip; step-hop.
   C. Creep, crawl, walk, slide, run, hop, leap, skip, gallop, jump; step-hop.
   D. Crawl, creep, walk, run, jump, hop, gallop, slide, leap, skip; step-hop.

(D.)

LOCOMOTOR SKILL: A skill that utilizes the feet and moves you from one place to another.

CRAWL: A form of locomotion where the person moves in a prone position with the body resting on or close to the ground or on the hands and knees.

CREEP: A slightly more advanced form of locomotion in which the person moves on the hands and knees.

WALK: A form of locomotion in which body weight is transferred alternately from the ball (toe) of one foot to the heel of the other. At times one foot is on the ground and during a brief phase, both feet are on the ground. There is no time when both feet are off the ground.

RUN: A form of locomotion much like the walk except that the tempo and body lean may differ. At times one foot is on the ground and during a brief phase both feet are off the ground. There is no time when both feet are on the ground simultaneously.

JUMP: A form of locomotion in which the body weight is projected from one or two feet and lands on two feet. Basic forms: for height, from height, distance, continuous, and rebounding.

HOP: A form of locomotion in which the body is projected from one foot to the same foot.

GALLOP: A form of locomotion that is a combination of an open step by the leading foot and a closed step by the trailing foot. The same foot leads throughout. The rhythm is uneven.

SLIDE: The same action as the gallop except that the direction of travel is sideways instead of forward. The rhythm is uneven.

LEAP: An exaggerated running step. There is a transfer of weight from one foot to the other and a phase when neither foot is in contact with the ground.

SKIP: A locomotor skill that combines a hop and a step (walk or run). The rhythm is uneven.

52. Having students pretend they are playing basketball or trying to catch a bus develops which locomotor skill?

- A. Galloping
- B. Running
- C. Leaping
- D. Skipping

(B.) Playing basketball involves near constant running up and down the court. In addition, chasing is a good example to use with children to illustrate the concept of running.

53. Having students play Fox and Hound develops:

- A. Galloping
- B. Hopping
- C. Stepping-hopping
- D. Skipping

(A.) Fox and Hound is an activity that emphasizes rapid running. The form of the exercise most closely resembles a gallop, especially in rhythm and rapidity. It can develop or progress at an accelerated rate.

54. Having students take off and land with both feet together develops which locomotor skill?

- A. Hopping
- B. Jumping
- C. Leaping
- D. Skipping

(B.) Jumping is a skill that most humans and many animals share. It is the process of getting one's body off of the ground for a short time using one's own power, usually by propelling oneself upward via contraction and then forceful extension of the legs. One can jump up to reach something high, jump over a fence or ditch, or jump down. One can also jump while dancing and as a sport in track and field.

55. What is the proper sequential order of development for the acquisition of nonlocomotor skills?

- A. Stretch, sit, bend, turn, swing, twist, shake, rock & sway, dodge; fall.
- B. Bend, stretch, turn, twist, swing, sit, rock & sway, shake, dodge; fall.
- C. Stretch, bend, sit, shake, turn, rock & sway, swing, twist, dodge; fall.
- D. Bend, stretch, sit, turn, twist, swing, sway, rock & sway, dodge; fall.

(C.) Each skill in the progression builds on the previous skills.

56. Activities such as pretending to pick fruit off a tree or reaching for a star develop which non-locomotor skill?

    A. Bending
    B. Stretching
    C. Turning
    D. Twisting

(B.) Stretching is the activity of gradually applying tensile force to lengthen, strengthen, and lubricate muscles, often performed in anticipation of physical exertion and to increase the range of motion within a joint. Stretching is an especially important accompaniment to activities that emphasize controlled muscular strength and flexibility. These include ballet, acrobatics or martial arts. Stretching also may help prevent injury to tendons, ligaments, and muscles by improving muscular elasticity and reducing the stretch reflex in greater ranges of motion that might cause injury to tissue. In addition, stretching can reduce delayed onset muscle soreness (DOMS).

57. Picking up coins, tying shoes, and petting animals develop this nonlocomotor skill.

    A. Bending
    B. Stretching
    C. Turning
    D. Twisting

(A.) Bending is the action of moving the body across a skeletal joint. In each of the sample activities, one must bend from the waist or knees to reach a low object.

58. Having students collapse in their own space or lower themselves as though they are a raindrop or snowflake develops this nonlocomotor skill.

    A. Dodging
    B. Shaking
    C. Swinging
    D. Falling

(D.) Falling is a major cause of personal injury in athletics. Athletic participants must learn how to fall in such a way as to limit the possibility of injury.

59. Which is the proper sequential order of development for the acquisition of manipulative skills?

A. Striking, throwing, bouncing, catching, trapping, kicking, ball rolling; volleying.
B. Striking, throwing, kicking, ball rolling, volleying, bouncing, catching; trapping.
C. Striking, throwing, catching, trapping, kicking, ball rolling, bouncing; volleying.
D. Striking, throwing, kicking, ball rolling, bouncing; volleying.

(B.) Striking, throwing, kicking, ball rolling, volleying, bouncing, catching, and trapping is the proper sequential order of development for the acquisition of manipulative skills. Each skill in this progression builds on the previous skill.

60. Having students hit a large balloon with both hands develops this manipulative skill?

A. Bouncing
B. Striking
C. Volleying
D. Trapping

(C.) In a number of ball games, a volley is the ball that a player receives and delivers without touching the ground. The ability to volley a ball back and forth requires great body control and spatial awareness.

61. Progressively decreasing the size of a target that balls are projected at develops which manipulative skill.

A. Throwing
B. Trapping
C. Volleying
D. Kicking

(A.) Children develop throwing skills (the ability to propel an object through the air with a rapid movement of the arm and wrist) by projecting balls at progressively smaller targets.

62. Hitting a stationary object while in a fixed position, then incorporating movement, develops this manipulative skill.

A. Bouncing
B. Trapping
C. Throwing
D. Striking

(D.) Striking is the process of hitting something sharply, as with the hand, the fist, or a weapon.

63. **A subjective, observational approach to identify errors in the form, style, or mechanics of a skill is accomplished by:**

    A. Product assessment
    B. Process assessment
    C. Standardized norm-referenced tests
    D. Criterion-referenced tests

(B.) Process assessment is one way to identify errors in the skills of an individual. It is one way to know the limitations and skills that every individual possesses.

64. **What type of assessment objectively measures skill performance?**

    A. Process assessment
    B. Product assessment
    C. Texas PE Test
    D. Iowa Brace Test

(B.) Product assessment measures the skills of an individual. This process is a methodical evaluation of the characteristics of your product or service in the eyes of potential users and customers. The two principle types of assessments are principle-based assessments and usability testing.

65. **Process assessment does not identify which of the following errors in skill performance?**

    A. Style
    B. Form
    C. End result
    D. Mechanics

(C.) Process assessment does not evaluate end results. Process assessment emphasizes analysis of style, form, and mechanics.

66. **Determining poor performance of a skill using process assessment can best be accomplished by:**

    A. Observing how fast a skill is performed.
    B. Observing how many skills are performed.
    C. Observing how far or how high a skill is performed.
    D. Observing several attributes comprising the entire performance of a skill.

(D.) To determine the source of the error in the poor performance of an individual, we use observations of several attributes that compromise the entire performance of a skill. Instructors should observe limitations and mistakes and determine how to best address these problems to improve future performance.

67. **Which of the following principles is not a factor to assess to correct errors in performance for process assessment?**

   A. Inertia
   B. Action/Reaction
   C. Force
   D. Acceleration

(C.) Force is not a factor to focus on in process assessment.

68. **Which of the following methods measures fundamental skills using product assessment?**

   A. Criterion-referenced tests
   B. Standardized norm-referenced tests
   C. Both A and B
   D. Neither A nor B

(C.) Criterion-referenced tests and standardized norm-referenced tests are both methods that can prove and measure skills in product assessment. They can help to prevent or lessen errors.

69. **Product assessment measures all of the following except:**

   A. How the student performs the mechanics of a skill.
   B. How many times the student performs a skill.
   C. How fast the student performs a skill.
   D. How far or high the student performs a skill.

(A.) Product assessment evaluates student performance and gives insight into how students can correct errors. Product assessment measures results. Thus, how the student performs the mechanics of a skill is not relevant to product assessment.

70. **Instructors can evaluate skill level of achievement in archery by:**

   A. Giving students a written exam on terminology.
   B. Having students demonstrate the correct tension of arrow feathers.
   C. Totaling a student's score obtained on the target's face.
   D. Time how long a student takes to shoot all arrows.

(C.) **Archery** is the practice of using a bow to shoot arrows. Totaling a student's score is the only method, of the possible choices, that evaluates skill level. Choices A and B test knowledge and choice D is an arbitrary measure.

71. Instructors can determine skill level achievement in golf by:

    A. The number of "birdies" that were made.
    B. The number of "bogies" that were made.
    C. The score obtained after several rounds.
    D. The total score achieved throughout the school year.

(C.) Instructors can determine skill level in golf by evaluating a golfer's score after several rounds. The number of bogies or birdies is not necessarily indicative of skill level because they are isolated events (i.e. the score on one hole). The player who consistently scores the lowest likely has the most impressive golf skills. Therefore, a player's score is the best way to determine his/her skill level. Finally, several rounds is a sufficient sample to determine skill level. An entire year's worth of scores is not necessary.

72. Instructors can determine skill level achievement in swimming by:

    A. How long a student can float.
    B. How many strokes it takes to swim a specified distance.
    C. How long a student can stay under the water without moving.
    D. How many times a student can dive in five minutes.

(B.) Instructors can determine skill level in swimming by counting the strokes a swimmer takes when covering a certain distance. The arm movement, the strength, and the tactic to move quickly gives the swimmer an ability to swim faster. The ability to float, stay under water, and dive quickly are not relevant to swimming ability.

73. Instructors can assess skill level achievement in bowling by:

    A. Calculating a student's average.
    B. Calculating how many gutter-balls were thrown.
    C. Calculating how many strikes were thrown.
    D. Calculating how many spares were thrown.

(A.) Instructors can determine the skill level of a bowler by calculating the student's average game score. There is a possibility that some coincidences take place (e.g., bowling a strike). To check the consistency, we determine the average instead of looking at only the score from a single game.

TEACHER CERTIFICATION STUDY GUIDE

74. **Although they are still hitting the target, the score of some students practicing archery has decreased as the distance between them and the target has increased. Which of the following adjustments will improve their scores?**

    A. Increasing the velocity of their arrows.
    B. Increasing the students' base of support.
    C. Increasing the weight of the arrows.
    D. Increasing the parabolic path of the arrows.

(D.) Increasing the parabolic path of the arrows will increase accuracy and precision at greater distances.

75. **Some students practicing basketball are having difficulty with "free throws," even though the shots make it to and over the hoop. What adjustment will improve their "free throws?"**

    A. Increasing the height of release (i.e. jump shot).
    B. Increasing the vertical path of the ball.
    C. Increasing the velocity of the release.
    D. Increasing the base of support.

(B.) In this case, increasing the vertical path of the ball will help the students make more free throws. Increased vertical path provides greater margin for error, allowing the ball to drop more easily through the hoop. Increasing the velocity cannot work due to common sense. Finally, increasing the height of release and base of support are not viable options in this case because the students are having no problem getting the ball to the basket.

76. **An archery student's arrow bounced off the red part of the target face. What is the correct ruling?**

    A. No score.
    B. Re-shoot arrow.
    C. 7 points awarded.
    D. Shot receives same score as highest arrow shot that did not bounce off the target.

(C.) When an arrow bounces off the red area of a target, the archer receives 7 points, the value of the shot had the arrow stuck in the target.

PHYSICAL EDUCATION

TEACHER CERTIFICATION STUDY GUIDE

77. **A student playing badminton believed that the shuttlecock was going to land out-of-bounds. The shuttlecock landed on the line. What is the correct ruling?**

    A. The shuttlecock is out-of-bounds.
    B. The shuttlecock is in-bounds.
    C. The point is replayed.
    D. That player is charged with a feint.

(**B.**) If a shuttlecock lands on the line, it is inbounds by the rules of badminton.

78. **A mechanical pinsetter accidentally knocked down the only bowling pin left standing for a spare attempt, after clearing all the other pins knocked down by the first ball thrown. What is the correct ruling?**

    A. Foul
    B. Spare
    C. Frame is replayed
    D. No count for that pin

(**D.**) When the mechanical pinsetter touches a pin and knocks it down, there is no count for the pin because the pin fell because of mechanical fault and the player had nothing to do with it. The other pins count and there is no foul for the player.

79. **The ball served in racquetball hits the front line and lands in front of the short line. What is the ruling?**

    A. Fault
    B. Reserve
    C. Out-of-bounds
    D. Fair ball

(**A.**) If a served ball falls in front of the short line, it is a fault according to a rule that states that a ball must fall within the short line frame at the time of serving. It is not out-of-bounds, as it is still within the limits of the pitch. However, it is also not a fair ball due to the service rule.

80. **Two opposing soccer players are trying to gain control of the ball when one player "knees" the other. What is the ruling?**

    A. Direct free kick
    B. Indirect free kick
    C. Fair play
    D. Ejection from a game

(**A.**) Assuming that the soccer player didn't intentionally hit the other player's knee, the result would be a direct free kick. If the foul was intentional, the referee can eject the offender from the game. Minor offenses and offenses not involving contact result in indirect free kicks.

PHYSICAL EDUCATION

TEACHER CERTIFICATION STUDY GUIDE

81. **Two students are playing badminton. When receiving the shuttlecock, one student consistently stands too deep in the receiving court. What strategy should the server use to serve the shuttlecock?**

    A. Smash serve
    B. Clear serve
    C. Overhead serve
    D. Short serve

(D.) The short serve would give land short in the court so the opponent would not be able to reach the shuttlecock. Therefore, the short serve would win the point. A clear or overhead serve enables the opponent to hit the shuttlecock and continue the game. A smash serve runs a higher risk of falling out-of-bounds. Neither of these scenarios are goals of the server.

82. **A basketball team has an outstanding rebounder. In order to keep this player near the opponent's basket, which strategy should the coach implement?**

    A. Pick-and-Roll
    B. Give-and-Go
    C. Zone defense
    D. Free-lancing

(C.) A zone defense, where each player guards an area of the court rather than an individual player, allows an outstanding rebounder to remain near the basket. The give-and-go, pick-and-roll, and free-lancing are offensive strategies that do not affect rebounding.

83. **When a defensive tennis player needs more time to return to his position, what strategy should he apply?**

    A. Drop shot
    B. Dink shot
    C. Lob shot
    D. Down-the-line shot

(C.) When a tennis player is off the court and needs time to return to his position, the player should play a lob shot. Down-the-line shots and drop shots are offensive shots and are too risky in this situation. The dink shot would allow the opponent to take control of the point.

84. An overhead badminton stroke used to hit a forehand-like overhead stroke that is on the backhand side of the body is called:

A. Around-the-head-shot
B. Down-the-line shot
C. Lifting the shuttle
D. Under hand shuttle

(A.) A shot played from the backhand side and over the head is known as an around-the-head shot. It is played when the shuttlecock is high and cannot be reached any other way.

85. A maneuver when an offensive player passes to a teammate and then immediately cuts in toward the basket for a return pass is:

A. Charging
B. Pick
C. Give-and-go
D. Switching

(C.) In the game of basketball, a give-and-go is an offensive play where a player passes to a teammate and immediately cuts toward the basket for a return pass. Charging is an offensive foul, a pick is a maneuver to free up a teammate for a pass or shot, and switching is a defensive maneuver.

86. A bowling pin that remains standing after an apparently perfect hit is called a:

A. Tap
B. Turkey
C. Blow
D. Leave

(A.) A bowling pin that remains standing, even after a perfect shot, is a tap. Other options, like turkeys and blows, are not relevant to the standing pin.

87. A soccer pass from the outside of the field near the end line to a position in front of the goal is called:

A. Chip
B. Settle
C. Through
D. Cross

(D.) Any long pass from the sides of the field toward the middle is a cross, since the hitter hits it across the field. A chip is a high touch pass or shot. A through pass travels the length of the field through many players. Finally, settling is the act of controlling the ball after receiving a pass.

88. **A volleyball that is simultaneously contacted above the net by opponents and momentarily held upon contact is a(n):**
    A. Double fault
    B. Play over
    C. Overlap
    D. Held ball

(D.) In volleyball, if two players simultaneously contact the ball above the net, the ball is a held ball.

89. **Volleyball player LB on team A digs a spiked ball. The ball deflects off of LB's shoulder. What is the ruling?**
    A. Fault
    B. Legal hit
    C. Double foul
    D. Play over

(B.) Since the spiked ball does not touch the ground and instead deflects off LB's shoulder, it is a legal hit. In order for a point to end, the ball must touch the ground. In this instance, it does not.

90. **A teacher who modifies and develops tasks for a class is demonstrating knowledge of which appropriate behavior in physical education activities.**
    A. Appropriate management behavior
    B. Appropriate student behavior
    C. Appropriate administration behavior
    D. Appropriate content behavior

(D.) In this case, the teacher is demonstrating knowledge of a behavior in reference to physical activity. It is known as appropriate content behavior. The other options are not related to physical activities.

91. **To enhance skill and strategy performance for striking or throwing objects, for catching or collecting objects, and for carrying and propelling objects, students must first learn techniques for:**
    A. Offense
    B. Defense
    C. Controlling objects
    D. Continuous play of objects

(C.) For enhancing the catching, throwing, carrying, or propelling of objects, a student must learn how to control the objects. The control gives the player a sense of the object. Thus, offense, defense, and continuous play come naturally, as they are part of the controlling process.

92. Which of the following is not a type of tournament?

A. Spiderweb
B. Pyramid
C. Spiral
D. Round Robin

(C.) A spiral is not a type of tournament.

93. Which of the following is not a type of meet?

A. Extramural
B. Intramural
C. Interscholastic
D. Ladder

(D.) A ladder is not a type of meet.

94. An instructor used a similar movement from a skill learned in a different activity to teach a skill for a new activity. The technique used to facilitate cognitive learning was:

A. Conceptual thinking
B. Transfer of learning
C. Longer instruction
D. Appropriate language

(B.) Using a previously used movement to facilitate a new task is a transfer of learning. The individual relates the past activity to the new one, enabling him/her to learn it more easily. Conceptual thinking is related to the transfer of learning, but it does not give the exact idea. Rather, it emphasizes the history of all learning.

95. A teacher rewards students for completing tasks. Which method is the teacher using to facilitate psychomotor learning?

A. Task/Reciprocal
B. Command/Direct
C. Contingency/Contract
D. Physical/Reflex

(C.) Since the teacher is rewarding the student, the contingency/contract method is in place. The command/direct method involves the interaction between student and teacher when the student fails to fulfill the requirements.

96. All of the following are Systematic Observational Evaluations except:

- A. Reflective Recording
- B. Event Recording
- C. Duration Recording
- D. Self Recording

(A.) Reflective recording is not a type of systematic observational evaluation. Event, duration, and self recordings are all methods used in systematic observational evaluations.

97. The ability for a muscle(s) to repeatedly contract over a period of time is:

- A. Cardiovascular endurance
- B. Muscle endurance
- C. Muscle strength
- D. Muscle force

(B.) Muscle endurance gives the muscle the ability to contract over a period of time. Muscle strength is a prerequisite for the endurance of muscle. Cardiovascular endurance involves aerobic exercise.

98. The ability to change rapidly the direction of the body is:

- A. Coordination
- B. Reaction time
- C. Speed
- D. Agility

(D.) Agility is the ability of the body to change position quickly. Reaction time, coordination, and speed are not the right words to describe the ability to move quickly, as we always say that the goalkeeper is agile.

99. Students are performing the vertical jump. What component of fitness does this activity assess?

- A. Muscle strength
- B. Balance
- C. Power
- D. Muscle endurance

(C.) Vertical jumping assesses the power of the entire body. It shows the potential of the legs to hold the upper body and the strength in the joints of the legs. Balance and muscle strength are secondary requirements. Power automatically ensures these secondary requirements.

100. Students are performing trunk extensions. What component of fitness does this activity assess?

   A. Balance
   B. Flexibility
   C. Body Composition
   D. Coordination

(B.) The core component of trunk extensions is flexibility. Trunk extensions also indicate the body's capacity for full expansion and emphasizes areas such as the stomach, arms, and shoulder joints.

101. Working at a level that is above normal is which exercise training principle?

   A. Intensity
   B. Progression
   C. Specificity
   D. Overload

(D.) Overloading is exercising above normal capacities. Intensity and progression are supporting principles in the process of overload. Overloading can cause serious issues within the body, either immediately or after some time.

102. Students on a running program to improve cardio-respiratory fitness apply which exercise principle.

   A. Aerobic
   B. Progression
   C. Specificity
   D. Overload

(C.) Running to improve cardio-respiratory fitness is an example of specificity. Specificity is the selection of activities that isolate a specific body part or system. Aerobics is also a good option, but it deals with the entire body, including areas not specific to cardio-respiratory fitness.

103. Adding more reps to a weightlifting set applies which exercise principle.

   A. Anaerobic
   B. Progression
   C. Overload
   D. Specificity

(B.) Adding more repetitions (reps) to sets when weightlifting is an example of progression. Adding reps can result in overload, but the guiding principle is progression.

104. Which of the following does not modify overload?

   A. Frequency
   B. Perceived exertion
   C. Time
   D. Intensity

(B.) Time extension, frequency of movement, and intensity are all indicators of overload. However, exertion is not a good indicator of overload, because measuring exertion is subjective and difficult to monitor.

105. Using the Karvonen Formula, compute the 60% - 80% THR for a 16-year old student with a RHR of 60.

   A. 122-163 beats per minute
   B. 130-168 beats per minute
   C. 142-170 beats per minute
   D. 146-175 beats per minute

(D.)

220 – 16 (age) = 204, 204 – 60 (RHR) = 144, 144 x .60 (low end of heart range) = 86, 86 + 60 (RHR) = **146 (bottom of THR)**

220 – 16 (age) = 204, 204 – 60 (RHR) = 144, 144 x 0.80 (high end of heart range) = 115, 115 + (RHR) = **175 (top of THR)**

146-175 beats per minute is the 60%-80% THR.

106. Using Cooper's Formula, compute the THR for a 15-year old student.

   A. 120-153 beats per minute
   B. 123-164 beats per minute
   C. 135-169 beats per minute
   D. 147-176 beats per minute

(B.) 123-164 beats per minute.

107. Prior to activity, students perform a 5-10 minute warm-up. Which is not recommended as part of the warm-up?

   A. Using the muscles that will be utilized in the following activity.
   B. Using a gradual aerobic warm-up.
   C. Using a gradual anaerobic warm-up.
   D. Stretching the major muscle groups to be used in the activity.

(C.) Warm-up is always necessary, but it should not be an anaerobic warm-up. The muscle exercises, the stretching, and even the aerobics are all helpful and athletes should complete these exercises within the normal breathing conditions. In fact, athletes should focus more closely on proper breathing. Athletes should engage in anaerobic stretching after activity, when muscles are loose and less prone to injury.

108. Which is not a benefit of warming up?

   A. Releasing hydrogen from myoglobin.
   B. Reducing the risk of musculoskeletal injuries.
   C. Raising the body's core temperature in preparation for activity.
   D. Stretching the major muscle groups to be used in the activity.

(A.) Warm-up can reduce the risk of musculoskeletal injuries, raise the body's temperature in preparation for activity, and stretch the major muscle groups. However, a warm-up does not release hydrogen from myoglobin. Myoglobin binds oxygen, not hydrogen.

109. Which is not a benefit of cooling down?

   A. Preventing dizziness.
   B. Redistributing circulation.
   C. Removing lactic acid.
   D. Removing myoglobin.

(D.) Cooling down helps the body to regain blood circulation and to remove lactic acid. It also prevents dizziness, which may occur after extensive exercises. The only thing that cooling down does not support is removing myoglobin. However, it can help myoglobin get a strong hold in the muscles.

110. Activities to specifically develop cardiovascular fitness must be:

   A. Performed without developing an oxygen debt
   B. Performed twice daily.
   C. Performed every day.
   D. Performed for a minimum of 10 minutes.

(A.) The development of cardiovascular fitness is not dependent on specific time limits or routine schedules. Participants should perform aerobic activities without developing an oxygen debt.

111. Overloading for muscle strength includes all of the following except:

   A. Lifting heart rate to an intense level.
   B. Lifting weights every other day.
   C. Lifting with high resistance and low reps.
   D. Lifting 60% to 90% of assessed muscle strength.

(A.) Overloading muscle strength is possible by lifting the weights every other day or by lifting weights with high resistance and low repetition. Overloading does not cause or require an intense increase in heart rate. However, overloading has many other possibilities.

112. Which of the following applies the concept of progression?

- A. Beginning a stretching program every day.
- B. Beginning a stretching program with 3 sets of reps.
- C. Beginning a stretching program with ballistic stretching.
- D. Beginning a stretching program holding stretches for 15 seconds and work up to holding stretches for 60 seconds.

(D.) Progression is the process of starting an exercise program slowly and cautiously before proceeding to more rigorous training. Answer D is the only answer that exemplifies progression.

113. Which of following overload principles does not apply to improving body composition?

- A. Aerobic exercise three times per week.
- B. Aerobic exercise at a low intensity.
- C. Aerobic exercise for about an hour.
- D. Aerobic exercise in intervals of high intensity.

(A.) To improve body composition, a person should engage in aerobic exercise daily, not three times per week. However, an individual can do aerobics for at least half an hour daily, he/she can exercise at a low intensity, or he/she can train with intervals of high intensity.

114. Which of the following principles of progression applies to improving muscle endurance?

- A. Lifting weights every day.
- B. Lifting weights at 20% to 30% of assessed muscle strength.
- C. Lifting weights with low resistance and low reps.
- D. Lifting weights starting at 60% of assessed muscle strength.

(B.) To improve muscle endurance, a person should lift weights at 20 to 30% of the assessed muscle strength. Lifting weights daily is counterproductive because it does not allow for adequate rest. In addition, lifting at 60% of the assessed muscle strength can damage the muscle.

115. Aerobic dance develops or improves each of the following skills or health components except...

   A. Cardio-respiratory function
   B. Body composition
   C. Coordination
   D. Flexibility

(D.) Aerobic dance does not develop flexibility, as flexibility results from stretching and not aerobic exercise. Ballet dancing, however, does develop flexibility. Aerobic dance develops cardio-respiratory function due to the unusual body movements performed. It also improves body composition and coordination due to the movement of various body parts.

116. Rowing develops which health or skill related component of fitness?

   A. Muscle endurance
   B. Flexibility
   C. Balance
   D. Reaction time

(A.) Rowing helps develop muscle endurance because of the continuous arm movement against the force of the water. However, flexibility, balance, and reaction time are not important components of rowing. Rowing also develops the lower abdominal muscles while the individual is in the sitting position when rowing.

117. Calisthenics develops all of the following health and skill related components of fitness except:

   A. Muscle strength
   B. Body composition
   C. Power
   D. Agility

(C.) Calisthenics is a sport that actually helps to keep a body fit in by combining gymnastic and aerobic activities. Calisthenics develop muscle strength and agility and improves body composition. However, calisthenics do not develop power because they do not involve resistance training or explosiveness.

118. **Which health or skill related component of fitness is developed by rope jumping?**

    A. Muscle Force
    B. Coordination
    C. Flexibility
    D. Muscle strength

(B.) Rope jumping is a good mental exercise and it improves coordination. Many athletes (e.g. boxers, tennis players) jump rope to improve coordination and quickness. Muscle strength is secondary to that.

119. **Swimming does not improve which health or skill related component of fitness?**

    A. Cardio-respiratory function
    B. Flexibility
    C. Muscle strength
    D. Foot Speed

(D.) Swimming involves every part of the body. It works on the cardio-respiratory system and it develops flexibility because of the intense body movement in the water. It also improves muscle strength as swimmers must move their bodies against the force of water. Increased foot speed is not an outcome of swimming.

120. **Data from a cardio-respiratory assessment can identify and predict all of the following except:**

    A. Functional aerobic capacity
    B. Natural over-fatness
    C. Running ability
    D. Motivation

(B.) The data from cardio-respiratory assessment can identify and predict running ability, motivation, and functional aerobic capacity. However, it cannot predict natural over-fatness, as natural over-fatness is a part of the human body. It is not artificially developed like running ability and motivation.

121. **Data from assessing _____ identifies an individual's potential of developing musculoskeletal problems and an individual's potential of performing activities of daily living.**

    A. Flexibility
    B. Muscle endurance
    C. Muscle strength
    D. Motor performance

(A.) Flexibility.

122. **A 17-year-old male student performed 20 sit-ups, ran a mile in 8 minutes, and has a body fat composition of 17%. Which is the best interpretation of his fitness level?**

    A. Average muscular endurance, good cardiovascular endurance; appropriate body fat composition.
    B. Low muscular endurance, average cardiovascular endurance; high body fat composition.
    C. Low muscular endurance, average cardiovascular endurance; appropriate body fat composition.
    D. Low muscular endurance, low cardiovascular endurance; appropriate body fat composition.

(**C.**) A 17-year-old male who performs 20 sit-ups, runs a mile in 8 minutes and has 17% fat composition has low muscular endurance, average cardiovascular endurance, and appropriate fat composition. 20 sit-ups is a relatively low number. An 8-minute mile is an average time for a 17-year-old male. Finally, a body fat composition of 17% is appropriate.

123. **Based on the information given in the previous question, what changes would you recommend to improve this person's level of fitness?**

    A. Muscle endurance training and cardiovascular endurance training.
    B. Muscle endurance training, cardiovascular endurance training, and reduction of caloric intake.
    C. Muscle strength training and cardio-vascular endurance training.
    D. No changes necessary.

(**A.**) The person requires both muscle endurance and cardiovascular training while keeping the other bodily intakes normal. An appropriate program would include moderate weightlifting and regular aerobic activity.

124. **An obese student's fitness assessments were poor for every component of fitness. Which would you recommend first?**

    A. A jogging program.
    B. A weight lifting program.
    C. A walking program.
    D. A stretching program.

(**C.**) An obese person should begin by walking and then progress to jogging. Weightlifting and stretching are not as important initially. They are also dangerous because the student may not have the ability to complete such strenuous tasks safely.

PHYSICAL EDUCATION

125. Which of the following body types is the most capable of motor performance involving endurance?

   A. Endomorph
   B. Ectomorph
   C. Mesomorph
   D. Metamorph

(B.) Characteristically, ectomorphs are lean and slender with little body fat and musculature. Ectomorphs are usually capable of performing at high levels in endurance events.

126. Which is not a sign of stress?

   A. Irritability
   B. Assertiveness
   C. Insomnia
   D. Stomach problems

(B.) Assertiveness is not a sign of stress. Irritability, insomnia, and stomach problems are all related to stress.

127. Which is not a common negative stressor?

   A. Loss of significant other
   B. Personal illness or injury.
   C. Moving to a new state.
   D. Landing a new job.

(D.) Landing a new job is generally not a cause of worry or stress. In fact, it is a positive event. Personal illness, loss of a significant other, or moving to a strange state can cause negative stress.

128. Which of the following is a negative coping strategy for dealing with stress?

   A. Recreational diversions
   B. Active thinking
   C. Alcohol use
   D. Imagery

(C.) The use of alcohol is a negative coping strategy for dealing with stress. Alcohol causes the brain to lose the stressful data thus soothing the individual, but it can be highly detrimental in the long run. Positive ways to deal with stress include active thinking, imagery, and recreational diversions.

129. **The most important nutrient the body requires, without which life can only be sustained for a few days, is:**

   A. Vitamins
   B. Minerals
   C. Water
   D. Carbohydrates

(C.) Although the body requires vitamins, minerals, and carbohydrates to achieve proper growth and shape, water is essential. Without it, the body gets dehydrated and death is a possibility. Water should be pure, as seawater can cause kidney failure and death.

130. **With regard to protein content, foods from animal sources are usually:**

   A. Complete
   B. Essential
   C. Nonessential
   D. Incidental

(A.) Animal protein is complete, meaning it provides all of the amino acids that the human body requires. Although animal meat is not essential to a person's diet, it is an excellent source of protein.

131. **Fats with room for two or more hydrogen atoms per molecule-fatty acid chain are:**

   A. Monounsaturated
   B. Polyunsaturated
   C. Hydrosaturated
   D. Saturated

(B.) Polyunsaturated fatty acids contain multiple carbon-carbon double bonds. Thus, there is room for two or more hydrogens. Polyunsaturated fats are healthier than saturated fats.

132. **An adequate diet to meet nutritional needs consists of:**

   A. No more than 30% caloric intake from fats, no more than 50 % caloric intake from proteins, and at least 20% caloric intake from carbohydrates.
   B. No more than 30% caloric intake from fats, no more than 40% caloric intake from proteins, and at least 30% caloric intake from carbohydrates.
   C. No more than 30% caloric intake from fats, no more than 15% caloric intake from proteins, and at least 55% caloric intake from carbohydrates.
   D. No more than 30 % caloric intake from fats, no more than 30% caloric intake from proteins, and at least 40% caloric intake from carbohydrates.

(C.) General guidelines for nutritionally sound diets are 30% caloric intake from fats, no more than 15% caloric intake from proteins, and at least 55% caloric intake from carbohydrates.

133. Maintaining body weight is best accomplished by:

   A. Dieting
   B. Aerobic exercise
   C. Lifting weights
   D. Equalizing caloric intake relative to output

(D.) The best way to maintain a body weight is by balancing caloric intake and output. Extensive dieting (caloric restriction) is not a good option as this would result in weakness. Exercise is part of the output process that helps balance caloric input and output.

134. Most high-protein diets:

   A. Are high in cholesterol
   B. Are high in saturated fats
   C. Require vitamin and mineral supplements
   D. All of the above

(D.) High-protein diets are high in cholesterol, saturated fats, and they require vitamin and mineral supplements.

135. Which one of the following statements about low-calorie diets is false?

   A. Most people who "diet only" regain the weight they lose.
   B. They are the way most people try to lose weight.
   C. They make weight control easier.
   D. They lead to excess worry about weight, food, and eating.

(C.) People who participate in low-calorie diets do not control their weight easily. They must work more and utilize their bodies in many other ways (e.g., walking) to keep themselves fit.

136. Physiological benefits of exercise include all of the following except:

   A. Reducing mental tension
   B. Improving muscle strength
   C. Cardiac hypertrophy
   D. Quicker recovery rate

(A.) Physical exercises can help improve muscle strength by making the body move and they can help provide quicker recovery between exercise sessions and from injuries. However, physical activity does not directly relieve mental tension. It might reduce tension temporarily, but chances are the tension will persist.

137. Psychological benefits of exercise include all of the following except:

    A. Improved sleeping patterns
    B. Improved energy regulation
    C. Improved appearance
    D. Improved quality of life

(B.) The psychological benefits of exercise include improved sleeping patterns, improved appearances, and an improved quality of life. Improved energy regulation is a physical benefit, not a psychological one.

138. Which of the following conditions is not associated with a lack of physical activity?

    A. Atherosclerosis
    B. Longer life expectancy
    C. Osteoporosis
    D. Certain cancers

(B.) A lack of physical activity can contribute to atherosclerosis, osteoporosis, and certain cancers. Conversely, regular physical activity can contribute to longer life expectancy.

139. Which of the following pieces of exercise equipment best applies the physiological principles?

    A. Rolling machine
    B. Electrical muscle stimulator
    C. Stationary Bicycle
    D. Motor-driven rowing machine

(C.) A stationary bicycle is the best option to support the body physically as it includes all of the operations related to an individual's body (e.g., movement of legs, position of arms, back exercise, stomach movement). Electrical muscle stimulators are very dangerous as they can cause muscles to loosen too much. Other machines may provide an unnecessarily extensive workout that is dangerous for muscle.

Sample Written Assignment

The sample written assignment consists of a brief scenario followed by a sequence of questions or topics to discuss. You should draft an essay of 150-300 words addressing all of the topics or questions. It is important that you organize your response and demonstrate a thorough understanding of the subject matter. Content is more important than writing style, though poor grammar, punctuation, spelling, and sentence structure can detract from your response.

Use the information below to complete the exercise that follows.

Evan is a 10-year-old fifth grade student who recently completed a physical fitness evaluation in his physical education class. Evan was able to perform 6 push-ups and no pull-ups. He completed the mile run in 6:58. The evaluation also showed that Evan had below average flexibility.

Evan is a physically active child, participating in tennis and soccer outside of school. Evan is a very talented athlete looking to improve his performance in his sporting activities. Evan is also a very reserved, shy child who does not make friends easily or interact much with other children. In addition, Evan's parents feel Evan is an unusually gifted tennis player and should stop playing soccer to focus on tennis.

Based on your knowledge of physical fitness construct a written response that addresses the following:

- interpret the results of Evan's fitness evaluation; determine the components of fitness that Evan needs to address

- identify two age-appropriate fitness activities that will help Evan achieve his goals

- advise Evan's parents on their desire to have Evan focus on tennis taking into account the social and psychological aspects of participation in sports and fitness activities

Strong Response to the Sample Written Assignment

The results of Evan's physical fitness assessment show that he has a high level of cardiovascular endurance (good mile run time), a low level of muscular endurance (poor results on push-up and pull-up test), and a low level of flexibility. Thus, a fitness program for Evan should focus on developing muscular endurance and flexibility. In addition, because Evan participates in soccer and tennis, he likely receives more than enough aerobic activity in these aerobically intensive sports.

Flexibility and muscular endurance are important, and often overlooked, aspects of tennis and soccer. Thus, developing these areas will improve Evan's athletic performance. Because Evan is only 10-years-old, I would recommend he engage in body support exercises, rather than resistance training exercises, to increase his muscular endurance. Such exercises include push-ups, pull-ups, sit-ups, lunges, and squats. I would not recommend weight training for a 10-year-old because lifting weights is dangerous and possibly detrimental for developing bodies. Evan should also engage in a regular stretching program after his tennis and soccer practices and matches. Stretching improves flexibility and stretching after physical activity is safest and most effective.

Finally, I would advise Evan's parents that he should continue to play both soccer and tennis. Sport specialization is not necessary at Evan's age to maximize performance and asking Evan to give up soccer could have other detrimental effects. Because Evan is shy and reserved, the social aspects of a team sport like soccer are important to his development. Participation in team sports promotes the development of social skills, leadership, teamwork, and interpersonal relationships. Evan will benefit from such interaction with other children and will improve his self-esteem, especially because he is a talented player. While tennis is an excellent sport, it is mainly an individual sport, and the opportunity for socialization and the development of friendships is limited.

XAMonline, INC. 21 Orient Ave. Melrose, MA 02176

Toll Free number 800-509-4128

TO ORDER Fax 781-662-9268 OR www.XAMonline.com

MASSACHUSETTS TEST FOR EDUCATOR LICENTURE - MTEL - 2007

PO# Store/School:

Address 1:

Address 2 (Ship to other):

City, State Zip

Credit card number_____-_____-_____-_____ expiration_____

EMAIL _____

PHONE   **FAX**

13# ISBN 2007	TITLE	Qty	Retail	Total
978-1-58197-884-1	MTEL Biology 13			
978-1-58197-883-4	MTEL Chemistry 12			
978-1-58197-875-9	MTEL Communication and Literacy Skills 01			
978-1-58197-893-3	MTEL Visual Art Sample Test 17			
978-1-58197-683-0	MTEL Earth Science 14			
978-1-58197-879-7	MTEL English 07			
978-1-58197-892-6	MTEL Foundations of Reading 90 (requirement all El. Ed)			
978-1-58197-887-2	MTEL French 26			
978-1-58197-876-6	MTEL General Curriculum (formerly Elementary) 03			
978-1-58197-877-3	MTEL General Curriculum (formerly Elementary) 03 Sample Questions			
978-1-58197-881-0	MTEL General Science 10			
978-1-58197-878-0	MTEL History 06 (Social Science)			
978-1-58197-196-5	MTEL Latin & Classical Humanities 15			
978-1-58197-880-3	MTEL Mathematics 09			
978-1-58197-890-2	MTEL Middle School Humanities 50			
978-1-58197-889-6	MTEL Middle School Mathematics 47			
978-1-58197-891-9	MTEL Middle School Mathematics-Science 51			
978-1-58197-886-5	MTEL Physical Education 22			
978-1-58197-684-7	MTEL Physics 11			
978-1-58197-898-8	MTEL Political Science/Political Philosophy 48			
978-1-58197-888-9	MTEL Spanish 28			
			SUBTOTAL	
	FOR PRODUCT PRICES VISIT WWW.XAMONLINE.COM		**Ship**	$8.25
			TOTAL	

www.ingramcontent.com/pod-product-compliance
Lightning Source LLC
Chambersburg PA
CBHW080535300426
44111CB00017B/2738